AIN'T I A BEAUTY QUEEN?

Ain't I a Beauty Queen?

BLACK WOMEN, BEAUTY, AND

THE POLITICS OF RACE

Maxine Leeds Craig

To Carolyn
with best wishes

Maxine Leeds Craig

OXFORD
UNIVERSITY PRESS

2002

OXFORD

UNIVERSITY PRESS

Oxford   New York

Auckland   Bangkok   Buenos Aires   Cape Town   Chennai
Dar es Salaam   Delhi   Hong Kong   Istanbul   Karachi   Kolkata
Kuala Lumpur   Madrid   Melbourne   Mexico City   Mumbai   Nairobi
São Paulo   Shanghai   Singapore   Taipei   Tokyo   Toronto

and an associated company in Berlin

Copyright © 2002 by Maxine Leeds Craig

Published by Oxford University Press, Inc.
198 Madison Avenue, New York, New York 10016

www.oup.com

Oxford is a registered trademark of Oxford University Press

Material in chapter 6 was previously published in Maxine Craig,
"The Decline and Fall of the Conk; or, How to Read a Process," *Fashion Theory* 1 (December 1997):
399–420. Berg Publishers kindly grants permission to republish this material.

Lyric excerpt from "Say It Loud, I'm Black and I'm Proud," by James Brown and Alfred James Ellis,
©1968 (Renewed) Dynatone Publishing Company. All rights reserved on behalf of Dynatone Publishing
Company. Administered by Unichappell Music, Inc. All rights reserved. Used by permission. Warner
Bros. Publications U.S. Inc., Miami, Fla. 33014

Lyric excerpt from "Bald Head," written by Henry Roeland Byrd, ©1950 Professor Longhair Music.
All rights reserved. Used by permission.

Library of Congress Cataloging-in-Publication Data
Craig, Maxine Leeds.
Ain't I a beauty queen? : black women, beauty, and the politics of race / Maxine Leeds Craig.
p.   cm.
Includes bibliographical references (p.) and index.
ISBN 0-19-514267-5; ISBN 0-19-515262-X (pbk.)
1. Beauty contests—Social aspects—United States.   2. African American women—
Social conditions. 3. African Americans—Race identity.   4. Feminine beauty (Aesthetics)—
United States.   5. Civil rights movements—United States.   I. Title.
HQ1220.U5 C73   2002
305.48'896'073—dc21   2001051007

3 5 7 9 8 6 4 2

Printed in the United States of America
on acid-free paper

In memory of my parents,
Marjorie and Oliver Leeds

ACKNOWLEDGMENTS

The interviews I conducted between 1992 and 1995 constitute the heart of this book. I am deeply grateful to the women and men who graciously gave me their time, spoke candidly about their experiences, introduced me to friends who would also become interview subjects, and even in some cases extended the hospitality of their homes as I traveled throughout the country to ask people about the intersection of beauty and politics in their lives.

The journey from idea to dissertation to book has been a long one, and I received help from many people along the way. Todd Gitlin, Troy Duster, and Waldo Martin, the members of my dissertation committee, were encouraging from the very beginning. Waldo Martin met regularly with me to discuss the connection between culture and social movements and introduced me to Michael Rossman, a collector of social movement posters, to whom I am grateful for allowing me to view and study posters of Angela Davis in his private collection. Todd Gitlin, chair of the committee, read countless drafts and gave invaluable criticism. Barbara Christian helped me to begin the project by introducing me to women who had participated in the Civil Rights Movement.

The Institute for the Study of Social Change at the University of California, Berkeley, was my home base when I was a graduate student. The race theory discussion group facilitated by David Minkus at the institute gave me my grounding in theory about race. The institute is also where the Dissters, my most important source of intellectual community, was formed. Nadine Gartrell, Deborah Gerson, and Ann Ferguson were my Dissters. The writing group was for me an ideal source of critical feedback, encouragement, and friendship, and without it I could not have finished the dissertation. Elizabeth Wheeler was a great housemate, fan, and source of inspiration. Susan Ferber, my insightful editor at Oxford University Press, helped me to transform a rough manuscript into this book.

Sometimes a person can have a great impact with a few words spoken at the right moment. At a time when I was considering not pursuing a career of teaching and research, Catherine Macklin advised me that, whatever I decided about work, I should write my book and then the relatives in Brooklyn would be proud no matter what my job was. Her advice meant that I had to finish this book.

I appreciate the help I received from several people in my search for illustrative photographs. Jesse Byrd of the San Francisco African American Historical and Cultural Society and librarians Patricia Akre, photography curator at the San Francisco History Center, San Francisco Public Library, and Susan Snyder of the Bancroft Library at the University of California, Berkeley, helped me to locate treasures in their collections. Lewis Watts generously gave me permission to use a great photograph of a processing shop from the Red Powell/Reggie Pettis Archive. I thank Kathy Sloane for her technical assistance and for her encouragement throughout this project. I am grateful to my cousin Althea Buckner for granting me permission to include in this book a photograph of her wearing her beautiful Afro.

This book is dedicated to the memory of my parents, who raised me in the Civil Rights Movement and taught me to love language. My mother pushed me in the stroller on picket lines and let me practice my printing making signs. I learned the power of the pen reading my father's sharp and frequent letters to the editor in the *New York Times*. They both knew how to tell a story.

I am very grateful to Beverly Leeds for her lifelong friendship and her belief in her sister. My husband, Mitch, helped me to think through the beginning of ideas, improved my messy drafts with his meticulous editing, and offered untiring encouragement. Throughout the years he has been by my side, my dearest friend.

CONTENTS

AIN'T I A BEAUTY QUEEN?

Chapter One

RIDICULE AND CELEBRATION:

BLACK WOMEN AS SYMBOLS IN THE

REARTICULATION OF RACE

In September 1968, as a panel of beauty experts prepared to select the forty-eighth consecutive white Miss America, two protests were under way.[1] One protest denounced beauty contests. The other *was* a beauty contest. On the boardwalk in front of Atlantic City's Convention Center roughly one hundred women who identified themselves as members of Women's Liberation dumped bras, girdles, and false eyelashes into a trash can. Several blocks away, at the Ritz Carlton Hotel, the National Association for the Advancement of Colored People (NAACP) staged the first Miss Black America pageant as a "positive protest" against the exclusion of black women from the Miss America title. As the day progressed, a counterprotest and a breakaway action added to the commotion that transformed the 1968 Miss America pageant from a cliché-ridden celebration of American beauty ideals into the symbolic beginning point of a new movement. Provoked by the Women's Liberation protest, three spectators, including a former Miss Green Bay, Wisconsin, stepped forward from the boardwalk crowd to form a counterpicket in the contest's defense, while inside the Convention Center Peggy Dobbins, a Women's Liberation protester, hurled a stench bomb from the audience.

The Women's Liberation protest captured the attention if not the sympathies of the national media. The image of unruly women mocking symbols of American beauty was broadcast widely by the media, and as a result the 1968 Miss America contest protest lives in the nation's memory as the action that announced the arrival of a new women's movement. The press erroneously reported that bras had been burned at the protest, providing the "bra-burner" image that, for years, allowed critics to place the women's movement on the incendiary fringe along with flag and draft-card burners.[2]

In the nation's black press, the preponderance of articles published about the events surrounding the Miss America pageant focused on the new Miss Black America contest.[3] They described how the winner, Saundra Williams, dazzled the contest's judges with her performance of an African dance she called the "Fiji." Meeting with reporters after her victory, crown nestled in her Afro hairstyle, she described her parents as middle-class Negroes and proudly listed among her prior accomplishments participation in a protest to integrate segregated businesses in Prince Anne, Maryland. Wearing an Afro, performing an "African" dance created in America, claiming middle-class status, putting her body on the line in civil rights demonstrations, and placing her beauty on display to demonstrate racial pride, Saundra Williams breathed life into the symbols and practices of an emergent black identity.

The women who heaped bras and girdles into the trash can at the Convention Center were awkwardly aware of the NAACP protest contest that was taking place a few blocks away. Many of the white women who were early members of the women's movement had been active participants in the Civil Rights Movement during its racially integrated years and had long-standing commitments to the cause of racial equality.[4] Their Civil Rights Movement participation made them sensitive to racial issues and familiar with African American protest. They denounced the Miss America pageant's racism as well as its sexism, handing out leaflets that listed racism as one of ten points of protest against the pageant and what it represented. Their actions on the day of the protest were steeped in metaphors drawn from the black experience of oppression and borrowed from the protest traditions of the Civil Rights Movement. They spoke of the "enslavement" of all women to the demands of beauty standards. As they picketed they sang, "We shall not be used," an adaption of "We shall not be moved," which was frequently sung at Civil Rights Movement protests. One of the women on the picket line was Robin Morgan, who would later emerge as a leader of the women's movement. The *New York Times* introduced her as a poet who was also a "housewife who uses her maiden name." Commenting on the NAACP protest, Morgan said, "We deplore Miss Black America as much as Miss White America but we understand the black issue involved."[5]

The divergence of the Women's Liberation and NAACP protests is striking. It is indicative of the gulf that existed by 1968 between the largely white Left (including the burgeoning women's movement) and even the more integrationist segments of black movements. The first Miss Black America pageant was a demonstration that existed on the cusp between the Civil Rights and Black Power movements. It celebrated black women by creating an all-black contest while maintaining that its goal was to protest the exclusionary practices of the Miss America pageant. By 1968, the Civil Rights Movement had been shattered and the growing Black Power Movement had been fragmented into groups pursuing widely varied courses. Despite the variety of goals and strategies of competing black political organizations, some commonalities existed. From virtually all positions within African American political movements at that time, regardless of location with respect to strategy for black liberation, there was scant room for a separate women's politics.

A *New York Times* reporter covering both demonstrations focused on Bonnie Allen, one of the few black participants in the Women's Liberation protest. Though picketing at the Miss America contest, she said, "I'm for beauty contests, but then again maybe I'm against them. I think black people have a right to protest."[6] The quote, seemingly full of contradictions, is most probably a reporter's composite. Nonetheless, it expresses the difficulty Allen had as she tried to formulate an opinion about these two protests, neither of which adequately addressed her situation. As a black woman in a movement that was established primarily by white women and ignored, viewed with suspicion, or mocked by many African Americans, Allen suggested an uneasy allegiance to both protests. Her inability to explain her position stemmed from what legal scholar Kimberlé Crenshaw has described as black women's "intersectional disempowerment."[7] Caught in the intersection of domination by race and by gender, Bonnie Allen could stand with the NAACP protest by ignoring its objectification of women or stand with the Women's Liberation protest and feel disloyal for not joining her brothers and sisters in unified protest at the Ritz Carlton Hotel.

The Women's Liberation protesters selected the 1968 Miss America pageant as the target of their action because it epitomized the objectification of women within a male dominated culture. Several studies have analyzed the ways in which beauty ideals serve to reinforce male supremacy.[8] These works demonstrate how beauty standards required all women to judge themselves in relation to unrealistic physical ideals but do not explain how Eurocentric standards placed black women and white women in very different situations vis-à-vis beauty as an ideal. In 1968, black women and white women stood in different locations in relation to the institutions that established and perpetuated national beauty ideals: national beauty contests, media advertising, women's magazines, Hollywood movies, and television programming. White women were objectified in these venues; black women were either excluded from them or included in images that reinforced Eurocentric beauty ideals. Black women had to contest their wholesale definition as non-beauties. In response to the exclusion of black women from dominant representations of beauty, African American women's beauty became part of the symbolic repertoire with which champions of the race sought to assert racial pride.

From the perspective of the achievement-oriented NAACP, the Miss America title was a symbol of success worth fighting for. In the Miss America contest's early days, racial exclusion was written into its by-laws.[9] Long after the racist by-law was rescinded the contest remained, in practice, closed to all but white women. To the extent that the annual spectacle of white women established the reigning definition of beauty, it reinforced cultural codes that placed black women outside of the beauty ideal. In the wider culture, black women had been excluded from all that was celebrated in the crowning of Miss America. Where Miss America represented a contradictory ideal of sexualized beauty and chastity, black women had been portrayed in mainstream depictions as ugly and sexually available, a diametrically opposed set of images.

Exclusion from the dominant beauty ideal did not mean that black women had been spared objectification in either dominant or minority culture. On the contrary, whether facing disparagement of their bodies in dominant cultural images or the mixture of appreciation (where alternative standards prevailed) and ridicule (where dominant standards prevailed) within African American communities, black women were diminished when their general worth was determined by their physical appearance. On that basis, black women potentially shared grievances with the white women at the Miss America protest. But Miss America, the symbolic target of the protest, had never stood for black women. Few black women in 1968 were willing to voice protest against the Miss America pageant for what it supposedly said about women generally.

The colliding protests at the Miss America pageant dramatized the complexity of the situation of black women in relation to images of beauty. In order to comprehend the positions of both Saundra Williams, the first Miss Black America, and Bonnie Allen, an isolated black woman in the Women's Liberation protest, one displaying her beauty as a protest, the other picketing displays of beauty, we must take account of the ways in which African American women have been depicted by the dominant culture. We should also consider the often divergent ways African American women have been depicted in African American cultural representations, the ways African Americans have used images of African American women to challenge cultural domination, and the subjective experiences of black women, whose bodies were the objects of ridicule and celebration.

SOCIAL SOURCES OF RESISTANCE

When the NAACP staged the first Miss Black America contest, they challenged centuries of stereotypically racist depictions of black women as ugly and vulgar. The staging of the Miss Black America contest was one act of intervention in a long struggle over the representation of the race in which the image of the black woman was a focal point. Through the years, as black spokesmen transformed the rhetoric of black racial pride, the black woman was in turn represented as the irreproachable symbol of successful assimilation, the beautiful face of defiant revolution, or the contemporary descendant of lost African empires.

Images of black women also figured in the efforts of white feminists to establish new representations of women. A vibrant feminist scholarship grew out of the women's movement of the 1960s and 1970s. Though these works were ostensibly about the lives of "women" generally, they most often described the experiences of white, middle-class women.[10] Feminists of the late 1960s and early 1970s did not completely exclude black women from their vision, however. Historian Phyllis Palmer argues that, in the iconography of the women's movement, certain black women were appropriated as models of strength.[11] Again and again, twentieth-century feminists pointed to the nineteenth-century black abolitionist Sojourner Truth as a source of inspiration. As the epitome of the strong black woman, Truth represented an alternative construction of womanhood. I use "womanhood" here rather than "femininity," because Truth was so often celebrated by feminists precisely because she was a woman but not feminine. Twentieth-century feminists knew her through early feminist and abolitionist accounts of her 1851 speech in which she was reported to have followed descriptions of the brutality she had survived as a slave with the repeated question, "and arn't I a woman?" She became an icon of the women's movement because her question so clearly articulated a nonfeminine way of being a woman. Historian Nell Painter's careful recovering of the details of Truth's life has demonstrated that the image of Sojourner Truth which was appropriated and celebrated by twentieth-century feminists was, in many ways, a creation of nineteenth-century feminists and abolitionists.[12] The phrase "arn't I a woman," which in many twentieth-century renditions became "ain't I a woman," was an embellishment added by white feminist abolitionist Frances Dana Gage in her 1863 account of Truth's 1851 speech. Neither the words "arn't I a woman" nor "ain't I a woman" were in Truth's speech. Gage wrote them and thus created her own image of Truth. Through an analysis of photographic portraits of Sojourner Truth, Painter shows that in contrast to the strong and folksy ex-slave that emerges from abolitionist descriptions, Truth preferred to represent herself to the world as a middle-class lady.

The image of the strong black woman, though usually presented in a sympathetic light, is itself limiting. At its core is a racialized construction of gender that excludes black women from more generally accepted ideals of womanhood. Differences in the public meaning of white womanhood and black womanhood were partly grounded in divergent experiences of work and in the disproportionately black experience of poverty. The polarization that was rooted in experience was exacerbated because dominant images of white women had been, at times, molded in specific opposition to real and mythical black women. The position of lady was distinguished by those it excluded—men, prostitutes, and black women.[13] Black females, defined as they were by either their assumed capacity for arduous labor or their supposed lack of morals, were not, in the dominant culture, ladies. In the South, the white woman's exclusive right to the position of lady was exercised in the customs and laws of the Jim Crow order. Jim Crow laws excluded black women from female public toilets, commonly known as ladies' rooms, and from the preferred seating at the front of the bus.

Racialized representations of femininity lingered well beyond the end of legal segregation. *New York Times* coverage of the 1968 Miss America and Miss Black America pageants relied upon and reinforced the image of the fragile white lady versus the strong black woman. Captions under photographs of the two winners pointedly noted that Miss America cried when her title was announced but Miss Black America shed no tears.[14] One of the first black feminist anthologies, edited by Gloria Hull, Patricia Bell Scott, and Barbara Smith and published in 1982, was entitled *All the Women Are White, All the Blacks Are Men, but Some of Us Are Brave*. The title aptly summarized dominant racialized constructions of gender. Here I acknowledge the history of the labor and struggles of black women while maintaining that black womanhood cannot and should not be reduced to the strong black woman celebrated in the image of Sojourner Truth. Many previous studies of portrayals of African American women have focused on the derogatory and limited set of images produced by white racists.[15] This approach, while important, ignores the ways in which African Americans have seen themselves. Alongside the huge onslaught of degrading imagery produced by whites stood an alternative set of images produced by a spirited black press who documented and celebrated the goings-on of black women. African Americans all over the country received their news and entertainment from the magazines *Jet, Tan, Sepia, Ebony*, and *Our World* and a host of black newspapers. These publications were filled with beauties, and in their pages, all the women were black.

Black institutions quite deliberately fought degrading images, albeit frequently by promoting atypical images drawn from ideals of black, middle-class life. Alternatives to white racist representations of blacks arose from myriad black community institutions. The chapters that follow will take the reader into hair straightening salons and late night political meetings, into cheering crowds at Harlem beauty pageants, and through some painfully dated poetry. This book will follow the triumphant entrance of black women into formerly glamorous careers just as the limitations of those careers were being exposed by a growing women's movement. These excursions into the processes and products of cultural production are taken to make a general argument about the dynamics of race, culture, and social movements.

Racial boundaries and the social meanings of racial identities are continually reconstituted in response to changing social structures and political projects. Since their mutual inception in the crucible of slavery, the boundaries and meanings of the categories "black" and "white" in the United States have been fluid and contested.[16] This book begins with the premise that race is socially constructed, not a product of nature, and that it is coconstructed with gender and class. If race was an essence, entirely constituted biologically in the body, then its meaning would be stable throughout time. But race, for all of the intransigence of racial domination, is much more fluid than that. It is a set of socially constructed boundaries, practices, and commonly held meanings mapped onto a population whose members themselves represent wide physical and social diversity. Physical differences can be used to distinguish racial groups, but it is the social meaning of those differences that make race matter and that carve the defining boundaries between races. The social meanings, practices, and boundaries of race have indeed changed, change continually, and are inevitably the sites of struggle.

Racial identities are defined through a continual interplay of individual practice and collective action. Each day of their lives, black women rearticulate the meaning of black racial identity as they position themselves in relation to culturally available images of black womanhood. Such culturally available meanings are the outcome of prior struggles against racism. Sociologists Michael Omi and Howard Winant suggest the use of the term "rearticulation" to describe the process by which racial social identities are redefined.[17] Racial rearticulation proceeds via the reorganization of familiar concepts. Omi and Winant emphasize the role "intellectuals" (broadly defined to include religious leaders, sports figures, and entertainers) play in the process of rearticulation. I extend the concept of rearticulation to include the remaking of racial meaning in day-to-day life. Race is continually rearticulated in culture. Racial meaning is revised from the bottom up in the practice of day-to-day living as well as from the top downward through imagery and language used in the mass media and the legal categories imposed by the state. Social movements play a particularly forceful role in the reshaping of racial identities by fostering the development of new practices and symbols that convey new racial meanings.

Sociologist Ann Swidler introduced the image of culture as a "tool kit" comprised of "styles" or "strategies" of action.[18] She proposed that cultures have "settled" and "unsettled" periods and that new cultural practices—styles and strategies of action—emerge during unsettled times. I argue that social movements are very often the sources of "unsettled" times and serve as wellsprings of new social practices. All social movements mobilize in and reshape culture. This is as true for what are thought of as traditional (class-based) movements as it is for the identity-based movements frequently referred to as New Social Movements.[19] Newly described, newly bounded, and newly practiced identities are among the products of social movements.[20] Rarely are these rearticulated identities the intended results of deliberate cultural work: Civil Rights Movement leaders did not plan to produce the transformation in identity that led to the formation of the Black Power Movement. My research on the Civil Rights and Black Power movements documents a mixture of intentional cultural work and unintended cultural outcomes.

The years between 1962 and 1972, when demands for black power supplanted demands for civil rights, form a decade of accelerated rearticulation of racial meanings. During those years, African Americans explicitly and self-consciously reconsidered what being black meant as they rejected timeworn language, oriented themselves toward Africa, adopted new names, created new rituals, and found new beauty in dark brown skin and the natural texture of African American hair. This book focuses on the last two facets of the new black self, beauty and hair. Changes in beliefs and practices related to these mundane aspects of life reveal racial rearticulation and collective self-definition at the most popular level. What was at stake in those cultural struggles? What does one win with the establishment of new practices and meanings of racial identity? Sociologist Pierre Bourdieu has suggested a framework for looking at such issues of culture, power, social reproduction, and social change.[21] The emphasis of his work has been to show how cultural practices generally reinforce social hierarchies.[22] By elaborating on Bourdieu's work, I will suggest a way of thinking about how, in racialized situations, gaps form in the cycle of social reproduction, creating spaces for change in the racial order.[23]

Bourdieu developed a compelling model of how cultural reproduction works to reinforce inequalities. He argues that the poor and working classes are excluded from cultural as well as financial capital. Lacking cultural capital, they fail in school. When they fail, societal hierarchies of privilege appear, to both the winners and the losers, to be natural hierarchies based on merit.[24] Bourdieu argues that capital exists in multiple forms, including economic, cultural, and social, and that the forms of capital are potentially convertible.[25] Economic capital is what is most conventionally considered wealth, that is, money, property, or whatever is the primary material resource in a given society. Cultural capital can be information or even modes of perception that give those who possess them advantages within certain social contexts. Social capital is the advantage that comes from one's connections to other people. Through institutions such as schools, economic capital begets cultural capital in a cycle of reproduction that usually strengthens and naturalizes existing forms of domination.

Bourdieu employs the concept of "habitus" to show how individuals or collective actors become endowed with and use various forms of capital to advance their positions within particular fields. Bourdieu's "habitus" is a concept that is closely related to Swidler's "tool kit," which contains styles and strategies for action. In Bourdieu's work, the habitus is the social source of strategies, categories, dispositions, and modes of perception. A woman's gender and social class profoundly and enduringly shape her goals and the very strategies through which she attempts to achieve them. As "the product of a particular class of objective regularities, the habitus tends to generate all the 'reasonable,' 'common-sense' behaviors (and only those)."[26] Reasonable behavior usually complies with the constraints of an individual's social location.

When the concepts of capital and habitus are applied to African American lives, two issues become apparent. The first is that racial discrimination has prevented blacks from converting one form of capital into another. Throughout much of American history, the black middle class has been thwarted by its inability to translate economic capital into generally recognized social honor. Conversely, in many instances discussed in this book, battles won for the recognition of the value of black culture were not translatable into a stronger economic position for most African Americans.

The second issue is the contradictory nature of the African American habitus. Black "common sense" has generally rejected white racism. Social reproduction rests upon a certain naturalization of the social order, but African Americans have never wholeheartedly accepted the racial order as natural, inevitable, or just. The ability of a dominant class to reproduce itself by naturalizing its position is most visible and efficient in those institutions controlled by the state. Those who do not speak with the accents of the dominant class are harshly disadvantaged in classrooms and courtrooms. Members of dominated groups, however, do not always sit in classrooms being judged by standardized tests. Outside of classrooms, they read their own newspapers in their own barbershops and worship in their own ways in their own churches. In these locations, on their own turf, they establish their own social orders. Ebenezer Baptist Church was not only a haven for alternative discourse; as Martin Luther King's church, it provided the birthplace for a social movement.

In societies structured in racial domination, race forms a basis for communities of identity that provide fertile ground for counterhegemonic cultural production. The African American habitus has largely been shaped in semiautonomous social locations, in institutions and spaces that, as the result of a combination of black preference and white segregation, were all black. Historian Evelyn Brooks Higginbotham has written about the black Baptist church as an institution through which blacks actively contested dominant images of the race.[27] African Americans also established newspapers, schools, social protest organizations, benevolent societies, and social clubs. Such semiautonomous social locations fostered everyday critical readings of the dominant culture.[28] Along with a host of strategies, categories, dispositions, and modes of perception that tended to reproduce elements of the social order, the African American habitus nurtured an enduring disposition to resist racial domination.

African Americans were themselves a heterogeneous group, and that heterogeneity shaped the forms that black resistance would take. There has never been a singular African American habitus. The intricate interplay of gender and class in African American lives produced particular rearticulations of race that grew out of specific racialized gender and class positions. These rearticulations stemmed from what I term "embedded agency," the freely chosen actions of men and women who worked within the constraints and privileges of particular social locations that shaped the terms of their struggles and the contours of their goals.[29] The racial projects initiated by black political organizations reflected the gender and class locations of the organization's leaders and had distinctly different consequences in the lives of black men and women, the poor and the middle class. As this book traces organized efforts to rearticulate the meaning of race, it will consider how hierarchies of class and gender shaped successive imaginings of the meaning of black.

THE VALUE OF SOCIAL HONOR

Battles for social honor have important consequences in the lives of those who are positioned at the bottom of a social hierarchy by structures of inequality. Historian George Mosse has argued that racism is practiced as a visual hatred.[30] Race is an embodied identity, that is, one is considered a member of a race because of the physical appearance or the genetic makeup of one's body. African American bodies, male and female, have alternately been despised, ridiculed, and feared as white popular representations of them have changed over time.[31] Black men and women have been represented as criminals, buffoons, simpletons, beasts, rapists, and whores.[32] In 1781, Thomas Jefferson, slaveholder and champion of the rights of man, began with what he considered the black man's ugliness when he set out to explain why emancipated slaves could not be permitted to remain in the United States. "The circumstances of superior beauty, is thought worthy attention in the propagation of our horses, dogs, and other domestic animals; why not in that of man?"[33] He further speculated about the black man's talents and deficits and concluded that the colored race was "inferior to the whites in the endowment both of body and of mind."[34] His opinions about race were typical, even moderate among eighteenth-century whites, and such views provided justification for continuing the inhuman institution of slavery. As the structure of racial inequality changed, dominant images of blacks were revised. After the Civil War, as whites faced the reality of living with free blacks, viciously rearticulated portrayals of the black race emerged alongside new mechanisms for maintaining white social control. From the post-Reconstruction era through the 1930s, black men were typically depicted as sexual predators, black women as lacking in sexual virtue, characterizations that served as justification for the lynching of black men and the rape of black women. As African Americans won greater inclusion in all aspects of American life, white popular portrayals of blacks were moderated. Yet in the contemporary period, in popular and even in purportedly scholarly works, African Americans have been described as having a propensity for violence, a reluctance to work, and an inability to achieve. Just as earlier derogatory images supported the institution of slavery and the practice of lynching, these updated images can have life or death consequences. Blacks are disproportionately subjected to police searches and police violence based on racial profiling and face routine discrimination in employment and housing as a consequence of dominant images of black criminality and black inferiority.[35] Revisions of the representation of blacks by whites have moved in sync with changes in the social, political, and economic position of blacks in relation to whites. Black struggles against slavery, wanton violence against blacks, and economic discrimination advanced on many fronts. To the extent that cultural struggles revised the image of blacks in the white imagination, they subverted the normalization of injustice.

For the majority of blacks, celebrations of black culture, inclusion of blacks in advertisements and Hollywood movies, selection of black beauty queens in formerly segregated pageants, and diversification of school curricula brought no change in their economic situation yet nonetheless positively transformed the quality of day-to-day life. This study is based on interviews with African Americans who experienced the transformation in black identity that followed the Civil Rights Movement. Many of the women I interviewed recalled how painful it was to live with degrading imagery of blacks and how exhilarating to see those images overthrown. Their testimony documents the value of winning struggles for the right to everyday dignity.

For some, general recognition of the value of black culture, language, artistry, or beauty has translated into economic opportunities. In the language of Bourdieu's framework, some blacks were able to convert newly valued cultural capital into economic capital. These conversions occurred most often when a challenge to the social order led to the opening or restructuring of an institution. The opening of formally closed professions and the establishment of black studies departments institutionalized shifts in the generally accepted value of African American cultural capital. Throughout the 1960s and 1970s, as victories of this sort accumulated, the class dynamics of racial rearticulation were revealed. Members of the more privileged class fractions of black communities were more likely to be able to translate the dominant culture's recognition of the value of black culture into stronger economic positions.

The most widespread victories of counterhegemonic cultural struggles are the changes in the day-to-day experience of living in a racially marked body. Can such cultural victories endure? Cultural capital is not hard currency. In the late 1960s, blacks throughout the country celebrated black culture, proclaimed "black is beautiful," and flaunted black beauty by wearing Afro hairstyles. A decade later, most black women returned to straightening their hair. Corporations can trademark cultural productions and maneuver to support the value of their brands, but communities cannot. Bourdieu argues that in order to successfully secure their positions challenging groups must objectify symbolic capital in institutions.[36] Symbols that emerge from social movement communities and express rejection of a dominant social order are rarely institutionalized. They exist in unbounded public space where their meaning can only be sustained by the context that surrounds them. By their very nature, social movements create periods of accelerated cultural change that rapidly alter the context surrounding any symbol. Additionally, in a capitalist economy, the power of any counterhegemonic symbol can be nullified as the symbol is repackaged and sold as the latest trend. My answer to the question of the durability of cultural change is that, ultimately, any particular symbol or practice matters little, but the process of self-definition matters a great deal. Black men and, I would argue, all women live in what might be considered "marked" or stigmatized bodies. Only the unmarked can trivialize the fleeting, joyous, cultural victory experienced when dominant meaning is subverted and what was formerly ridiculed is finally celebrated.

THE MULTIDIMENSIONALITY OF RACIAL REARTICULATION

African Americans have ceaselessly reinterpreted dominant culture. They have contested and revised the social meanings of black racial identity through spectacles, protests, and daily acts of self-presentation. Since race is constructed as an embodied identity, challenges to racist hierarchies are often expressed as contests over the representation of racialized bodies. Though both black men and women live in "marked" bodies, many African American efforts to reclaim the honor due to the race have particularly focused on celebrating and defending the beauty or dignity of black women.[37]

When social movement leaders use culture as a resource for mobilization, their rhetoric draws on themes that they believe will resonate with their constituencies. Culture is not simply a neutral pool of resources available to be harnessed by clever organizers. Activists who draw upon culturally available symbols and language to advance a movement use material that is embedded in multiple structures of inequality. The racialized symbols and practices that were challenged by the Civil Rights and Black Power movements never conveyed race alone. They were simultaneously expressive of meanings about class and gender. As black activists sought to forge new meanings of the identity black, they did so by incorporating and reorganizing existing social meanings of gender and class. When in 1968 the NAACP organized the first Miss Black America pageant as a protest against racism and as a celebration of black pride, they incorporated very conventional gender ideology. They created a spectacle about which Bonnie Allen, who wanted to fight both racism and sexism, could not easily comment when asked about her "sister" being crowned Miss Black America (see figure 1.1). The first Miss Black America pageant challenged racial conventions, reinforced gender norms, and celebrated middle-class aspirations all at the same moment.

Images of beauty and beauty practices can serve as a focal point for view-

Figure 1.1. Saundra Williams, the first Miss Black America, 1968.
New York Times Pictures.

ing the complex project of racial rearticulation. In the early decades of the twentieth century, most African Americans viewed hair straightening as a modern and attractive practice of female grooming. As such, a woman's straightened hair was seen as good grooming and was a symbol of personal and racial pride. Hair straightening was overwhelmingly a black female practice in the 1920s and 1930s. Their black male contemporaries were not expected to chemically alter the texture of their hair. In the 1940s, as black men belonging to particular subcultures began to straighten their hair, the meaning of straightened hair was bifurcated by gender. Straightened hair continued to represent pride and modernity for women, but a man with a straightened hairstyle was considered dangerous. In the lingo of the time, he was a "player." By 1965, straightened hair had been transformed into a symbol of racial shame for both men and women, but by 1980, straightened hair was again acceptable for women. In the 1980s, most black women, regardless of their political orientations, wore straightened hair. Journalist Lisa Jones wrote, "Everything I know about American history I learned from looking at black people's hair."[38] In this book I follow the transformations in black self-presentation in order to show how, with each change, black men and women were positioning themselves in relation to available meanings of race, class, and gender. Their hair transformations and the contemporaneous revisions of definitions of beauty provide a window on the rearticulation of race.

This book begins with the lively history of African American beauty contests and continues through the emergence, in the mid-1960s, of a new standard of beauty that found common expression in the words "black is beautiful." I document the practice of racial identity in everyday life by examining the period from the emergence of the Civil Rights Movement to the fragmentation of African American activism in the black power politics of the early 1970s. Beauty contests, explicit attempts to rebuild a lost black culture and implicit acts of self-love, played parts in the rearticulation of race during those years.

As black power politics took shape around a variety of competing political strategies, black activists and intellectuals engaged in passionate debates about the role culture might play in the fight against inequality. In his widely read polemic, *The Crisis of the Negro Intellectual* (1967), Harold Cruse argued that the black movement would not advance without the development of black cultural institutions led by black intellectuals. At the time of the publication of his book, Cruse allied himself with no contemporary black political organization. He wrote of black political and cultural activities from the perspective of Harlem and the East Coast, where conflicts between cultural activists, such as Amiri Baraka, and more traditional civil rights leaders, such as Roy Wilkins of the NAACP, remained at the level of verbal barbs.

On the West Coast, the rift that developed between those who viewed themselves as cultural activists and those who eschewed self-consciously cultural politics exploded into a deadly battle on the night of January 17, 1969. On the University of California at Los Angeles campus a gunfight broke out between followers of cultural nationalist leader Maulana Ron Karenga (whose organization was called US, for United Slaves) and members of the Black Panther Party, who ascribed to what they called "revolutionary nationalism." Black Panthers Alprentice "Bunchy" Carter and John Huggins were killed.

As the leader of US, Karenga sought to give black Americans a way to regain lost African traditions through African-inspired rituals of his own creation. If, in Karenga's analysis, blacks had been robbed of their culture and suffered as a people severed from the sustaining power of their roots, the solution was to reconnect with those roots by reviving and reinventing lost traditions. By contrast, the stated aim of the Black Panther Party was to provide self-defense for the black community by monitoring police activity and arming themselves in preparation for confrontations with the police. The divide between "cultural" and "revolutionary" activism was the frame through which many African Americans involved in black social movements described the competing participants in a crowded and strategically stymied movement field. Regardless of the movement frames through which they viewed themselves, I argue that they all participated in the reshaping of racialized culture.

In the 1960s, as a by-product of the Civil Rights Movement, African American men and women challenged long-standing racial codes in their daily lives. In that decade, any African American woman negotiated a changing world of racial meanings that framed each day from when she combed her hair in the morning until she went to bed at night. Racial rearticulation proceeded as men and women embodied and, through their embodiment, altered racial categories. Whether or not an African American woman was directly involved in protests and even if she reaped none of the benefits that came as educational and employment opportunities expanded, she knew that the country was being changed by a vast social movement that was waged by and for African Americans. At a minimum, she saw the Civil Rights Movement on television and read about the movement's victories and setbacks in the black press. Some of the decade's most powerful media images of personal courage and organized resistance flowed from that battle being fought on her behalf. Recorded and disseminated by the media, protests were no longer isolated, local events. Through television, African Americans across the country witnessed protesters being attacked with fire hoses in Birmingham and marchers twenty-five thousand strong arriving in Montgomery, Alabama. Distant victories of "the movement" were brought home, when in diverse locations; often only after a picket line or boycott, a downtown bakery or department store hired a black woman. Cultural offshoots of "the movement" spread to cities around the nation as entrepreneurial activists opened small shops to sell African or African-inspired goods and books by black authors. Some African Americans felt momentum building and believed that great changes were coming. Others felt that the improvements in race relations were insignificant, and their anger at white supremacy deepened. Emotions varied, but it was impossible to have no feelings about a movement waged in one's name.

As that decade of hope, pride, unity, anger, and polarization unfolded, the most personal practices began to be seen as expressions of a political stance vis-à-vis the movement for black rights. Members of civil rights and black power social movement organizations, participants in protests, and those close to them can be thought of as a "black movement community."[39] This heterogeneous community of commitment provided semiautonomous social spaces where dramatic changes in the everyday practices and meanings of racial identity could be formed. As a result of participation in a social movement, many members of the black movement community experienced personal transformation; they began to see themselves in new ways and, as a result, formed new interpretations of their own behavior. For members of the black movement community, one of the consequences of personal transformation was the politicization of their bodies and of behavior that was formerly considered private.

Cultural changes that had roots in the black movement community also affected black men and women outside of the movement. Many African Americans only knew the movement indirectly through televised images. As a visual medium, television emphasizes the surface. The televised mediation of the movement encouraged those who were introduced to it through television to substitute the televised image for the movement itself and to express their identification with the movement by adopting the look of "militants" they had seen on television. Thus, for African Americans inside and outside of the movement community presentation of self could express where a person stood in relation to the struggle against racism.

In day-to-day life, the politicization of bodies came down to choices about how activists and their supporters wore their hair, whom they slept with, and whom they loved. In the polarized culture of the mid-1960s, being black and proud meant not straightening one's hair, holding a standard of beauty that favored dark skin, and deliberately choosing black men and women as lovers. The practices of the new black identity were experienced as political, difficult, exhilarating, and liberating because they took place in a field of accumulated imagery in which sex, gender, class, and race were deeply intertwined. One of the results of the reassessment of racial meanings and practices was that by the late 1960s a new and more inclusive beauty standard had been established. The changes that ensued in the publicly available images of beauty, in practices of self-presentation, and in the meaning of the word and identity "black" affected the lives of all African American women. The following chapters chronicle the way in which a social movement unseated (if only temporarily and within limits) the old beauty standard.

Chapter 2 introduces the reader to four aspects of African American life that formed the sociocultural context in which new standards of beauty emerged—the disparagement of black women in dominant cultural images, an African American discourse of race and respectability, the broad acceptance of theories of black self-hatred, and the close connection between social class and skin tone within black communities. These four social contexts made beauty something worth fighting about and shaped the internal conflicts that would arise within black communities about the meaning of black and beautiful.

Chapter 3 presents the history of early African American beauty contests, which were black institutional responses to racist depictions of black women. They constitute evidence that African Americans did not accept the dominant racial order as natural. With few exceptions, the contests were produced by black institutions exclusively for black audiences. Separate by design, these contests can be considered nationalist, though they should not be automatically grouped analytically with later expressions of black separatism. The early black beauty contests were produced in an era of white racist segregation. In that context, black social institutions did not, in and of themselves, present a direct or immediate challenge to whites. Beauty pageants were generally sponsored by members of the black middle class and reflected the biases characteristic of the class. Black newspapers and social clubs established separate black beauty pageants as nonconfrontational ways of expressing racial pride, but they often reinforced hierarchies of gender, class, and color in their challenges to white supremacy.

Chapter 4 chronicles African American attempts to integrate white beauty contests. These attempts were rarely individual efforts. The contestants often received support from organizations, such as the NAACP, that viewed beauty crowns as worthy goals. Black efforts to integrate white contests paralleled the trajectory of twentieth-century African American protest movements, rising in number as the Civil Rights Movement broke down other institutional barriers to blacks. As certain kinds of civil rights victories became commonplace, many African Americans questioned the significance and value of attempts to win formerly white contests of beauty. African American institutions, often representing a broader class base than the earlier middle-class sponsors of all-black pageants, returned their attention to celebrating black women's beauty within African American contexts.

Chapter 5 traces the development of the natural or Afro hairstyle from its origins, among activists in social movement organizations and on college campuses, to its transformation into a popular commodity. The chapter is based on interviews with women who, as early participants in the Civil Rights Movement, were among the first to stop straightening their hair to wear what eventually became known as naturals or Afros. I document the ways in which meanings and practices that emerged in social movement communities spread beyond the movement community to nonactivists. The chapter follows these meanings and practices beyond the borders of the movement to analyze what happens to the products of social movements when they are no longer embedded in and sustained by a social movement culture.

Chapter 6 looks at the rearticulation of race in light of gender differences. The new meanings and practices of race had different consequences for black men and black women. In 1964, very few African American men straightened their hair and virtually all African American women did. When men gave up straightened hairdos, they became more conventionally masculine. Women who ceased straightening their hair did so at the risk of sacrificing their femininity. Though the experience and meaning of wearing straightened hair was quite different for men and for women, a gender-neutral discourse of racial pride masked the differences.

Chapter 7 considers how the rearticulation of race began to incorporate an antagonistic stance toward a vaguely defined middle class. Women figured prominently as symbols in the ensuing rhetorical conflicts. Across time periods and cultures, men have employed images of women in political rhetoric.[40] Prior to the 1970s, race leaders called on black women to represent the dignity of the race through a particularly middle-class mode of deportment. With the rise of the Black Power Movement, that female style of presentation-of-self began to represent the despised "bourgeois black woman." A new generation of black leaders used a gendered rhetoric of racial pride to excoriate "bourgeois" black women for "acting" white. Chapter 7 discusses the burden of being a living symbol. Black women, who were expected to embody rapidly changing reformulations of racial pride, were in difficult positions.

Chapter 8 follows the use of women as symbols in the fractured politics of the Black Power Movement. As the movement for black liberation fragmented, images of the beautiful black woman and calls for stylistic conformity were frequently employed in attempts to forge a unified black identity and to maintain solidarity within black political organizations.

Each of these chapters reveals the process of racial rearticulation in action. Racial rearticulation advances at many levels. Sometimes a change in racial meaning is launched as the result of deliberate cultural work. Social movement leaders and community spokespersons challenge existing social constructions via spectacles, speeches, and writing. When they perform such cultural work they frequently incorporate existing social meanings of gender and class into their reformulated constructions of race. Race is also rearticulated in day-to-day practice as men and women embody, struggle against, embrace, and, as a result, reshape socially available racial categories. Sociology is very often the study of the unintended consequences of social action.[41] Civil rights workers organizing in the South to end racial terror and inequality discovered that, somewhere along the way, their identities had changed. Cultural change was a by-product of their political struggles. Chapter 9 proposes a model of the process of racial rearticulation that accounts for its dynamics at the institutional and individual levels and for the incorporation of class and gender into the production of new meanings about race. It returns to the questions raised in this chapter about the value of cultural struggles in light of the difficulty of sustaining cultural change.

Writing a book about race, I, too, participate in racial rearticulation with the very words I use. Part of the saga of people of African descent in the United States has been the ongoing effort to find a suitable name for the race. In the past several years "African American" has increasingly come into use, replacing "black," the term that proud activists of the 1960s adopted when they rejected "Negro" and "colored" as euphemisms of a bygone era of racial timidity. African American, by reasserting the race's African origins, identifies American blacks as other American ethnic groups are known—by place of origin rather than by color. I find both "black" and "African American" acceptable and use both throughout the text. In a few places in the text, when describing historical events, I use "Negro" or "colored" as the term in use at the time.

The hairstyles that emerged in contrast to straightened hair in the 1960s became known as "Afros" or "naturals." As nonstraightened but shaped and combed styles proliferated, the word "Afro" was used most often to describe hair cut into a large round shape, while "natural" meant any of a variety of unstraightened cuts and shapes. Maintaining a "natural" requires shaping, combing, and often the application of hair care products, so a "natural" is not merely hair left in an untouched state.

The legacy of Eurocentric beauty standards leaves no neutral words with which to describe black hair textures. Before the mid-1960s, straight hair was known as "good" hair, as opposed to "kinky" or "nappy" "bad" hair. As a term of added derision, hair could be called "peasy," which connoted kinky hair that was not conventionally groomed and lacked uniform texture. "Kinky" and "nappy" were pejorative terms until the late 1960s, when the popularity of natural hairstyles reversed what were considered good and bad hair textures. I use "kinky" as a neutral term, "nappy" with irony, and "tightly curled" in an attempt to find language that is merely descriptive.

With the widespread acceptance of Afro hairstyles, "kinky" and "nappy" became good attributes, but the word "nappy" retained a certain bite and could only be used with some irony. The ironic use of "nappy" continues to be effective today. For instance, a popular black beauty salon in Oakland, California, is called "Oh My Nappy Hair." The tongue-in-cheek use of "nappy," however, is an insider's joke. The ongoing sensitivity of many African Americans to the derogatory connotations of the word was revealed in a controversy that arose in the fall of 1998 at a predominantly black and Latino elementary school in the Bushwick section of Brooklyn.[42] A white teacher, Ruth Sherman, developed a lesson plan around a children's book entitled *Nappy Hair*.[43] The award-winning book, written by black author Carolivia Herron, uses the image of kinky, nappy hair to upend the negative connotations of the word "nappy" and celebrate the resilience and beauty of black women. Ruth Sherman read it to her third-grade class because she appreciated the book's positive message. A parent who saw photocopied pages of the book among her daughter's school papers was angered to learn that a white teacher was using the derogatory word "nappy" in her child's classroom, and she distributed photocopies of the material throughout the neighborhood with a note expressing her feelings. A number of her neighbors shared her reaction, and in short time the group was demanding Sherman's removal. Although school officials ultimately decided that Sherman had done nothing wrong, the teacher felt uncomfortable continuing to work in the community after the conflict and transferred out of the school.

"Nappy" is a word that can produce a smile when used by black sisters. Its meaning can be played with and turned upside down by black beauticians and authors, but the word remains provocative, particularly when used by someone who is not black. When she introduced *Nappy Hair* into her classroom, the well-meaning Ruth Sherman became caught in a thicket of painful and still unresolved issues about race, beauty, self-worth, and self-definition, the very issues she had sought to address by introducing the book to her class.

Two issues contributed to the intensity of the reaction against Sherman's use of *Nappy Hair*. The first and most obvious is the continuing pain caused by the persistent dominance of Eurocentric standards of beauty.[44] Had that been the only issue present, the controversy might have been resolved when those protesting the book's use were shown the book in its entirety and the curricular context in which Sherman had placed it. To some degree, such a resolution did not follow because when disputes begin in highly polarized situations, it is difficult for antagonists to withdraw their complaints. A cooling of the *Nappy Hair* conflict was particularly unlikely because a second set of issues was involved: ownership and control of culture. Interlaced with the protesters' anger about the word "nappy" itself were their feelings that only African Americans could use it.

The passionate feelings that came to the fore in the *Nappy Hair* controversy are central to this study. My primary focus is on the 1960s and 1970s, a period in which the rise of the Civil Rights and Black Power movements fostered an accelerated reexamination of the meanings and practices of racial identity. Using oral history interviews and African American publications as my main sources, I study the ways in which African Americans contested and reshaped classed and gendered racial meaning.[45] Counterhegemonic cultural production is simultaneously an effort to redefine symbols and create new practices and a struggle to claim and retain ownership of and control over what is produced. These were the issues at stake when black college students cut their unstraightened hair into Afros and when black activists later picketed wig stores to protest imported, synthetic "black pride" Afro wigs. Sociologists trying to understand social change and activists seeking to dismantle oppression have asked whether members of subordinated groups can successfully contest domination through culture. This study finds answers to those questions by looking at the emergence and trajectory of a set of beliefs and practices that were popularly summed up in three words: "black is beautiful." How was something as taken for granted as a beauty standard challenged and what were the consequences for American lives?

Chapter Two

CONTEXTS FOR THE EMERGENCE

OF "BLACK IS BEAUTIFUL"

The phrase "black is beautiful" was never synonymous with any one political organization. No group stood behind the slogan in any formal way, though activists in many organizations used the words. For a brief span in the mid-1960s, "black is beautiful" expressed the spirit of self-love and exuberance felt by a generation that had found a new way to see itself. I use the words "black is beautiful" to refer to the new practices of self-presentation and the newly expressed appreciation of dark skin and tightly curled hair that became widespread in African American communities in the late 1960s and early 1970s. This chapter introduces four contexts that provide background for understanding the emergence of and black community reactions to "black is beautiful."

The first context was the historic widespread disparagement of dark skin, tightly curled hair, and African facial features. A new standard of beauty that celebrated dark skin, naturally kinky hair, and full lips offered redress to those women who had been devalued by earlier beauty standards. A second context was an African American culture of presentation-of-self that viewed good grooming as an avenue for the achievement of respect. In the 1960s, generational conflict erupted in households throughout black communities because the unstraightened hairstyles that signified racial pride to young activists represented heedless bad grooming to their elders. A third context, which facilitated the emergence of beauty as a political issue, was the influence of sociological and psychological theories of black self-hatred. As a final consideration, I discuss patterns of privilege within black communities based on skin color. These four contexts provide background for understanding the politicization, during the 1960s, of the beauty of black women.

For a few years in the late 1960s a black woman could feel exhilaration just by walking down the street wearing unstraightened hair, her glorious Afro hairstyle exemplifying beauty, defiance, and pride. One can only understand her joy by knowing how disparaged black women's bodies had been in the past. Numerous scholars have documented the grotesque portrayal of black men and women in artifacts, literature, advertisements, and films produced by whites.[1] Racist images focused particularly on the body. Over and over again, in brutal caricatures, physical attributes of blacks were associated with negative character traits and low social positions. Racist ideologies created social hierarchies based on visible physical differences. Blacks were stigmatized on the basis of their skin color, the texture of their hair, and the shape of their lips. Countless reproduction of derogatory images of blacks in the form of cartoon drawings, figurines, or burlesqued portrayals by white actors in blackface established and reinforced the widespread association of dark skin, kinky hair, and African facial features with ugliness, comedy, sin, or danger. The most blatant forms of caricature diminished in the decades after the Second World War, but the core images lived on in updated and softened revisions. In the dominant media, the most common image of the black woman was the domestic servant, usually portrayed as a fat, dark-skinned woman wearing a head wrap in a setting that valorized thin, pale women with flowing hair. The domestic servant, as portrayed by the media, may have been a sympathetic character, either an all-suffering helper or the sassy deliverer of comic relief, but she was never situated in a context that would encourage viewers to see her as a beauty. In visual amusements produced by and for whites, black women were also portrayed as overbearing and aggressive wives or girlfriends and as prostitutes. The "mammy," the domineering woman, and the whore defined the narrow yet contradictory field of white popular representation in which a black woman was variously asexual, out-of-control, or oversexed but never beautiful.

The degradation of black bodies was particularly painful for African American women. In a male supremacist society in which women were valued as much for beauty as men were for their accomplishments, an ugly woman was a failure.[2] The cosmetics industry magnate Helena Rubenstein once declared that "there are no ugly women, only lazy ones."[3] Rubenstein expressed what historian Lois Banner described as the ideology of the democracy of beauty.[4] According to this belief, beauty was available to any woman who worked to achieve it. However, as long as dominant standards of beauty excluded brown skin and short, tightly curled hair, beauty status was unavailable to most black women. Mass media images of black women may have been produced for the amusement of whites, but blacks could not avoid seeing them. Added to the burden of suffering unequal access to education, housing, employment, and justice, black women bore the shame of being women in unacceptable bodies.

African Americans are an extraordinarily diverse population. In the words of Civil Rights Movement veteran Juadine Henderson, black people "claim everybody."[5] Henderson grew up in rural Mississippi, but the inclusiveness of the category "black" is true nationwide. Unlike whites who define themselves through exclusion, African Americans consider all who have some African ancestry their brothers and sisters. As a result of more than two hundred years of intermixing of African peoples with Europeans and Native Americans, African Americans have a wide range of complexions, facial features, eye and hair colors, and hair textures. Some African American women are closer to hegemonic beauty ideals than others, and beauty standards that favored light skin and long hair operated within African American communities. The ranking of African American women according to the shade of their skin has been a frequent theme in African American fiction. *The Blacker the Berry*, Wallace Thurman's satirical treatment of African American skin color prejudice, was extremely popular and controversial when it was published in 1929. Toni Morrison's powerful work, *The Bluest Eye*, is a contemporary treatment of the same issue. Originally published in 1970, it again rose to great popularity when television talk show host Oprah Winfrey featured it in her book club in 2000. Its sustained power to move readers attests to the persistence of strong feelings about skin tone within black communities.

The ranking of women by skin color emerged as a frequent theme in interviews I conducted with African American women. I was told of the myriad ways in which they learned that dark skin, kinky hair, and full lips were considered ugly. Some spoke of painful, stinging incidents. Others couched their testimony in humor. Most descriptions were of lessons learned within all-black settings at home or in school. Two dark-skinned women told me that they were encouraged by female relatives to apply themselves at school because they had slim chances of finding husbands to support them:

> [My grandmother] would say, "Your chance of getting a good husband who's going to be able to take care of you is much less than somebody else. So you're going to have to be prepared educationally. That way you can make sure you live a comfortable life. You'll be educated. You'll have a good job. You'll be able to take care of yourself." But she attached it to the fact that I was not pretty. You know what kind of an impact that has on you. Because here's somebody whom you love and who was so very good to me, and I clearly knew was in my corner, every step of the way. But a part of being in my corner in her mind was to be frank with me. And I'm darker than my grandmother and father. I can see that a lot of why I was fed "You're

not pretty" had to do with coloring and hair texture and length of hair.[6]

Another woman recalled how her female relatives treated her dark skin color as a problem they could not hide:

> [There was] always this apologetic formulation around, "well, you're black, so you better study hard because you probably won't get a man." That this was a problematic area that they couldn't quite cover up or twist into any kind of shape. The women were really conflicted behind, "Oh God. What have we got here? We can't do anything with her." They would [use] clothespins to try to squeeze my nose to make it real sharp. Because if my features weren't so African, there'd be some compensation [for my dark complexion].[7]

Pearl Marsh, whose family raised her to appreciate the attractiveness of her dark complexion, encountered color prejudice when she attended a black college. During her first year as a student, Marsh was summoned by the dean to receive the suggestion that she abstain from wearing bright colors that accentuated her dark skin.

> The women's dean called me in when I first came to school. I had bought two sweaters: one was a bright orange mohair sweater and one was a bright yellow one. I know she was being nice. She called me in and said I was really too dark to wear those colors and that I really should wear navy blues, browns, and black.[8]

Facial features also were ranked in a racially laden hierarchy. One woman recalled feeling that her lips were too big to be considered beautiful: "I remember as a young girl, feeling like my lips were too big. I think about it now. It's very strange. I really did believe that. Compared to what? I don't know, but obviously as compared to some sense of European loveliness."[9]

Over-the-counter bleaching creams were sold in great quantity, although they could not actually transform a dark complexion into a light one. Plastic surgery was beyond the means of most black women. The average black woman could not alter her skin color or facial features, but she could effectively remove the curl from her hair. After the First World War, techniques for straightening black hair became widely available and increasing numbers of African American women regularly straightened their hair.[10] As the Great Migration brought large numbers of black women from the rural South to the urban North, straightened hair became the norm. While it is difficult to date precisely when hair straightening moved from popular practice to an expectation of normal black female grooming, the evidence indicates that, for the generation of black women living before the Civil Rights Movement, hair straightening was essentially mandatory. Kinky hair was rarely seen in public. It was considered shameful. Sheila Head of Oakland, California, recalled, "When you got your hair washed you'd quickly try to plait it up so you didn't see the massiveness of your kink."[11] Almost without exception, a girl's hair was braided until she became old enough to have it straightened, and then it was straightened over and over for the rest of her life (see figures 2.1 and 2.2). Hair was straightened in the privacy of a kitchen, a woman's domain and, if outside the home, in a black beauty shop. Whites were not supposed to see nappy hair.

The most common method used by black women to straighten their hair was to dress it with a protective coat of pomade, known colloquially as "grease," and then comb it with a metal "hot comb" that had been heated in the flames of a kitchen stove. Straightened hair remained straight until it had contact with moisture through rain, shampooing, swimming, or sweating. To prevent their hair from "going back" between straightenings, black women did their best to avoid letting their hair get wet. They wore plastic rain scarves, never went for a swim, and washed their hair every two weeks just before straightening it again. Linda Burnham recalled being ridiculed for having "Brillo" hair after enjoying a swim without wearing a swimming cap as a child. In her words, "You know the bane of all little black girls is the water."[12]

Regular hair straightening that began in late childhood was one way that almost all of the women I interviewed learned that straightened hair was an unquestionable norm. Brenda Winstead of Washington, D.C., explained that hair straightening was a basic part of growing up: "That's the way you grew up. When you got to be seven or eight, straighten your hair."[13] The practice of straightening hair was so thoroughly accepted that it was a norm even for those black women who, because of mixed racial heritage, did not have tightly curled hair. Jean Wiley could not remember knowing any black women who did not straighten their hair in the 1950s, regardless of their hair texture. "Almost everybody was [straightening their hair.] Even people who didn't need to go near it. I don't know of any women who weren't."[14] Black women whose hair was naturally straight straightened their hair because having it greased and pressed was the only way to look well groomed. The rigidity of the norm led, on occasion, to comic improvisation and tragic limitation. Letisha Wadsworth laughed when she recalled the following childhood experiment:

> Straightening hair was such a ritual. It's like, how straight could it be? How long could it last? I remember one time we ran out of grease to straighten our hair and my mother used Crisco and [that was] the straightest our hair had ever been. But then my sister came home and said, "Somebody told me my hair smelled like fried chicken!" So we would never let her do our hair with Crisco again. But at first we thought we'd really stumbled onto something.[15]

Figure 2.1. Elementary school girls who were too young to have their hair straightened. San Francisco. San Francisco History Center, San Francisco Public Library.

Figure 2.2. Adult women and older girls straightened their hair. San Francisco, circa 1950s. San Francisco History Center, San Francisco Public Library.

One woman, who requested anonymity, told about being the only black woman at her college in the early 1960s and living in a dormitory with a public kitchen. Standing in the cooking area pressing her hair in front of her white fellow dormitory residents would have been mortifying, but having unstraightened hair was equally disgraceful. Her quandary was intensified because the college had a swimming requirement that most students passed during their first year. She dropped out of the swimming class after the first weeks because of the difficulty of finding privacy to straighten her hair several times a week. As each year passed, the swimming requirement remained unfulfilled. In her last year, on a trip to a big city, she found a barber who gave her a professional chemical straightener that kept hair straight even after contact with water. She used the straightener in the dormitory, learned to swim, and graduated.

Hegemonic standards of beauty were taught and retaught to African American women as they were introduced to grooming practices by their relatives, through polite suggestions about flattering colors, in the reactions and expectations of adults around them, in the experience of attention or neglect from men, via the unintentionally hurtful concern of guardians, and from the rude taunts of playmates. The humorous insult has a long tradition in African American culture. Often taking the form of an insulting description of the opponent's mother, this tradition is known as the "dozens."[16] A game of the dozens begins among a group of black schoolchildren when one yells out a humorous insult about another. The unwritten schoolyard rules compel the recipient to respond with a returned insult as funny, original, and disparaging as the first. These ritualized insults teach toughness while schooling children in social rankings. Poverty, family scandals, and physical traits were typical points of ridicule. Dark skin was a frequent target. Historian Lawrence Levine quoted the following two examples in his study of black folk culture:

> "If electricity was black, your mother would be a walking powerhouse."
> "Your mother so black, she sweat chocolate."[17]

The humor in both of these examples lies in the mother's quantity or intensity of blackness. Since the form implies an insult, the negative value of black is taken for granted by the speaker and reinforced in the mind of the listener.

When girls matured into young women, they encountered color prejudices in dating. Male supremacy operated in black communities no less than in the larger society. As women waited to be asked to dance, to be invited on a date, or to receive affection from men, they were vulnerable to and dependent on male assessments of their beauty. More often than not, male choices were shaped by racialized standards of beauty. Pearl Marsh lamented that a dark-skinned woman had to wait until the end of the semester to get a date at the black college she attended in Huntsville, Alabama: "We always laughed in my dorm that the first month of school really light-skinned girls got dates. Then the brown-skinned girls started getting dates. And finally by Christmas when all these relationships were breaking up maybe the dark-skinned girls would get a date."[18]

In addition to learning hegemonic standards from grooming routines, from the protective strategies of family members and teachers, from the cruel teasing of friends, and from romantic rejections, the women I interviewed encountered Eurocentric standards of beauty in popular culture. Through movies, magazines, and television, they saw and learned from pictures that excluded or ridiculed dark-skinned women.

I asked the women I interviewed if, when they were growing up, there were any stars they found beautiful or with whom they identified. Many said there were no famous beauties with whom they could identify. The most frequently named beautiful women were Lena Horne, Dorothy Dandridge, and Diahann Carroll, each one a light-skinned black woman with European features. Images of attractive women available through the media reinforced the message that beauty was found in light skin, straight long hair, thin lips, and a narrow nose.

It is against this background that one can comprehend the sense of delight many black women felt at seeing dark-skinned women with unstraightened hair hailed as beautiful. Yet when black women stopped straightening their hair to wear the new unstraightened styles, many of their harshest critics were black. What explains the hostility within black communities toward the first black women who proudly wore unstraightened hair? In the early 1960s, mothers and daughters, professors and students, and fraternity brothers and coeds clashed over what young "militant" women were doing with their hair. Why did mothers, teachers, and fraternity brothers consider a hairstyle worth fighting about? What did straightened hair represent? To an older generation, a black woman's straightened hair represented good grooming, and thus it was a way to defend her dignity. The next section considers the meaning of straightened hair for different generations of black women, all of whom needed strategies for achieving respect in a society that devalued them.

RACE AND RESPECTABILITY

Above all let the Negro know that the elevation of his race can come only, and will come surely, through the elevation of its women.
—*Kletzing and Crogman*, Progress of a Race

In order to understand the social meanings of straightened hair, it is necessary to view grooming practices as many black women saw them, as personal actions that could be taken to win respect despite living in a hostile environment. These strategies for asserting dignity have roots in the nineteenth century, when black activists, entrepreneurs, and intellectuals frequently organized such personal strategies into collective racial projects. The epigraph to this section is typical of nineteenth-century African American discourse of "racial uplift." Incorporating prevailing sentiments that women were the caretakers of morality, black writers of the day stressed the importance of the position of women in the progress of the race.[19] Women had special roles in these racial projects: as activists, as the group targeted for services, and as designated bearers of racial dignity.[20] Black leaders exhorted women to deport themselves with dignity because the race had to defend itself against the slurs of white racists. The good character of the race had to be visibly demonstrated by every black woman.

The gendered discourse of race and respectability developed in the context of the poverty, demeaning work, and vulnerability to sexual victimization that characterized most black women's lives. Usually denied the limited judicial protection offered to white women, black women had no recourse when they were victims of rape or sexual abuse.[21] Despite black women's sexual victimization, whites commonly portrayed them as utterly lacking in moral virtue.[22] An indication of the differing social status of black women's versus white women's bodies at the end of the nineteenth century can be seen in the use of a black woman as the model in the first medical textbook photograph of a vagina.[23] John Montgomery Baldy's gynecology textbook, published in 1896, trained white doctors through the use of an image of a black woman's vagina at a time when prevailing white opinion would have been scandalized by the exposure of a white woman. The photograph did not shock because white scientists and entrepreneurs had previously established the practice of exhibiting the sexual parts of black bodies, sometimes for the edification and other times for the amusement of fellow whites.[24] Within a Victorian society that is generally characterized as highly protective of women, black women were vulnerable, defamed, and exposed. In response to white treatment of black women, black writers and social activists employed a discourse of race and respectability to reclaim the sanctity of black women.

One of the clearest examples of the institutionalization of the African American discourse of race and respectability is the work of the clubs of the National Association of Colored Women (NACW). Historian Darlene Clark Hine has shown how chaste modes of self-presentation were institutionalized into racial projects as modesty became the hallmark bearing of members of the NACW.[25] Formed in 1896, the NACW fought lynching with protest and campaigned against false characterizations of black women's sexuality. The meeting that brought leaders of black women's clubs together and ultimately led to the NACW's formation was instigated by a published letter in which a white male author disparaged the honor of black women as part of his justification for the lynching of black men. NACW campaigns were wide-ranging. They strengthened black educational institutions, worked to build economic opportunities for blacks, and organized to improve the living conditions of black women who migrated to northern cities. Throughout their campaigns, they maintained a commitment to establishing a place of honor in American society for black women. Club members expected black women themselves to contribute to establishing that place through their sexual virtue, education, temperance, industriousness, spirituality, and generosity to charitable organizations. Appearance, too, had its role in the struggle to win respect. Mary Church Terrell, the first president of the NACW, aware of the power of the gaze of the racist, emphasized the importance of what could be seen. In an 1898 speech, she described the startled reactions of white women who witnessed the dignified bearing and tasteful attire of black women at NACW conventions. She noted that "even the white people who think they know all about colored people and are perfectly just in their estimate of them are surprised when they have an ocular demonstration of the rapidity with which a large number of colored women has advanced."[26] Each NACW member had the responsibility to be an "ocular demonstration" of the swift advancement of the race.

The discourse of race and respectability can be viewed as a product of the aspirations and fears of a particular segment of the black population. The increasing numbers of black southern migrants in northern cities jeopardized black, middle-class dominance within their own communities and threatened to disrupt their precariously harmonious relationships with whites. Feminist literary critic Hazel Carby argues that the growing urban working class, particularly the surge of black women moving to cities, threatened a male-dominated social order and so became the focus of a "moral panic" among the black bourgeoisie.[27] Hence the emphasis on the role of women in middle-class calls for racial uplift. The motto of the NACW, "lifting as we climb," captures the members' upwardly mobile aspirations as well as their commitment to leave none behind as they rose. In one of her addresses, Terrell reminded members that the NACW must come "into closer touch with the masses of our women, by whom, whether we will or not, the world will always judge the womanhood of the race."[28] The racist's gaze would judge the black race on the basis of the least of its members, and thus dignified self-presentation was a racial project in which all black women could and must participate.

The rhetoric of Negro uplift reflects the embedded agency of a male-dominated, black middle class, yet the strategies of personal presentation its members proposed had appeal to a broad spectrum of black women. While black intellectuals were crafting and promoting an image of upstanding black womanhood, the white media generally offered two stock images: the hypersexual black woman and that asexual black woman workhorse, the "mammy." The kernal of truth in the image of the mammy is that throughout most of American history the great majority of black women worked in menial jobs. Having entered the United States as slaves, black women have had a more continuous history of employment than white women.[29] Because of a pattern of exclusion of black men from skilled employment, the labor of black women has often been essential to their family's economic survival. Work in itself can be an avenue for achieving status and dignity, but until the mid-1960s, discrimination in employment and unequal access to education limited most black women to employment as farm workers, domestics, or restaurant and hotel workers. The image of the "mammy," however, distorted the meaning of work in black women's lives. In popular culture, a working black woman was an ugly drudge. In real life, black women did what they could to prove that the dichotomy between female labor and female attractiveness was a false one. Many poor, black women who labored in occupations that garnered little respect outside of black communities were receptive to the message that dignity could be claimed through personal actions of behavior and self-presentation—even if the message came from the black elite.

The discourse of race and respectability, institutionalized by the women of the NACW at the end of the nineteenth century, continued in subsequent decades and serves as a foundation for understanding black community conflicts about self-presentation that arose in the 1960s. Black educators and writers of the 1920s extolled the virtues of black women. In 1923, G. W. Rigler, the president of Hartshorn (a black women's college in Virginia), hailed the mission of educated black women: "The salvation and uplift of the Negro race, as of any other, and of the nation and civilization of which they are a part, will be found dependent largely upon the character of the women."[30] Later writers used images of decadent white flappers to demonstrate, by means of contrast, the superior nature of black women. In 1927, proclaiming the virtues of African women, the *Baltimore Afro-American* reported that "African Girls Wear More Clothes than U.S. Flappers," and the *Boston Guardian* used the headline "Colored Women Modest" to lead a story about a black cook who risked death rather than tear off her clothes that were aflame: "In contrast to her conduct, we recall the white girl who stripped off everything and took a bath in a tub filled with wine, for the delectation of white men and women in New York."[31] The black press continually tried to rewrite the image of the black woman as racism kept the majority of African Americans in poverty. Despite massive black migration and enormous changes in the nation's economy, black women remained trapped in the least desirable occupations. In 1930, the majority of black women worked either as farmhands or as domestics.[32] As African Americans migrated from the South to flee brutality and rising unemployment, black women found jobs predominantly as domestics and institutional cleaning women in northern cities. As late as 1950, 41 percent of black working women were employed as household servants, and only 5 percent of black working women (as compared to 40 percent of white working women) were clerical or sales workers.[33]

Black women of the generation that preceded the emergence of the Civil Rights Movement did what they could to obtain respect. Many, laboring at hard and socially undervalued work, presented themselves, when they could, with as much propriety as they could afford.[34] Donning fabulous hats on Sunday at church; wearing clean, pretty dresses; and having their hair straightened and styled to motionless perfection were ways of displaying dignity. Grooming was used to convey personal and racial pride. The association of good grooming with racial pride was fostered especially by entrepreneurial black women in the hair care business. Annie Turnbo Malone and Madam C. J. Walker, two outstanding black businesswomen of the early twentieth century, built their businesses by selling hair care products to black women and were civic leaders in their communities. Franchises of their products provided thousands of black women an entrée into small business. Malone's Poro products and Walker's eponymous line of hair care treatments represented the great success of two black, female entrepreneurs and carried the aura of racial pride. Promotional materials for the Madam C. J. Walker line of hair products in 1944 stated that "the products this company manufactures have meant much to the women of our race. It has become a rare thing to see a woman who has not a beautiful and well kept head of hair and a lovely smooth skin, much of this new self-pride and personal ambition is born of the proven merit and unquestioned effectiveness of Madam C. J. Walker's Wonderful Hair and Scalp preparation."[35] From the 1920s onward, the hair care business provided an opportunity for black women to gain a small measure of independence by selling hair care services in their homes or in small beauty shops. Though the businesses were small, they provided an alternative to domestic work. The legions of small entrepreneurs as well as the renowned Malone and Walker encouraged the association of good grooming with independence and pride (see figure 2.3).

Neat attire, conventional hairstyles, and even prudishness battled degrading images born of racist stereotypes and the actual working conditions of most black women. The importance of grooming as a way to defy the racist assumptions of whites was conveyed from mother to daughter and woman to woman. Caught between degrading portrayals of black women in dominant culture and constraining invitations to embody honorable black womanhood, black women may have felt compelled, in the name of racial and individual pride, to embrace the latter and impose constraining definitions of black womanhood upon their daughters.

The persistence, in the 1950s and 1960s, of the belief in the importance of good grooming and deportment was evident in my interviews with women who grew up during those years.[36] Barbara Christian came to the United States from St. Thomas, Virgin Islands, in 1959 to attend a predominantly white college in Milwaukee, Wisconsin. She described the social pressure she felt to maintain her dignity as a black woman by conforming to conventional standards of

Figure 2.3. Beautician's Club, a professional group that met once
a month in San Francisco, circa 1939. San Francisco History
Center, San Francisco Public Library.

grooming: "When I came to Marquette University, I didn't get my hair straightened regularly. And a group of girls, African Americans, came to me and said,
'You can't do that here. People will think of us as country.' There was this sense
of good hair and bad hair and looking groomed."[37]

"People [that is, whites] will think of us as country." The condition of the
hair on Christian's head reflected not only her own appearance but also that
of the women of the race. "Country" connoted the rural poverty and lack of
sophistication that her fellow students had escaped by attending a predominantly white midwestern university, and she was expected to maintain that distinction in her appearance. Straightened hair represented access to hair products, sanitation, leisure, and relative prosperity. A woman who put time and
money into her appearance was dignified, and her dignity spoke well of the race.
Grooming was a weapon in the battle to defeat racist depictions of blacks.

Good grooming was socially encouraged for all women during the 1950s and
early 1960s.[38] Black mothers incorporated existing gender norms into their efforts to properly raise daughters amid the hostility of white racism. Many
young African American girls learned to behave and appear well groomed in
the context of lessons about their obligation to the race. A well-behaved, at-

tractive, young black lady with neat pressed hair was an asset to her race. Though middle-class black leaders championed the connection between deportment and dignity, it was embraced as a strategy by working-class blacks as well. Letisha Wadsworth's father was employed as a janitor in a public library while working part-time at the post office. She recalled her mother's admonitions against appearing unruly in public: "I remember lots of stuff about when you're going out, how you conduct yourself and carry yourself. Because people are watching you and you represent all black people. You know, [laughs] the burden of the whole black race. Conduct yourself so that people will know you're upstanding and that's how black people are."[39]

In 1968, when *Ebony*, the popular chronicler of Negro achievement, featured models wearing Afros, distraught female readers sent letters to the editor. Shirley Drake wrote, "Each time I walk down the street and see another woman of my race wearing one of those hideous 'naturals' I am so humiliated I could cry."[40] Similarly, Mrs. K. E. Williams wrote, "I am attempting to rear my children to be proud of their race . . . all the 'naturals' do is accentuate the negatives."[41] When, in the late 1960s and early 1970s, members of the older generation saw the way young blacks flaunted nappy hair, they were aghast at what they saw as a reckless rejection of appearances. In 1969, during a student strike in Harlem, a group of black female City University students formed a workshop to talk about their concerns. They ardently discussed the direction of the black movement, sexism, and, with just as much passion, generational conflicts about hair. Adele Jones told the others, "I have a girlfriend whose mother actually went into fits when her daughter walked in with an Afro. Laid down on the floor and cried." The mother, Jones explained, wanted her daughter to look "presentable," a word that implied both employable and non-threatening to whites. In the mother's view, straightened hair was the only way to achieve that look. Cenen Moreno, another student present at the gathering, agreed: "They're afraid for us. Afraid of the reaction against us."[42] Some daughters resorted to deception to avoid arguments at home. Linda Burnham recalled "women who had to wear wigs, straight wigs till they got to the bus stop and then [took] their wigs off where they had a natural underneath. They really got a lot of flack at home."[43]

Black women of the older generation knew that whites would very likely look down on them, and they were accustomed to using personal appearance as a way to assert some control over how they would be perceived. Black journalists, ministers, and community leaders had preached that women could have some measure of control over the way they were treated if they presented themselves well. Many black women took that message to heart and earnestly tried to teach it to their daughters. When I interviewed writer and activist Frances Beal in the 1990s, she wore her hair unstraightened. I asked her if she had straightened her hair prior to the 1960s. "Absolutely!" she answered and linked it to the common belief at the time that self-presentation would make a difference in the way black people were treated.

> Certainly it was the thing to do. You know it's really hard to explain. There was a certain consciousness about being Negro. . . . If you'd be good, people wouldn't be racist against Negroes. If you act just like a lady then. . . . It's beyond this type of orientation to think that there's something wrong with the system. There's something wrong with Negroes if we don't get treated right. Therefore if you act right you will be treated right.[44]

An older generation of women saw no contradiction between straightening their hair and racial pride. The hot comb was nothing more than a tool for exerting proper self-control. When a woman pressed the wild kinks out of her hair, she made herself presentable in a world that was ever ready to severely judge her. I interviewed a woman whose skills as a beautician had never lifted her out of poverty. The flawlessness of her pressed hair was for her a source of pride:

> So many people are struggling so hard they don't have time to put all this extra time into their hair. You have to take your kids to school. You have to worry about the PG&E [utility bills]. You don't have time to fool with the hair no more. You just want to do something and go. Yet we have to keep ourselves looking nice all the time. Somebody asked me do my hair ever go out of place? I said no.[45]

Motionless hair was the way she flaunted her self-control, discipline, and skill. Her hot comb was a primary tool through which she made her self. Black women who arrived at their teen years in the 1960s began to view the hot comb in an entirely different way. To the young, hair straightening was a self-inflicted technology of oppression. The change in perception was enormous, and as a result some mothers worried and cried as they watched their daughters step outside with nappy hair.

THE CONSEQUENCES OF COLOR

Before many mothers had a chance to adjust, it seemed that new rules had been written that invested hair with a highly politicized meaning. What was formerly a source of pride had been transformed into a mark of shame as a new rhetoric and associated new practices for fashioning a self gained wide currency. One of the underpinnings of the new rhetoric was the popularization of reform-minded social science research on race, color, and self-esteem. Much of this research concluded that African Americans suffered from low self-esteem. Black psychologists Kenneth Clark and Mamie Clark, who studied issues of skin color and self-esteem among black children, published the foundational piece of research in 1947.[46] They reported that when young black children were given a choice between black dolls and white dolls they favored the white dolls and made disparaging comments about the brown-tone dolls. At that time, their findings were seen primarily as evidence of the negative psychological consequences of segregation and racial inequality. Thurgood Marshall, who at the time was a lawyer representing the NAACP before the Supreme Court, employed the evidence of the Clarks' studies to argue effectively in 1954 for an end to school segregation.[47] A decade later, black intellectuals and activists who were frustrated at the pace of change also drew inspiration from the psychological literature of race and self-esteem. Black power advocates cited anticolonial activist Frantz Fanon's descriptions of psychologically damaged colonized people to justify ideologies of redemption through consciousness-raising.[48] The tenor of Fanon's writing was worlds apart from that of Kenneth and Mamie Clark. Yet his work and theirs form part of a sustained literature that argued that racism had had devastating consequences on black self-esteem. By the mid-1960s, the problem of self-hatred among blacks was accepted as common wisdom. In keeping with that perspective, sociologists J. Richard Udry, Karl Bauman, and Charles Chase opened an article about patterns of marriage and skin color with the assertion that "constant playing of the Negro role has produced a damaged self-concept, one of low self-esteem and self-contempt."[49] The widespread acceptance of the self-hatred paradigm and the consequent black popular desire to overcome alleged self-hatred gave an impetus, weight, and seriousness to emerging "black is beautiful" practices. Black activists drew upon the assumption of widespread black self-hatred when they called on blacks to throw off their mental shackles and embrace black identity. Yet a close look at the research of race and self-esteem reveals a more complicated picture than universal black shame.

Although the Clarks' study was not the first that purported to study Negro self-esteem, its influence far outpaced any studies that preceded it. Working in northern and southern nurseries and kindergartens in 1940 and 1941, Kenneth and Mamie Clark asked 253 black children to choose between two dolls: one beige, the other brown.[50] Beginning with four tests that sought to elicit racial preference (i.e., "Give me the doll that looks bad") followed by three tests of the child's ability to distinguish between races (i.e., "Give me the doll that looks like a colored child"), the Clarks culminated each experiment by asking the child to "give me the doll that looks like you." The Clarks found that 60 percent of the young black subjects identified the white doll as the "nice doll" with the "nice color." The same percentage of children said the black doll was the one that "looks bad." Children who rejected the brown doll explained their choices in the following ways: "Cause he ugly," "Cause it don't look pretty," "Cause him black," and "Got black on him."[51] These findings were accepted by social scientists of the 1950s as proof of black self-hatred and were cited in the

1954 Supreme Court decision *Brown v. Board of Education of Topeka* as evidence of the psychological destruction wrought by segregation. The public concern about the role of dolls in the mental health of black children can be seen by the involvement, in 1951, of diplomat Ralph Bunche and former first lady Eleanor Roosevelt in the development of an "anthropologically correct Negro doll." Eleanor Roosevelt explained her support for the development of "Saralee" by saying that "a really beautiful Negro doll would give joy to Negro children and add to their self-respect."[52]

The pathos of the Clarks' findings compelled psychologists to use picture and doll racial preference tests with young children again and again. Not until the 1970s were the data reconsidered by social scientists and the black self-hatred paradigm challenged. Literature reviews published in the 1970s began to question whether self-hatred had been as widespread among African Americans as had been reported.[53] In 1984, child psychologist Margaret Spencer reexamined the question by designing a study to distinguish between self-esteem and racial identification.[54] She found that black children effectively compartmentalized self-esteem and racial identification and suggested that they may retain a positive self-image while making choices that demonstrated a white cultural orientation. In 1991, William Cross published a comprehensive study that reassessed four decades of experimental research on black racial identity.[55] He concluded that the early doll studies purported to measure mental health, but they actually measured reference group orientation. Cross defined reference group orientation as "how a child or adult orients himself toward his or her socially ascribed group."[56] Reexamining the evidence of the years of accumulated doll studies, some of which found black children of the black power era choosing black dolls, Cross found that the tests always demonstrated diversity rather than uniform preferences. Black children often showed a lack of preference, choosing white dolls as often as black dolls. The absence of ethnocentrism had, in the past, been interpreted as self-hatred, but Cross suggested that it could be viewed instead as biculturalism. His reanalysis of the foundational studies and survey of more recent work called into question the long-standing assumption that most black children suffered from low self-esteem. Critics have stressed the diversity of the findings, even in the Clarks' classic study; the inadequacy of doll and similar tests as measures of self-esteem; and the tests' questionable application to adult psychology.

The doll studies were investigations of the preferences of young children. Another body of literature attempted to assess the attitudes toward skin color held by black youths and adults. One of the earliest sociological assessments of adult African American attitudes toward skin color was published as part of St. Clair Drake and Horace Cayton's ethnographic study of black Chicago in the 1940s.[57] They found widespread rejection of dark brown skin and a beauty standard that favored light-skinned women. But, despite the favored position of light-skinned women—or perhaps because of it—many respondents told the researchers that they would prefer a spouse with a medium-brown skin tone.

Later investigators found similar results. In a survey conducted in 1950, the majority of students at a black high school in St. Louis, when asked about their skin color preferences, stated that they preferred to be brown (as opposed to light or dark) and preferred to marry a brown-skinned spouse.[58] In a report published in 1952 based on a survey of black students attending a North Carolina college, Joseph Himes and R. E. Edwards found that four-fifths of the students stated that light skin and straight hair were "not important" in a future spouse.[59] More men than women (17.4 versus 8.4 percent) expressed a preference for a light-skinned spouse. Like the students who in 1950 said that brown skin was the most desirable, the majority of these students answered that light skin was "not important" as a characteristic for a mate.

In a later study based on research conducted in North Carolina in 1957, Himes joined with another psychologist, Charles Anderson, to ask black male and female undergraduates what attributes they sought in a dating partner.[60] Among the twenty-eight qualities, including "friendliness and cheerfulness" and "good conversational ability," Anderson and Himes listed four attributes that might be construed as physical: "sex appeal," "taller and older men," "handsomeness," and "redbone" (light complexion). The students placed "redbone" relatively low on the list, at position twenty-two, two notches above "plenty of money." Rather than concluding that in North Carolina in 1957 neither money nor light skin won any advantage in obtaining a date, it would seem just as plausible that these findings indicate what students deemed self-respecting answers. In the 1950s, before the black pride movement of the 1960s, young, educated, black Americans knew that it was inappropriate to favor light skin.

In 1970, researchers returned to the St. Louis high school where the study of skin color preference had been conducted in 1950 in order to measure changes in attitudes between cohorts.[61] Again, the majority of respondents claimed that they preferred to be brown and would prefer a brown-skinned spouse. Between 1950 and 1970, the percentage of subjects who said they preferred a dark spouse rose from 2.8 to 16.6.[62]

These findings cannot tell us whether the rejection of dark skin reflected black self-hatred or what respondents made of the consequences of having dark skin, but what is striking here, as in Drake and Cayton's work, is the consistent popularity of the choice of brown. If these responses can be accepted as accurate assessments of the regard with which brown skin was held, they counter a simple black self-hatred thesis. If, instead, they represent what were deemed by the respondents as appropriate answers, they indicate that, years before the Black Power Movement, many African Americans felt that it was important to demonstrate racial pride.

Despite ambiguous evidence, theories of black self-hatred carried the authority of established fact in the 1940s, 1950s, and 1960s. In 1968, black psychiatrists William Grier and Price Cobbs articulated it in their widely read psychological portrait of black America, *Black Rage*. Touted on its cover as the book in which "two black psychologists tell it as it is—in the first book to reveal the full dimensions of the inner conflicts and the desperation of the black man's life in America," *Black Rage* generalized from case studies of mentally troubled patients to the general population. This work, along with earlier studies that concluded that black self-hatred was widespread, provided an intellectual tradition that was incorporated into the political discourse of the Black Power Movement, paving the way for the politicization of beauty and of black women's bodies.

The material consequences of meeting or failing to meet beauty ideals constituted a fourth context that set the stage for the emergence of "black is beautiful." There were serious social consequences for those who did not conform to dominant standards of beauty. The force of hegemonic standards was exerted most powerfully in the two realms of life that establish social position: marriage and work. Beginning in the 1960s, an increasing number of sociologists measured the effect of skin color on opportunities for marriage or employment. These studies found that, despite answers recorded in the attitude surveys just outlined, lighter skin brought concrete advantages.

The majority of studies of the effects of skin color on the life chances of black women has focused on one aspect of life: marriage. Howard Freeman and his colleagues, reporting in the mid-1960s on data obtained in a survey conducted in Boston that considered the skin color and class background of both spouses, found that in the marriage market, light skin enhanced status for men and for women.[63] Light skin allowed African American, blue-collar men to marry women from white-collar backgrounds and women from blue-collar backgrounds to marry white-collar men. In a study of two age cohorts of black married couples conducted in the late 1960s, Richard Udry and his coauthors reported an increase in the frequency of dark-skinned men marrying lighter women.[64] With regard to marriage, the emerging Black Power Movement lessened the stigma of dark skin for men, yet no similar trend was evident for dark-skinned women. Though the rhetoric claimed that "black is beautiful," darker black women continued to face rejection. In a study of a sample selected from the 1978 edition of *Who's Who among Black Americans,* Elizabeth Mullins and Paul Sites found that, as a group, the sample was lighter-skinned than the general population of African Americans and that the wives were frequently lighter than their husbands.[65]

How does position in the spectrum of African American skin tone affect employment? Most of the research on skin tone and employment surveyed only men, ignoring the importance of paid employment in black women's lives. Though these studies did not directly survey women, the patterns of male employment they documented had indirect effects on the lives of dark-skinned women because dark-skinned women were more likely to marry dark-skinned men. Researchers have surveyed the employment status of black men of various shades and found that men with dark skin are at a disadvantage in the job market. Sociologist Edward Ransford found in a 1965 survey of black men in Los Angeles that dark-skinned men with less than a high school education were significantly more likely to be unemployed than lighter men with the same level of education.[66] Dark-skinned men with high school diplomas or some college were less likely than lighter men with the same levels of education to have white-collar jobs. Verna Keith and Cedric Herring included gender in their analysis of skin color and employment and found that dark-skinned women were at a disadvantage. Analyzing data from a 1979–1980 survey, Keith and Herring found a correlation between female light skin color and status of occupation.[67] Over a decade later, sociologists James Johnson and Walter Farrell surveyed black men in Los Angeles and found that dark-skinned men were still at a disadvantage when they sought jobs.[68] In a study of African American men with thirteen or more years of education, the authors found that 19.4 percent of dark-skinned men were unemployed, compared to 10.3 percent of light-skinned men. The studies all point to a similar conclusion. Darker men and women faced greater obstacles in the labor market.

When considered together, what do the results of studies of attitudes and of outcomes tell us? Survey data regarding adult attitudes toward skin color indicate that at least since the mid-1940s the majority of African Americans either reject light skin or say that it is not an important trait. Yet these findings are undercut by studies of actual patterns of marriage that show that, more often than not, economically successful black men chose to marry light-skinned women. Lighter-skinned blacks had greater opportunities to accumulate advantages. They were favored with regard to opportunities for marriage and for employment. As a result, it became difficult to separate questions of skin tone and class within black communities. The research findings on patterns of marriage indicate that among African Americans preferences for light skin existed and that the standard that favored light skin weighed most heavily on women. However, black preferences for light skin were continually challenged within black communities. Few educated blacks would tell a survey researcher that they preferred light skin. Norms of racial pride that were refuted by contradictory practices and a beauty standard that was powerful but contested complicate the emergence of "black is beautiful" in the 1960s. When African Americans of all shades declared that "black is beautiful," they were defying a racial order that had held all blacks down but had granted some advantage to blacks who were physically closer to whites. By embracing the word "black," and not "brown," "colored," or "yellow," "black is beautiful" subverted white supremacist social rankings. There had been no linear progression from black self-hatred or "colonized minds" to the black pride voiced in the words "black is beautiful." Before and after the words emerged as a popular phrase, there was evidence of black racial pride, black racial shame, love among blacks that had no explicit reference to race, and instances of human frailty that produced splits between words and deeds.

I have outlined four facets of the cultural milieu out of which "black is beautiful" grew. First, "black is beautiful" arose in angry reaction to a dominant beauty standard that had favored light skin and long straight hair. Second, youths who adopted the new beauty standard and its accompanying practices encountered resistance from those who maintained older notions of what constituted proper presentation-of-self. Third, a tradition of social science research that accepted black self-hatred as a paradigm provided support for the belief that what one did with one's hair was a political concern. Finally, a pattern of privilege based on skin color established what has been called a "pigmentocracy" in black communities. Because lighter-skinned African Americans had greater chances in both marriage and employment markets, class stratification within African American communities was intimately intertwined with color stratification.

The remainder of this book looks at how African Americans created new social meanings and practices by subjecting existing cultural material to everyday critical readings. As a new generation of blacks critically examined practices that had been accepted as the way to be a proud colored person, long-standing black community conflicts reemerged. Conflicts between African American classes, evident in the discourse of early projects of "racial uplift," repeatedly arose with greater clarity in subsequent decades of black activism. Such conflicts were expressed as refusals to accept the leadership of those who appeared to be representing the interests of a privileged or limited segment. During those same years, conflicts between black men and women remained private troubles, making it extremely difficult for black women to refuse the calls by black leadership to accept and embody particular images of black womanhood. Those who did refuse black gender norms acted as individuals, and as individuals could be seen as abandoning the racial project, as failures as women, or, when the two agendas were intertwined, as a disgrace to the race because they failed as women.

Black communities created their own institutions that served as sites of cultural production. The leaders of these newspapers, churches, women's clubs, and political organizations incorporated existing meanings as they promoted new, old, particular, and varied ways of interpreting race. In noninstitutional settings as well—in discussions in black homes between mothers and daughters, in gatherings of young friends—black men and women critically examined the culture they had inherited from the struggles of those who preceded them. They retained some and rejected other elements of dominant culture, cel-

ebrated pieces of African American culture, and cast off practices that were reinterpreted as remnants of a shame-filled past. The next chapter chronicles one
genre of cultural production, the beauty contest. These spectacles ranged from
nineteenth-century competitions promoted as testimonials to the beauty of the
race to raucous post–World War II entertainments held in halls full of catcall-
ing fans. All contributed to the serious project of making gender, race, and class.

Chapter Three

AIN'T I A BEAUTY QUEEN?

REPRESENTING THE IDEAL

BLACK WOMAN

See. Look at us. We have some beautiful black girls, too. Because
there was a time when blacks couldn't get into the white beauty contests,
so they developed their own and showed how beautiful we are.
—*Beautician Barbara Williams, recalling black beauty
queens in the era of segregation*

Before civil rights legislation brought limited racial integration to the United
States, African Americans lived and died in racially segregated settings. Under
the conditions imposed by segregation, blacks found ways to resist racial oppression. Excluded from or mistreated by white churches, schools, newspapers,
clubs, and funeral parlors, black men and women created their own institutions
wherever and whenever possible. By 1910, there were 35,000 black churches in
the United States.[1] African Americans established 106 colleges and more than
2,000 newspapers before 1950.[2] Black churches, newspapers, classrooms, radio
stations, funeral parlors, and the streets of black neighborhoods were sites of
cultural production. In these spaces and institutions, African Americans created
and sustained symbols, meanings, and cultural rankings that countered dominant white views of blacks.

Expressing anger is one way to challenge white supremacy; refusing to accept the white world's image of oneself is another. Historian James C. Scott
wrote about the ways in which slaves created, against all odds, safe places and
secure ways to express their anger against their masters. He described the expressions produced in those sites as the "hidden transcript" of resistance.[3] Post-
emancipation middle-class blacks were considerably less vulnerable than their

slave forebears. They were able to use black publications, colleges, and social clubs to disseminate alternatives to white portrayals of blacks. What they created was not so much hidden from whites as it was ignored by them. The black middle class produced a compelling record of racial pride, meaningless to their contemporary whites but vital to African Americans.

Members of the black middle class dominated black colleges, social organizations, newspapers, and large churches. Spokesmen for the black middle class were able to promote their versions of proud black identity through their dominance of these important sites of cultural production. As business owners or professionals serving black clientele, they had achieved some degree of material comfort but were still treated contemptuously by whites. Many members of the black middle class were eager to fight nonmaterial forms of racial domination. This chapter tells the story of a group of African Americans who, relative to other African Americans, were in advantaged positions. Their strategies of resistance sought to work within the disjuncture between black, middle-class life and the position of all blacks in a white supremacist symbolic order. A tension was built into these strategies of racial rearticulation that sought to elevate the position of the race by making claims of middle-class distinction. Efforts by elite blacks to assert the dignity of the race always drew upon dominant cultural codes that carried a host of conventional ways of thinking about class and gender. And, while contesting the racist devaluation of all blacks, many middle-class black cultural products reinforced the intraracial pigmentocracy that favored light-complexioned blacks. Photographs of glamorous and beautiful black women published by the black press circulated within black communities. Although many African Americans saw the photographs of beauty queens published in black newspapers and magazines, few had anything to do with their production. Though these images were part of black culture, they did not correspond to how all black men and women defined beauty. Nonetheless, they effectively communicated something simple: black women are beautiful, too. An African American woman who was simply showcased as pretty made an effective counterclaim to caricatures of black women as humorously or monstrously ugly.

Black beauty pageants constitute a complex history, stretching back over a century in which black institutions variously ignored, addressed, incorporated, contested, or rejected white standards of beauty and white depictions of blacks. Accounts of African American beauty contests, which predated attempts to integrate all-white contests, can be found in the black press as early as the 1890s. Articles on black beauty contests report sponsorship by black newspapers, black cosmetics or hair care companies, the music industry promoting black entertainers, fraternal orders, social clubs, the NAACP, and colleges. The contests varied according to whether or not they were explicitly framed as displays of racial pride, whether they incorporated images of Africa or Europe, whether or not they promoted explicitly middle-class images of women, and whether they challenged or reinforced the African American pigmentocracy. Tracing the discursive strategies employed by African American contest producers and the press that reported about the pageants they produced, I will detail some of the varied ways in which African Americans created a transcript of racial pride.

Beauty contests projected ideal images of African American women, ideals shaped by a particularly male-dominated black, middle-class worldview. Middle-class black men, as journalists and community leaders, had a greater role than women as spokespersons for the race. Middle-class black women had significant leadership roles within certain circumscribed areas, but men dominated the wider black public arena. From editorial pages and podiums they called on women to embody particular definitions of black womanhood. The record of black beauty pageants is very often a narrative of how black men as cultural agents constructed black women as cultural symbols.

In 1891, *The Appeal,* a black newspaper published in Chicago, launched a beauty contest. Announcing the contest, the newspaper asked, "Who is the Most Beautiful Afro-American Woman?," and solicited participation from its readers.[4] The contest was open to "every Colored woman in America" and was primarily a gimmick to build circulation. One married and one single woman were elected by write-in ballots available in each copy of the newspaper. Buying the election (along with copies of the newspaper) by repeatedly voting for the same candidate was encouraged. "See that your friends all get *The Appeal,* and if they do not wish to use the ballot, ask them to save it for you." The *Appeal* did not defend the beauty of African American women; it took it for granted. The newspaper's assumption of black women's beauty has to be seen in the context of contemporaneously prevalent images of black women. In 1891, the most widely available images of African Americans were generated in the viciously antiblack post-Reconstruction South. There, an ideology of "retrogression" was used to characterize emancipated African Americans. In this view, the consequence of the emancipation of slaves was that blacks had lost the civilizing influence of their slave masters. Left to their own impulses, blacks were destined for savagery. In speeches, newspaper accounts, caricatures printed as postcards and illustrations, and in fiction, blacks were described as reverting to a state of barbarism. The black man was "a fiend, a wild beast, seeking whom he may devour," according to South Carolina senator Benjamin Tillman.[5] Northern white newspapers echoed the white South's slander. Writing about the black women of St. Helena Island, South Carolina, where former slaves lived in relative isolation from whites and successfully maintained African customs, a *New York Sun* reporter claimed: "Almost without exception the women of these islands who have Negro blood in their veins, are prostitutes. It is a hopeless task to endeavor to elevate a people whose women are strumpets."[6] Publications produced by whites were saturated with the message that black men were beasts and black women were whores. The *Appeal*'s assumption that its entirely African American readership would be eager to honor the beauty of the women in their lives attests to the ability of African Americans to maintain a sense of their own worthiness. Despite the pervasiveness of gruesome white representations of blacks, the *Appeal* was so confident of black self-love that they sponsored a beauty contest to increase the paper's circulation.

From the 1890s to the early decades of the twentieth century, reader participation beauty contests were extremely popular, circulation-boosting features for newspapers throughout the country.[7] Photography studios and the Eastman company's new portable "Kodak" camera made it possible for members of the middle class to capture their own images in photographs. Newspapers took advantage of the widespread availability of snapshots by encouraging female readers to send in their photographs and be acclaimed as beauties. In 1914, the *New York Age*, one of the most prominent black newspapers in the country, joined the trend and infused their contest with a decided element of racial pride. They publicized the beginning of the contest with the declaration that "the most beautiful women in the world are those of the Negro race!" Unlike the earlier popularity contest sponsored by the *Appeal*, the *Age*'s "Chosen Fifteen Most Beautiful Negro Women in the United States" would be selected from photographs mailed in by the readers by a panel of twelve "disinterested and capable" judges. The two-column lead article closed by stressing the importance of the pageant: "The *New York Age* and the National Exhibition and Amusement Company are hoping that the contest will substantiate and prove beyond the slightest possibility of doubt that Negro women are the most beautiful women in the world."[8]

Week after week, from July through October, the *Age* built enthusiasm for the contest by reprinting photographs mailed in from places as varied as Pine Bluff, Arkansas, and Passaic, New Jersey. These pictures graced stories flagged with six and seven echoing headlines:

> Expressions of Approval and Commendation of Idea of Selecting Most Beautiful Woman of Race Are Received Daily
>
> "MOST IDEAL CONCEPTION"
>
> Correspondent Says Contest Is Most Ideal Conception Ever Inaugurated and That We Should Be Proud of Our Beautiful Women
>
> "I think that this Beauty Contest conducted by *The Age* is one of the most ideal conceptions ever inaugurated. It is all right. We should be proud of our beautiful women."[9]

In contrast to earlier contests that were produced by and for African Americans, the *Age* began to describe its pageant as if it were an event that could influence whites. They promoted the contest as an intervention in the process of collective definition: "The management of the Autumn Amusement and Advertising Festival, in connection with which the Beauty Contest is being conducted, furnish the information that they are being deluged with requests for information concerning the contest and there is every reason to believe that the eyes of the world will be opened as to the development of comely Negro women."[10] Coming from the contest's sponsors, the report of global interest in the contest was a mixture of optimism and self-promotion. Nonetheless, it reflects the aspirations of the editors and perhaps of their readers as well. The theme was repeated in the next week's beauty contest feature: "To show the world at large the development of physical and spiritual comeliness is an undertaking of considerable magnitude, but the results to be attained make the effort well worth while. It will counter-act the world's conception of the American Negro woman based on the caricatures and exaggerations published in the comic weeklies."[11]

The editors linked physical and spiritual comeliness, both of which were expected to be unmistakably evident in facial portraits. Beauty historically has been interpreted as a manifestation of inner moral qualities, and the belief in outer beauty as an expression of inner worth was particularly strong at the turn of the century.[12] In that context, demonstrating the beauty of the race was tantamount to establishing the inner worth of the race.

The *Appeal*'s 1891 contest did not explicitly present itself as a defense of the race. By contrast, the competition sponsored by the *New York Age* was promoted as a way to fight debased images of black women. Defending the race and defining the race go hand in hand. In the third week of the *Age*'s contest, Demond Lewis, one of the paper's readers, submitted a letter that was published on the front page.[13] Lewis suggested that the contest was an opportunity to establish an "ideal type of Negro beauty." In the ensuing weeks of the contest, the newspaper's coverage shifted from merely attesting to the beauty of the race to the establishment of an ideal representative who was not to be the most typical African American woman but her finest expression.

After publishing Lewis's letter, the *Age* featured a new caption under its weekly photographs of beauties that read: "Various types from which the Ideal American-Negro Beauty may be evolved." Prior to the publication of the letter written by Lewis, the *Age* used only the word "Negro" to describe the beauties sought. After his letter, the new captions under the pictures of contestants read "American-Negro." The letter Lewis submitted to steer the contest in the direction of finding an ideal type suggested what that type might be. The ideal Negro woman was of the "Egyptian" type, with a touch of the "Spirit of the New World." She would have

> a well balanced and symmetrical head, full slender neck, the features clear cut, with the appearance of being chiseled rather than cast; the

forehead broad and slightly expansive, a fine Negro nose with a trace of the Egyptian and a slight aquiline curve; the mouth fairly small but well proportioned and a slightly pointed, round, firm chin; the eyes should be large but slightly elongated; surmounted by a fine brow that is not too sharp, delicately arched, and last but not least, with the marvelously fine curving eyelash of which the Negro race can be justly proud.

This "Egyptian" touched by the New World was a woman of mixed racial heritage. Her mouth was small, her features chiseled. Hair texture and skin color, two features that were often the focus of black racial shame, went unmentioned, yet the six contestants showcased in that edition of the newspaper were light complexioned with long hair. In 1914, the desirability of lighter skin and longer hair was so firmly established among middle-class African Americans that it went without saying. The editors of the *New York Age* unproblematically accepted blacks of mixed racial heritage as representative of the race. The *Age*'s switch to the phrase "American-Negro" in its contest features, after Lewis's letter was published, suggests that the mulatto was the ideal representative they sought.

Lewis's description of the ideal American-Negro woman as a descendant of Egypt reflects an American, turn-of-the-century fascination with Egypt combined with what historian Wilson Moses describes as the nineteenth-century black leadership's attachment to the idea of "civilization."[14] Egypt stood for a civilized, distant, royal, and light-complexioned Africa. By supplanting the West African origins of most African Americans with Egypt, Lewis Africanized his preference for light skin. His conception of the ideal Negro woman was compatible with the dominant discourse of beauty, which had long included a place for mysterious exotic beauties.[15] In dominant culture, the beautiful exotic woman was Oriental, and in 1914, the Orient extended in the western mind from Asia through Egypt. In the popular imagination, Cleopatra was the Egyptian woman. Difference could be beautiful if it was embodied in the form of a fascinating exotic woman. By having Egypt represent the African in the American-Negro, the *Age* was responding directly to racist descriptions of American blacks as barbarians. Egypt evoked images of grand civilizations of great wealth. In the popular imagination, the remainder of Africa was merely the jungle home of backward people. Guided by the popular social mapping of the continent of Africa, the *Age* claimed Egyptian ancestry for its ideal Negro woman.

Burlesque houses and carnival beauty pageants alike relied on the appeal of pretty women to draw crowds. Beauty contests have always existed on a thin line between soft pornography and family entertainment. Contest producers have attempted to distinguish themselves from more tawdry entertainment by promoting beauty instead of sex, linking beauty itself to inner worth and to refinement, making appeals to national or racial pride, and surrounding contests in pageantry. The *Age* incorporated several of these strategies, fusing commercial interests, middle-class aspirations, and racial pride into a seamless whole. In the rhetoric of the *Age*'s contest, displays of refinement and wealth that the newspaper considered "culture" were evidence of the greatness of the race: "[An] effort [is] being made to let the world see the type of cultured and beautiful women developed in the race which has had to struggle for advancement and elevation under a handicap suffered by no other race in modern history."[16] Refinement, extravagance, and racial pride came together in the middle-class image it sought to promote. After months of build-up through the newspaper's pages, the *Age* encouraged its readers to attend the exhibition that would culminate with the selection of the "Chosen Fifteen" beauties. Readers were promised that it would be "without doubt the most pretentious venture ever promoted for the Negroes of New York."[17]

On a Friday night in October 1914 at the Manhattan Casino, the judges announced the "Chosen Fifteen" and presented local winners with solid gold "One of the Chosen Fifteen" pins. Photographs of the winners were displayed in the casino and reproduced on the front page of the *Age*. The winners were all, not surprisingly, light-skinned women. The accompanying article described the winner's jeweled prizes in detail and thanked the dedicated and "disinterested" judges for their efforts, which had produced a selection that was "universally conceded to be beyond criticism."[18]

That, however, was not the last word on the "ideal type" of the American-Negro woman. Isaac Fisher wrote a letter criticizing the contest's outcome for publication in the *Negro Farmer*, a newspaper he edited at Booker T. Washington's Tuskegee Institute. The *Age* published a copy of his letter in its section of out-of-town news.[19] Fisher questioned the selection of mixed-race women as the ideal representatives of the race: "Here was one with the winsome, dainty grace of the frozen North countries—light hair and blue eyes. She had to be considered. American caste said: 'She belongs to the Negroes.'" He was not willing to accept as ideal representatives women who represented so few black women. Presaging the cultural nationalists of the 1960s, he implored artists to

> select some definite race type or types—types that retain the features
> of the race in softened, chastened, refined outlines. And these types
> we are going to print often in our newspapers, use on our calendars,
> put on our Christmas cards, hang on the walls of our daughters'
> rooms, place in the students' rooms in colleges, hang on the walls of
> our churches until a little colored girl, just becoming conscious of her
> youthful beauty, will go and stand before a picture of a beautiful girl
> type of her own race and decide to be like her.

The *Age*, a New York newspaper published by relatively privileged African Americans, testified to the glory of the race by flaunting middle-class achievement and promoting light-skinned women. Their "disinterested and competent" contest judges reinforced an image in which class and color were unproblematically fused under the rubric of a "cultured representative" of the race. Even the preference for racially-mixed women was incorporated into a discourse of racial pride by representing the African roots of American blacks as Egyptian. Writing in the *Negro Farmer*, Fisher represented another voice, one that questioned the privileging of mixed-race blacks but that nonetheless validated an atypically middle-class vision of African Americans. Few African Americans attended college or sent printed greeting cards in 1914. But Fisher separated class from color and urged African Americans who had access to the means of cultural production to do the same. Both Fisher and the editors of the *Age* sought to defeat racist caricatures of blacks. Neither perspective had an audience outside of African American communities for a long time to come. Less than a year after the contest, D. W. Griffith's spectacular *Birth of a Nation* used blackfaced white actors to portray dreadful stereotypes of black men and women. President Woodrow Wilson was so captivated by the thoroughly racist extravaganza that he said, "It's like writing history with lightning!" African Americans in northern cities responded to the film with picket lines and editorial condemnation, demonstrating that the self-respect reflected in the ignored transcript of racial pride was ready to be mobilized when provoked.[20]

African Americans successfully built autonomous institutions that were Afrocentric in the sense that they did not address whites. At times, some black publications did not even acknowledge the presence of a dominant white world. A May 2, 1925, item in the black-owned *Chicago Defender* did not mention race in its description of a black beauty contest in Baltimore, calling it "the first contest held in that city."[21] In the same year, the *Chicago Defender* sponsored its own beauty competition, the contest for the "Prettiest Girl."[22] The absence of named race was a reportorial style used by some writers in the *Chicago Defender* and other black newspapers. As black writers writing for black readers inhabiting a black social world, there was no need for the racial qualifiers used by white authors to distinguish the nonwhite other. Often, however, as in the *Age*'s "Chosen Fifteen" contest, the rhetoric and staging of black beauty contests were explicitly racial. In some cases, the rhetoric grew out of a deliberate effort to demonstrate the falsehood of white depictions of the black race. In other instances, producers framed their contests in the rhetoric of racial pride in order to lend greater dignity and significance to a commercial venture. Even white owners of businesses that marketed to blacks could use black racial solidarity to sell.

Historian Kathy Peiss has shown how the white, male owners of the Golden Brown Chemical Company, producers of a line of cosmetics for black women, effectively created a false black identity for their firm. In 1925, the company sponsored the National Golden Brown Beauty Contest, which promoted Negro racial pride and, simultaneously, themselves as a "Negro" business.[23] The owners of the company masked their identity behind the fictional Madame Mamie Hightower, whose rags-to-riches biography echoed that of the real black cosmetics entrepreneur, Madam C. J. Walker. The Golden Brown competition combined a vote-buying popularity contest with a final selection by a panel of experts. Blank ballots came in bundles of fifty or one hundred with the purchase of varying sizes of Golden Brown cosmetics. The National Golden Brown Beauty Contest, which attracted more than one thousand mail-in entrants, is an early example of the manipulation of racial identity as a commodity. When the light-skinned Josephine Leggett, "striking artiste and star of the Shuffle Along Company," won the title by polling more than 300,000 votes, her achievement was extensively covered by the black press.[24] Promotional material for the competition hailed it as the first annual national Golden Brown contest. The first seems to have been the last.

National black contests were not seen again for decades, but local black beauty contests remained popular and continued to be venues for celebrating and thus defining black beauty. Throughout the 1920s, fraternal groups such as the Knights of Pythias sponsored pageants, northern black enclaves of Louisiana migrants crowned queens at Mardi Gras balls, and black newspapers continued to boost their sales by combining themes of racial pride with photographs of beauties (see figure 3.1). "Ladies, Girls Rescued at Last by Alluring Offer," proclaimed the *Oakland (Calif.) Western American* in 1927.[25] The paper purported to "save" the colored women of California by giving them the chance to be beauties in its Miss Golden State beauty and popularity contest. Each year, "seventy-five girls are chosen and sped to Atlantic City for the title of Miss America. Girls from hill and dale are entered . . . but what about the poor colored girl?" The editors asserted that the Miss Golden State contest would undo the annual insult of the exclusively white Miss America Pageant by creating an alternative for colored women.

Noting the proliferation of beauty contests in which "only the pecuniary returns are cared for," the *Western American* insisted that it had different goals. Its contest was "an exaltation of the womanhood of our group." Although they used the noble rhetoric of racial pride to generate interest in the competition, the contest was built atop a financial scheme. At a dance at the contest's end judges would select the winner of the beauty component of the contest. The winner of the popularity contest would be the young lady who could get her supporters to buy the greatest number of votes. Two dollars and fifty cents bought three hundred votes and a year's subscription to the *Western American*; nine dollars procured nine hundred votes and a four-year subscription.

Week after week, the newspaper featured a changing array of photographic

Figure 3.1. Amelia Ramey, "Mardi Gras Queen,"
Oakland, California, circa 1920s. Courtesy Oakland
History Room, Oakland Public Library.

portraits of the contestants along with their mounting tallies of votes. As a popularity competition, the contest recorded popular tastes and consequently showcased a spectrum of skin tones. The paper encouraged this visual challenge to the pigmentocracy in its promotional material: " 'Do you allow brown skin women to enter the contest?' inquired one attractive Miss. . . . The *Western American* . . . want[s] the women and girls of California to know that they stand solid against any form of racial bigotry and welcome all of our race regardless of color or complexion."[26] Text that accompanied the photographs highlighted the differences in skin color of the racial "types" who competed in the contest. The 1920s had been a decade in which the somewhat submerged conflicts about skin color within black communities were brought to the fore by "Back to Africa" movement leader Marcus Garvey, which may explain why the *Western American* questioned the pigmentocracy that had been silently reinforced by the producers of earlier contests. The editors played with the issue of pigment, at one point bemoaning the bleaching of the race yet at another writing effusively about the good looks of a society Creole. In the end, the pale-skinned Mrs. Richard York won the popularity contest by having her supporters buy the largest number of subscriptions.[27] The judges awarded the somewhat darker but still light-brown Marilyn Adams the beauty prize based on a formula that avoided the thorny issue of color: 40 percent posture, 25 percent gait, 15 percent facial expression, 10 percent personality, and 10 percent public opinion.

It has become commonplace to observe that until the ascendancy of the black consciousness movement in the late 1960s winners of African American beauty contests were light-skinned women. However, Isaac Fisher's 1914 letter of complaint regarding the light complexions of the *New York Age*'s "Chosen Fifteen" and the popularity of brown-skinned Miss Golden State contestants indicate that the prizing of light skin within black beauty contests was questioned long before the 1960s. African American critiques of their own community's preference for lighter-skinned women formed a steady counterhegemonic part of the complex picture of African American social rankings. These alternative valuations, usually muted by the dominant belief in the superiority of light skin, occasionally rang out. On those occasions, the diversity of African American views and the popular rejection of the pigmentocracy could be clearly heard.

One of these moments came in 1947, in Harlem's Golden Gate Ballroom. At the time Harlem was full of World War II veterans who were impatient with American racism after having fought to defend American freedom. In an upset to the pigmentocracy, a dark-complexioned woman was crowned as a beauty queen after a Harlem audience rose up in protest at a black beauty contest. Buddy Johnson, leader of the band that made the tune "Miss Fine Brown Frame" a hit, presided over Harlem's Miss Fine Brown Frame contest. Johnson and a panel of judges bypassed Evelyn Sanders, a curvaceous dark-complexioned woman who was the audience's favorite, to award the title to a light-complexioned woman.[28] As was reported in the May 1947 issue of *Ebony*, "The audience would have none of it, however, and articulately let Maestro Johnson and his judging board know that, for once, white standards of beauty would not be forced upon them." The judges attempted to quiet the audience by splitting the Miss Fine Brown Frame title from the contest's $300 prize by offering the title to the light-skinned contestant and the cash to Evelyn Sanders. The attempt to bribe the crowd's favorite while bestowing the honor of the title on the judges' light-skinned choice only further antagonized the spectators. When the judges saw fists waving in the audience, they capitulated and named Sanders Miss Fine Brown Frame.

In words and in pictures, *Ebony* reported the upset to the pigmentocracy in a manner that ultimately reinstated the African American class/color hierarchy. Sanders was described as the darkest among a decade of Harlem beauty queens and the most "exotic," a pairing of black skin tone with brazen sexuality that parallels the dominant white culture's association of purity with white women and uncontrolled sensuality with black. Evelyn Sanders was a high school graduate who seemed to be between jobs, an "ex-beautician" who aspired to be a model. She also wished to study dance with Katherine Dunham. She was defined by desire rather than by accomplishment. *Ebony* described her as a natural woman of the people who sewed her own daring bikini, loved to eat, and eschewed exercise and cosmetics. Sanders won on the basis of her body, a judgment graphically reinforced by *Ebony*. The lead photograph of the story was peculiarly cropped: The queen had no head. What readers saw was her fine brown frame labeled with boxes attached by pointers to the tip of one breast, her belly button, buttocks, and thigh reading 35", 23", 38", and 23".

Compare the way Sanders was portrayed to the images of women in the early black beauty contests. Those entrants were known by their faces, which were scrutinized by the judges for qualities of physical and spiritual beauty. When Demond Lewis described his detailed vision of the ideal Negro woman, he described a face. The value of having the right kind of face is evident in an advertisement found in the middle of *Ebony's* Fine Brown Frame story. The advertisement, which is for a skin bleaching cream, showed a woman's face but not her body. It was the face of a light-complexioned bride being kissed. Beauty Star Skin Whitener promised "thrilling new hope for lighter, brighter skin. . . . Here's your chance for a complexion that invites and holds romance."[29] The advertisement promised marriage, the right kind of love, for women who could achieve the right, light kind of face.

In the photograph that cropped off Sanders's head, she was a body only. According to *Ebony*, Sanders won on the basis of her sassy walk; her home-stitched, revealing bikini; and the raw sexiness of her natural body—she neither dieted nor exercised. Hers was a very different queendom than that ruled by "cultured" representatives of the race. *Ebony* reported this popular challenge to the pigmentocracy in a way that reinforced the association of dark skin with sex, light skin with goodness; dark skin with shameless sensuality, light with cultivation.

Though middle-class institutions like *Ebony* continued to uphold the pigmentocracy, by the late 1940s there was wide popular support for diverse images of beauty among African Americans. The crowd in the Golden Gate Ballroom showed their enthusiastic appreciation of a dark-skinned woman and revealed the heterogeneity of African American social rankings. In interviews with African American women who came of age in the 1950s and 1960s, I was told of many women who did not meet hegemonic beauty standards but who were considered beautiful by men and women in their communities. The upset at the 1947 Miss Fine Brown Frame contest indicates that by that year the connection between skin tone and beauty was no longer as tightly linked as it had been in 1914, when the *New York Age* speculated about an ideal type of black woman. The insurrection in the Golden Gate Ballroom differed from Isaac Fisher's 1914 letter of protest in yet another way. Not only did the audience refuse to allow the crowning of a light-skinned woman, but they also showed no respect for middle-class comportment. They had no desire to prove to the world that they were "cultured."

The controversy surrounding the Miss Fine Brown Frame contest was unusual. African American beauty contests, as described in the black press, continued to be conventional institutions that upheld middle-class propriety. *Our World* was a short-lived, New York–based magazine that attempted to compete with the Chicago-based *Ebony*.[30] In 1950, *Our World* launched the "Most Beautiful Negro Woman" contest. In most respects, this contest employed conventions and rhetoric that had been used in African American beauty contests since The *Appeal*'s 1891 search for the most beautiful Afro-American woman. *Our World* declared that the time had finally arrived for Negro beauties: "For centuries women of color have made their mark on history. Beautiful Candace, Queen of Ethiopia; sensuous Cleopatra; Josephine, the creole belle who roped the man who conquered Europe—Napoleon. Negro women here have never received the recognition they deserve for their beauty. . . . *Our World* is convinced that now is the time to glorify the Negro woman and make her proud of her unusual beauty."[31] One of the techniques beauty contests use to transform common-born women parading in rented halls into ersatz royalty is to evoke distant glamour. In *Our World*'s contest, racial pride was made compatible with glamorous Europe. The "Most Beautiful Negro Woman" would receive a "$1,000 wardrobe and a gown fashioned by one of Paris' greatest dress designers" along with a "trip to Paris, the Riviera, Rome and London." The only references to Africa were to Ethiopia and Egypt of long ago.

Like the organizers of the *Age's* 1914 contest, *Our World* named Cleopatra as the ancestor of modern Negro beauties. Yet times had changed since the *Age* sought to define a singular ideal type of American-Negro beauty. By 1950, even the middle-class black press accepted that there were multiple ways to define Negro beauty and that the beauty standard included a spectrum of skin shades. Writing about the development of the facial cosmetics industry, historian Kathy Peiss argues that the industry has "taken discourses of class, ethnicity, race and gender—discourses that generate deeply held conscious and unconscious feelings of fear, anxiety, and even self-hatred—and displaced them onto safe rhetorical fields, in this case a language of color and type."[32] In black beauty contests, color was potentially a huge issue. Many black pageants avoided public contestation of the issue by limiting participation to light-skinned women. When, after the Second World War, middle-class arbiters of Negro beauty began to acknowledge a broader definition of beauty by including an occasional dark-skinned woman among the larger group of light-skinned women, they made discursive room for her with the innocuous language of type.

Unlike the *Age*, which in 1914 sought to define one ideal type, *Our World* appeared to be more inclusive. They launched the contest with an article on the varieties of Negro beauty, illustrated by ten "types." "It's time to glorify the Negro woman. . . . The truth is Negro beauty has no pat definition. We refuse to accept it on the basis of a Roman nose, a Grecian Neck, or an olive skin." In the following captions, *Our World* employed an inclusive rhetoric of pride in all of the race's varieties to describe photographic portraits of ten "types" of Negro beauties:

> Barbara Trevigne, the light-skinned exotic type, obviously had Caucasian background.
> Lena Horne is the olive tan sophisticated type.
> Mary Smith, New York model, is the fair-to-white sexy type. Stacked in the right places, Mary is the kind that attracts many wolf-calls. She's often mistaken for white. Has no trouble passing.
> Mildred Smith is the light brown sparkling type.
> Edith Chandler is the sweet nut brown type.
> Carmen de Lavallade is the graceful creole type.
> Ann Lamb is the dark seductive type. Ann has that dreamy eyed quality, flawless complexion and a body to fit.
> Valencia Butler is the light fragile type.
> Jane White, daughter of NAACP secretary Walter White, is the light entertaining type.[33]

Our World's beauty typology is evidence of a black beauty standard, held by middle-class African Americans, that had become more inclusive than the "ideal type" described in the *New York Age* in 1914. Still, light-skinned women were disproportionately represented. Only two of the ten types had brown skin and only one of those two had a dark complexion. Complexions were stereotypically paired with personality traits. The typology's wording, such as "olive tan sophisticated type," implied that personality traits flowed naturally from complexions, a dangerous discursive strategy given the ways in which racist ideologies have relied on forging links between skin color and social rankings. Under closer examination, *Our World's* typology, when applied to light-skinned women, has little coherence. Light women are described as fragile types, sexy types, exotic types, and entertaining types. However, the position of the lone dark woman is disturbingly familiar. She is the dark, seductive type who has a flawless body, a description that harkens back to the depiction of the earlier dark-skinned queen—Miss Fine Brown Frame.

Black beauty queens of the 1950s and early 1960s shared the pages of black newspapers with coverage of the emergence of the Civil Rights Movement. Miss Negro Press Photographer's Ball, Miss Bronze California, and its offshoot, Miss Bronze Northern California developed into stable annual events (see figures 3.2, 3.3, and 3.4). Miss Negro Press Photographer's Ball began in the mid-1940s, Miss Bronze California in the 1960s. Both contests were slow to respond to political currents. Lee Gilliam, a hairstylist who groomed the participants in the Miss Bronze California contest, recalled that in the years of his involvement, between 1966 and 1974, all but two of the winners had light skin.[34] By the 1950s, the crowning of yet another light-skinned beauty queen no longer appeared to contest organizers, the press, or a wider audience as an event that defended the glory of Negro women. Discussion of the issue of skin color, even in the attenuated language of type, disappeared from reports of beauty contests. If controversies arose in the contests, they did not capture the interest of the black press. For almost twenty years after the 1947 Miss Fine Brown Frame revolt, neither *Ebony* nor *Jet*, the two most popular black magazines, discussed skin tone in a report of a beauty contest. The attentions of black reporters were focused elsewhere. Brief announcements of beauty contest winners were overshadowed in the black press by reports of civil rights victories and of the violence faced by civil rights activists. The black press reduced its coverage of all-black contests as their attention was drawn to what they considered more newsworthy racial breakthroughs in white contests. For almost two decades, black contests were treated as pleasant but insignificant events, rendered trivial by the efforts of black beauty queens to gain entrance to white contests.

One small newspaper item about an all-black contest of the 1950s did record a significant change. In 1957, a notice in the New York–based *Africa Weekly* announced that "Miss Danlyn Lee, 24 years old, and from the Bronx, was crowned Miss Africa 1957 in New York on Marcus Garvey Day"[35] The meaning of black and of Africa had so shifted that an American woman from the

Figure 3.2. "Miss Refreshing Smile," a part of "Miss Bronze
Northern California," circa 1964. Courtesy San Francisco African
American Historical and Cultural Society Library.

Figure 3.3. Program of the 1964 Miss Bronze Northern California beauty pageant. Courtesy San Francisco African American Historical and Cultural Society Library.

Figure 3.4. Program of the 1965 Miss Bronze Northern California beauty pageant. Courtesy San Francisco African American Historical and Cultural Society Library.

Bronx could be proud to be crowned "Miss Africa." Her identification was with the continent, not just the ancient civilizations of the Nile. The 1957 Miss Africa contest was substantially ahead of its time. In the 1950s, black media attention focused on beauties challenging segregated contests. All-black contests generally represented only the complacency of the black middle class. The all-black Miss Africa contest did not fit into either the integrationist frame or into the somewhat elite black social world that sponsored most black contests. The Miss Africa contest was neither a civil rights news item nor proper material for a newspaper's society pages, and so it was ignored by most of the black press.

This chapter looked at all-black contests from the end of the nineteenth century through the late 1950s. Middle-class blacks built separate black institutions as nonconfrontational ways of displaying racial pride during an era in which legal and de facto segregation was the norm. It is possible to divide black resistance to white domination into the two strategies of separatism and integrationism, though the categories are of limited use when considered without context. From the perspective of late twentieth-century black nationalism, separatism is the more radical stance, but in the context of legal segregation, blacks who built separate institutions were often taking the path of least resistance. Assimilation through integration has been considered an abandonment of race loyalty for the sake of individual achievement, yet the first occasions of integration were always the result of collective actions taken at great risk. The Civil Rights Movement and earlier strategies of "racial uplift" were most often simultaneously assimilationist and collective. Both the separatist and the integrationist strategies sought, either directly or indirectly, to regain control over social identity, and both, I would argue, met with some success. Many black leaders pursued both strategies, helping to maintain the strength of black institutions while fighting for integration. In 1954, *Brown v. Board of Education* signaled the start of a new era in which race leaders increasingly looked outside of the boundaries of their communities for symbols of achievement. The next chapter follows the efforts black women put forth to be recognized as what the entire nation celebrated as beautiful. The black press championed their ascent until hard-won fights to end racism changed the political landscape again and the all-black contest reemerged as a vehicle for racial pride.

This brief survey of black beauty contests demonstrates the multiplicity of cultural rankings available within black communities. The contests were the products of black institutions and provide strong evidence that African Americans prized their own beauty. By their very existence, black beauty contests countered depictions of African American women as ugly and indecent. The culture that the black middle class produced, as seen in beauty contests, was never a simple replica of the dominant culture, which itself was heterogeneous. As black community institutions, beauty contests were neither fully autonomous nor fully dominated; they incorporated but altered prevailing discourses of race, gender, and class. Searches for the ideal Negro woman maintained some connection with the African origins of the race, but the allusions were almost always to a mythical version of North Africa. They frequently created symbols of black achievement by reinforcing hierarchies of class and color. Their "disinterested" black, middle-class judges found beauty according to the tastes of their class. Research shows that middle-class men favored light-skinned women in that everyday beauty contest, the marriage market, and so it is not surprising that lighter women won formal contests of beauty. However, as public spectacles, beauty contests themselves were ultimately subject to the judgment of a black public, many of whom resented the continuous succession of light-skinned beauties. The record of black beauty contests up to the 1950s cannot simply be described as a legacy of self-love or self-hate. It is a record of a struggle against white characterizations of blacks and an internal dialogue about who represented the race. The contests conveyed, altered, and reinforced standards of beauty and shifted the cultural orientation of black identity toward the allure of the ancient Nile, European glamour, American citizenship, or the entire continent of Africa. They promoted particular class orientations. Although for many years in most contests light-complexioned women won the prizes, their victories represent only a partial view of the valuation of black women in black communities. The pigmentocracy was occasionally questioned inside contests and often outside of them. The next chapter chronicles the integration of formerly white beauty contests. In these contests, race took precedence, eclipsing issues of color and class.

Chapter Four

STANDING (IN HEELS)

FOR MY PEOPLE

Instead of powerful Sojourner Truth or dignified Rosa Parks, picture winsome Clintona Jackson, who was hailed in the September 1962 *Ebony* as a "20 year old Negro beauty," winner of a traditionally all-white beauty contest, the International Freedom Festival Pageant, in Detroit. As the daughter of a doctor and engaged to a Howard University engineering student, Jackson was the ideal woman to represent the race as exquisitely middle class and perfectly assimilable. According to *Ebony,* "At fiancé's request, Tona gave up thoughts of law 'to study something I could do at home while I was raising a family [painting].'" Like many black beauty queens of the era, she represented a collective effort, having been encouraged to enter the Miss Freedom Festival by the local chapter of the NAACP. Jackson was shown in *Ebony* outfitted in heels and a one-piece, tiger-skin swimsuit, with the caption beneath reading, "Tona told intimates after winning, 'I didn't do it for myself but for my people.'"[1] With that quote, *Ebony* framed Jackson's effort to integrate a white beauty pageant as an action in the larger struggle for racial equality. Some whites associated with the contest viewed her victory in just that way. *Ebony* reported that Jackson received no congratulations from the parents of white contestants and that sponsors seemed to be withholding gifts. *Ebony*'s cover featured her grouped in a portrait with two white contestants who placed but did not win. Demurely seated with her ankles crossed, wearing a white, tea-length dress, gloves, and a sparking tiara, Jackson was proof of one battle won for the social status of the race.

Before the Second World War, very few black women attempted to enter white beauty contests. One of the earliest reports of an integrated beauty contest was the sad story of a 1924 contest abruptly canceled by its white "society" sponsors when it appeared that the contestants of favored color were going to lose. Preliminary votes indicated that a young, black Hunter College student held second place. The item was treated as front-page news in the black-owned *New York Age* and was carried beyond the New York region by the Lincoln News Service.[2]

After the abruptly terminated 1924 contest, there were no reports of integrated contests until 1938. The first "International Beauty Contest," which included "scores of pretty girls both sepia and white," was held in what the black *Pittsburgh Courier* described as a "white hotel."[3] Six years later, in 1944, at a small, predominantly white teacher's college in Pennsylvania, an African American woman was selected to reign as the Coral Princess at the midwinter formal. Her minuscule victory was celebrated in the nationally read black newspaper the *Chicago Defender*.[4] Through the end of World War II, with rare and minor exceptions, African American women were excluded from participation in beauty or popularity contests with white women.

For many African Americans, beauty contests in which white women competed were the real contests. Compared to the Miss America pageant, whose early by-laws barred black women, black contests seemed to be mere imitations. Lee Gilliam, a hairdresser who had been involved in the production of the Miss Bronze California contests, described the appeal of white contests for the black women who entered all-black contests. "They all would liked to have gone into Miss America because they felt that, Miss America offered more opportunities. I think most of your local black contests made them feel like they were second class."[5] Sheila Head, who was born in Oakland, California, recalled looking at photographs of black college campus queens in black magazines but felt that these contests did not carry the status of the Miss America contest: "I always looked at the pictures [of campus queens in *Ebony*]. Always. But it was not as glorified [as Miss America] because it wasn't on TV. And it wasn't recognized as mainstream. We knew that it was college. I could be a homecoming queen. Miss America is something different."[6] Mary O'Neal, who in her early college days at Howard University was the winner of a popularity contest, expressed the difference between desiring the recognition of winning the Miss America contest and accepting white standards of beauty. She said, "I used to cry when they sang Miss America. I wanted to experience that. I wanted to be a winner. But I didn't want to look like anybody in that pageant. I would love to have had Bert Parks sing to me."[7]

Just as African Americans organized to fight racial exclusion at lunch counters, on public transportation, and in workplaces, African American women began to challenge the color line in beauty contests. Black beauty contestants and moderate civil rights organizations viewed efforts to integrate contests as politically significant. When African American women challenged segregation in beauty contests, they rarely did so as individuals. Black women who risked entering white beauty contests usually acted with the encouragement and support of the NAACP or other black community organizations. When they won or placed, the black press treated their personal victories, no matter how small the title, as accomplishments for the race.

In 1965, Sarah Pener, a black woman, was crowned Miss Rochester, which meant that she would compete in the Miss New York State competition and be on the path to the Miss America contest. *Ebony* devoted a lengthy article to her victory, headlined "Negro Girl in Miss America Race." The magazine quoted from one of her many fan letters, which read, "Congratulations! Your people are proud of you," signed, "A black woman."[8] The beauty contest was viewed as a site for contesting racism as much as it was a contest of the beauty of individual women.

One of the first organized challenges to a formerly white beauty contest was the effort to have a black woman selected as Miss Subways, which was established in 1941. Each month the John Robert Powers modeling agency selected Miss Subways, whose picture was displayed on train cars as a diversion for New York City's subway riders. In the second year of the contest, a black social club, the All-Ears, submitted photographs of attractive black women to the Powers agency, along with a stream of letters encouraging it to open the contest to black women. They were rebuffed. Later, in 1944, a Harlem youth center selected three young black women to attempt to win a spot. They were not chosen. The Powers agency claimed that they would welcome qualified black applicants but continued to select white women. The All-Ears increased its pressure on the agency by writing to the Transportation Board and the mayor. A New York City newspaper published the following letter to the editor in 1947, urging black women to apply:

> This is not just a question of getting a Negro girl chosen as Miss Subways, or even to get started getting modeling jobs open to Negro women in agencies that discriminate at present. This can be the beginning of getting pictures of Negroes in our magazines, newspapers, subway ads, etc. in [illegible] other than that of maids, butlers, or mamies [sic].[9]

The barrier fell in 1948 when the April Miss Subways title was awarded to a young black woman who was president of the Brooklyn Youth Council of the NAACP. She not only appeared on nine thousand subway posters, but her face was also on the cover of *Crisis*, the monthly journal of the NAACP. Her achievement of "beauty" status, briefly described on the first page, opened an issue of *Crisis* that contained articles on antidiscrimination efforts in the South, the military draft, legal injustice, and discrimination in education. Her victory was not merely personal. Lester Granger, executive secretary of the Urban

League, joined her on stage at an event to celebrate her victory. The Urban League and the NAACP treated barriers to the fame and recognition accorded beauty queens as a significant realm of discrimination.

After the naming of a black Miss Subways in 1948, African American women increasingly entered and placed in formerly all-white contests. Regular reports of African American women entering and placing in local, formerly white contests in the North and of brave African American beauties who entered formerly white contests in areas of the Deep South and Midwest appeared in the black press throughout the late 1950s and early 1960s.

At the same time that civil rights organizations supported aspiring beauty queens, they exerted pressure on airlines to drop barriers against black women in another "glamour" position for women: the airline stewardess. The Urban League enlisted the support of the New York State Commission against Discrimination to force airlines to begin hiring black stewardesses.[10] Despite an agreement made in 1956 between the commission and eighteen airlines, by 1957 not one airline had hired a black woman as a flight attendant. The commission investigated the case of Dorothy Franklin, a black woman whose application for a stewardess position had been rejected by TWA.[11] The outcome of her hearing rested on the establishment of one fact: The commission had to determine whether she held what all parties agreed was a necessary requirement for the position—beauty.

The men from TWA presented their case, arguing that they had not rejected her for her race but for her "appearance." The commissioner and his staff examined the evidence (Miss Franklin) and were unanimous in their belief that "the airlines' objections to her appearance are not factually accurate and cannot be accepted as valid reasons for her rejection." The commission's chief investigator charged that "respondent's stated reason for not hiring complainant is merely a contrived excuse for the purpose of concealing respondent's true reason for her rejection, mainly her color." These men regarded beauty as a fact upon which all reasonable men could agree. They discussed race as if it had nothing to do with appearance and beauty—as if beauty had never been racialized. Before they could rationally settle this beauty contest in a courtroom, Miss Franklin dropped her case.

The first big successes for black American beauties were won in France. Black beauty contestants, like African American musicians and writers, found France a more hospitable country than the United States. In 1959, an American black woman, Cecelia Cooper, won Miss Festival at Cannes, an event widely reported on in the black press. The following year the title was again won by an African American, LaJeune Hundley.[12] Her victory was celebrated in *Ebony* as a victory for all black Americans.

In 1966, following Clintona Jackson's success at the International Freedom Festival, the NAACP began to exert pressure on the Miss America pageant. Remaining true to its law abiding approach, the NAACP did not demand that a black woman be placed in the televised Miss America pageant, which would have required circumvention of the pyramid of smaller victories required of Miss America pageant contestants. Instead, it demanded that all commercial floats in the parade that accompanied the pageant have at least one "Negro beauty."[13] The white and black press viewed the parade as a minor sideshow, and the NAACP's efforts drew little press attention.

In the following years, more and more black women entered formerly white contests. The trend was particularly common on college and university campuses where young black students began to enter and win homecoming queen contests. Reports of their victories reached a peak in 1967. In many of these contests, the winners were the first black women to hold the title, their bids had been backed by some organized collective support, and the victory was celebrated as one more triumph of the integration of blacks into formerly white institutions. At that time, any attempt at integration in any realm was considered a civil rights action, and many of the contestants were committed to the Civil Rights Movement. Black beauty queens turned up in picket lines and in jail cells. Nancy Streets, the first black Miss Indiana University, was barred at gunpoint from entering a whites-only skating rink in Bloomington. Streets pressed charges but lost the case in a jury trial.[14] *Jet* magazine described Student Nonviolent Coordinating Committee (SNCC) member Diane Nash Bevel as "a former Chicago Miss America beauty contestant who quit Fisk [University] to join the sit-in movement" noting that she had been "arrested several times for her leadership in the Nashville boycotts, South Carolina sit-ins and the Mississippi Freedom Ride."[15] A 1963 *Jet* article praised another civil rights beauty queen with the photograph caption: "Cheer-leading beauty queen once headed NAACP youth branch, helped picket Newark store into fair hiring policy."[16]

The white winners of the Miss America contest were, by contrast, famously and scrupulously apolitical. When Judith Anne Ford, Miss America 1968, was asked about police brutality at the Chicago Democratic National Convention that year, she responded, "I hate to talk about this. It's so controversial."[17] One can find instances of white beauty queens who joined radical movements, but as activists they became fallen queens. Kathy Huppe, the 1969 Miss Montana, relinquished her title and her place in the Miss America pageant when pageant officials pressured her to keep silent about her participation in protests against the Vietnam War.[18] In 1988, Michelle Anderson, a white feminist activist, entered the Miss California contest in order to disrupt it.[19] Just before the announcement of the winner, Anderson revealed herself as not a true beauty contestant but a feminist when she pulled a protest banner out of her bra. As an activist, she ceased to be a beauty queen and was stripped of the Miss Santa Cruz title that had been her entrée to participation in the Miss California contest. Black beauty queens, however, carried their titles into protest demonstrations because their titles, in the first place, were emblems of racial pride. Unlike white beauty queens who wore their crowns for themselves, black beauty queens stood for the race.

Black contestants challenged the content of the contest but not its form. On the contrary, their demands for inclusion reinforced the legitimacy of beauty contests as institutions that celebrate women. Black beauty queens were always symbols of both defiance and conventionality. When they entered beauty contests, they challenged nothing about the construction of gender except the color of beauty and femininity. These women saw the Miss America title and the contest itself as a symbol and a ritual that could be claimed by black women and used to assert the dignity of the race.

By 1968, white supremacy had not been defeated in the most prestigious national beauty contest, the Miss America pageant. The NAACP sought to draw national attention to the exclusion of black women by staging its own contest in the same city at the same time. NAACP officials hoped that the presence of an all-black contest would reveal the whiteness that had been lightly covered by the Miss America pageant's official stance of racial neutrality. Protestors from Women's Liberation came to Atlantic City that year with very different aims. They saw the contest itself as degrading to all women, including the contest's winners, losers, and viewers, who were encouraged by the spectacle to compare themselves to the unrealistic ideals of beauty glorified by the pageant. The protests organized by the NAACP and Women's Liberation collided on the pages of the nation's newspapers. On one level, their actions were quite similar. Seasoned organizers in both groups chose the attention-gathering spectacle of the Miss America pageant as a target. Political strategists working within the media-conscious environment of the late 1960s could be certain that a protest at the pageant would be news, since the Miss America title was a symbol known to every American. Women's Liberation parodied Miss America, denounced the spectacle as a ritual that reinforced male supremacy, and characterized the pageant as an inherently sexist institution that should be ridiculed out of existence. Their leaflets proclaimed, "No More Miss America!" The NAACP, however, saw the ritual as one that valorized women. In their view, the contest was historically, not inherently, racist. While Women's Liberation protested the racism of the contest as one of the specific ways it oppressed women, the NAACP sought to fight that racism by having a black woman win the crown in the name of all black women. The victory would be won for black mothers and daughters who could watch the crowning of a black woman on national television. The NAACP was not ready to dispose of a symbol that seemed within reach.

The NAACP's protest for integration took the form of a racially separate contest. They created an alternative black contest rather than attempting the slow path through the hierarchy of contests that culminated in the Miss America pageant. Miss Black America was staged as what the NAACP called a "positive protest" against the racism of the Miss America contest. In the past, the organization had fought racism by steadily mounting legal challenges to the system of racial segregation. That strategy could not work in this situation. Racist regulations were no longer part of the Miss America structure, yet the title continued to be awarded to white women.

The black movement community had changed dramatically in less than a decade, and the NAACP's cautious strategies and integrationist goals were increasingly under attack. Two years before the NAACP created Miss Black America, Stokely Carmichael had shouted the name of a new movement: "black power." Black power called for the building of black institutions and rejected what its proponents saw as the failed strategy of integration. The message of black power resonated in the hearts and minds of young African Americans. Some of those youths were at historically black colleges and could take pride in their participation in some of the oldest of America's black institutions. What could black power mean to black college students at predominantly white institutions? In those institutions, contests over symbols grew in importance. In the name of black power, black students on predominantly white campuses introduced new meaning into homecoming queen pageants. Popularity contests became opportunities for demonstrating racial solidarity. As a result, black women won homecoming contests all over the country. At Northwestern University, the University of Illinois Circle Campus, Southern Illinois University, the University of Michigan, the College of San Mateo, San Jose State University, Thiel College in Pennsylvania, and Morehead State University in Kentucky, African American women were elected homecoming queen.[20] For black student participants in the burgeoning black student movements on integrated college campuses, beauty contests offered a highly symbolic and easily organized focus for their efforts.

As these victories mounted, and became less exceptional, and as integration generally began to represent a failed liberal strategy, the attention of the black press and the organizing strategy of civil rights organizations returned to black institutions. Miss Black America continued on in subsequent years as a pageant to celebrate black women, but it was no longer presented as a vehicle of protest against the whiteness of the Miss America pageant. A black woman's entrance into a formerly white beauty contest no longer carried the same weight as an act of protest. One of the last organized challenges to segregation in beauty pageants took the form of a disruptive protest rather than a singular bid for inclusion. In Mobile, Alabama, in 1969, a local black organization pledged to completely disrupt the America Junior Miss Pageant.[21] The authorities protected the sanctity of the contest and arrested one hundred protestors.

The logic that drove the collective effort behind attempts to integrate beauty contests was twofold: first, it was an attempt to secure an opportunity that had material consequences and, second, it sought to transform the image of black women in the collective imagination of the nation. The integrationist strategy was often pursued by civil rights organizations through the attempt to have one individual or a small group succeed in gaining entry to a formerly segregated institution. Such attempts to win "firsts" were limited victories. Attempts to integrate white beauty contests epitomized the limits of such strategies. African Americans watched and cheered as lone black men and women achieved the distinction of being the first black person in a particular university, corporation, government post, or occupation. These victories accumulated, but the lives of the majority of African Americans remained the same. By winning a formerly white beauty contest, a black woman gained fleeting inclusion in a trivially elite group. Integration efforts of any sort required recruitment of brave men, women, or children to serve as test cases. When, after the application of protest, pressure, and negotiation, they succeeded, the fruits of their efforts were too frequently limited to the winning of much heralded "firsts." The black press, eager to print good news, supported the strategy by reporting every "first" won.

Ebony viewed the reporting of black achievement in any field as essential to its mission. Summarizing the magazine's goals on its tenth anniversary, the editors wrote that "by portraying through words and pictures the success stories of great Negro Americans, we have proved for our youth that their dreams, too, can come true, and that any goal in life can be achieved if we put into it enough study, work and faith."[22] Writing in 1952, before the rise of the Civil Rights Movement, the editors of *Ebony* advocated study, work, and faith. Ten years later, any black journalist would have added protest and boycott to the list of required ingredients for advance. By the mid-1960s, after a decade of protest left the majority of African Americans mired in poverty despite countless success stories of the achievements of a new black elite, enthusiasm for celebrating individual success waned. Young black activists increasingly questioned the value of the integrationist strategy altogether since it had, so often, only resulted in winning places for a privileged few.

Though their orientation shifted away from integration as a goal, black activists continued to be concerned with recasting the image of the race. In fact, this concern intensified as segments of the Black Power Movement explicitly sought to redefine the meaning of black. To this end, celebrating the beauty of black women became a trope of the Black Power Movement. Influenced by the wide acceptance of theories of black self-hatred, black activists promoted the symbol of the beautiful black women as an antidote to centuries of disparagement. The organizers of the 1966 "Miss Weusi" contest advertised it with a poster of a beautiful black woman whose hair was shaped into an Afro.[23] By 1966, knowledge of a small vocabulary of Swahili words had become common among black Americans with a newly found interest in their African roots. "Weusi," meaning black, was one of the words in circulation. The winner of Miss Weusi, a contest typical of the times, was selected at Small's Paradise, a popular Harlem nightspot. Following the trajectory of black political move-ments, the black press returned its attention to contests sponsored by black in-stitutions as the movement shifted from civil rights to black power. All-black contests gained a significance they had not held for decades. In an era of black consciousness, these contests frequently challenged not only white supremacy but also the supremacy of lighter skin. In the coverage of these contests, the buried issue of skin color returned to the pages of the black press.[24] For many years after the report of the upset in Harlem's "Miss Fine Brown Frame" con-test, when the crowd insisted on giving the crown to its dark-skinned favorite, the black press lost interest in the issue. There is no reason to believe that African Americans ceased to care about social discrimination against dark-com-plexioned members of their community. But the black press, in its focus on the race (and not the color) of black contestants entering white contests, had ig-nored the light complexions of the civil rights contestants.

In its renewed coverage of all-black pageants, the black press deemed con-tests newsworthy when they indicated the arrival of a new black aesthetic. By 1967, the closely intertwined issues of class and skin tone had surfaced as issues of open conflict within black communities. *Jet*, always representative of a broader range of African American life than its deliberately middle-class elder sibling *Ebony*, raised the issue in 1967. Chester Higgins, *Jet*'s longtime savvy wit, placed the thorny issue on the safe ground of a humor column. In his March 9, 1967, column he wrote, "At a recent Detroit modeling contest, the light skinned lovelies were really chagrined when a stacked dark hued lass, with a natural yet, walked off with first prize."[25] That same year a *Jet* reporter noted that, judging by the winners of black campus beauty contests, "the Negro col-lege student body [has] broken from the 'blue-vein' tradition."[26] And, for the first time, the desirability of long straight or straightened hair was questioned in African American contests. Before 1966, straight or straightened hair was an unquestioned requirement for all well-groomed African American women, whether they were to be considered beauties or not. By 1966, unstraightened hair had become a symbol of racial pride. To proclaim their belief in the new look, students at Howard University that year elected Robin Gregory to be the first Howard homecoming queen with a natural hairdo.

Gregory's victory was explicitly political, the result of a collective effort. Black male students who had attended a civil rights seminar conducted a poll to build support for a "natural" queen. Gregory was chosen because she com-bined the traditional middle-class lineage of a Howard University homecoming queen with a record of involvement in the Selma to Montgomery march. Gre-gory and her supporters vigorously campaigned for her title. The importance of her challenge is reflected in the unfounded rumors that circulated on campus and were reported in the *New York Amsterdam News*: "Rumors that the Dean of Students refused to place the crown on her head, that teachers on the advisory committee resigned, and that demands were made for a recount plagued the homecoming festivities."[27] The *Amsterdam News* ran the story with a visual comment on trends in Howard's beauty queens. Their portraits, printed in chronological order, demonstrated the increasing number of dark-skinned queens.

In January 1968, the Afro-American Unity Movement, an organization described by *Jet* as "militant," called for the beginning of a "Black Beauty" pageant in Atlantic City to protest the exclusion of black women from the Miss America pageant.[28] The contest they proposed never materialized, but by the summer of 1968, the NAACP successfully adopted the same tactic. The NAACP's Miss Black America contest represents the point at which the trajectories of the separatist and integrationist black movements met and became one. As a protest against discrimination, the oldest pro-integration black social protest organization sponsored an all-black pageant.

I have argued that earlier all-black pageants were institutionalized expressions of black pride. Their parades of beauty queens sought to nullify the effect of white exclusion of blacks from beauty pageants with abundant displays of beautiful black women. The early black beauty contests were parallel institutions rather than protests. Given the racial terror of lynching and white mob violence common at the time, they did not operate within an environment in which direct protest for inclusion was possible.

In 1968, the NAACP took an old form and gave it new meaning. The contest as protest had little immediate effect on the Miss America pageant. In 1970, Miss Iowa, Cheryl Browne, became the first black woman in the Miss America contest. By that year, however, even the NAACP was taking the separatist path, having established the Miss Black America contest as an annual all-black event. Browne entered the Miss America contest without black organizational support. In the apolitical Miss America tradition, Browne represented her state and not her people. She told *Newsweek* reporters, "I hope this will show the radicals in the black power movement that things aren't so bad."[29] Attention slipped away from the goal of integrating Miss America, and white women continued to be chosen as winners until 1983.

The NAACP initiated Miss Black America as a protest against racial discrimination but inadvertently developed the contest as a new black institution. The contest's origins as a vehicle of protest remained evident in the composition of its judging panel. In contrast to the beauty and talent industry representatives who usually judge beauty contests, the early Miss Black America contest judges included politician Shirley Chisholm; former chair of the Congress of Racial Equality (CORE) and advocate for independent black economic development, Floyd McKissick; Betty Shabazz, the widow of Malcolm X; nationalist author John Killens; and Clifford Alexander, the former chair of the Equal Employment Opportunity Commission. The contest was sponsored by the National Association of Colored Women, which had a long tradition of promoting racial advancement by challenging degrading portrayals of black women.[30]

Similar pageants sprang up around the country. The same year that the Miss Black America pageant was organized by the NAACP, the Miss Black Beauty Contest was organized in Harlem. Its announcement made clear the link the organizers saw between celebrating black beauties, expressing racial pride, and showing solidarity with the growing Black Power Movement. The contest was billed as "a day dedicated to the embattled students of America," and its strict rules captured the spirit of the times in their insistence that to be beautifully black was to be as natural as possible. It cautioned contestants that this was "a natural beauty contest. Hair must be in its natural state whether kinky, curly, or lanky. No lipstick, eyebrow pencil or falsies."[31] As black beauty contests reemerged as newsworthy items in the late 1960s, contest promoters were explicit about the form's use as a vehicle for racial pride.

Many of the pre–black power era, all-black contests celebrated beauties who were incidentally "colored" or "Negro." The black power contests of the late 1960s expressly celebrated black beauty. Regardless of whether the contests implicitly or explicitly celebrated black women, all of them showed that black people never universally accepted the dominant culture's disregard for black women. African Americans maintained their own social rankings, which were heterogeneous, changing, and heavily influenced by the course of black social movements.

Attempts to integrate formerly white contests were assimilative efforts, typically collective in origin, quite often organized with the backing of a civil rights organization. Gains won were frequently viewed by the contestants, the black press, and fans as gains for the image of the community. The work of the integrationists succeeded in ending segregation that had ranged from the wholesale disenfranchisement of the black population in the southern states to the legal segregation practiced in the North via discriminatory hiring practices, restrictive covenants, and redlining. As the barriers fell, the limitations of ending discrimination by achieving "firsts" became more apparent. Each victory had less meaning. Black women entered formerly white beauty contests without direct social movement organization support and could adopt the individualist discourse that the contests promoted. In 1970, Miss Iowa, speaking to reporters about being the first black woman in the Miss America contest, said, "I was judged for me and not my color."[32]

Willing or not, and even if they used a discourse of racial neutrality, black contestants assimilated into dominant beauty institutions as black women. They continued to be subject to the consequences of being minorities within white majority institutions, and race continued to be a potential base for solidarity. In 1983, when Vanessa Williams became the first black Miss America, she repeated the theme of race-free individual achievement as, time and time again, journalists asked her about the significance of her race. Though she did not ask for their support, moderate black leaders cheered her victory as one for the race.[33] Since she was positioned as a "first," some black leaders criticized the selection of the light-skinned Williams because she was not representative of the race. Though she used the individualist discourse available to and even demanded of every Miss America winner before her, she could not escape the racialization of her position. Blacks claimed her and a few whites threatened her, but more whites looked to her victory as proof that America's racial problem was solved. When dated pornographic photographs of Williams appeared in *Penthouse,* forcing her to relinquish her crown, the shock and sense of loss were collective within the black community.

In black beauty parlors, through the pages of the black press, and in the myriad institutions of African American life, black women learn what it means to be beautiful. Black institutions are key locations of black cultural production, but nowhere in the United States do young black women live in an entirely African American world. For all of the black girls and their mothers who watched white women be selected as Miss America year after year, the civil rights beauty queen victories mattered. When they saw a nationally televised African American beauty, they learned the troubling good news that they, too, could be valued for their beauty alone.

Black women who entered contests with the support of the NAACP or other black organizations followed an assimilationist strategy as part of a collective effort to fight racism. This and the previous chapter looked at beauty contests as evidence of black community appreciation of black women and as rituals that celebrated and redefined racial identity. Whether it was expressed in the form of jokes about the white man, disparaging comments about white women (known collectively in the language of black cultural rankings as "Miss Ann"), or in the pride mothers felt for their own children, men and women in black communities maintained their own sense of social esteem. They ranked their own beauties according to black community standards, standards that shifted over time. Black social rankings were neither identical to the values of the dominant culture nor entirely distinct from them. Black cultural rankings never constituted a singular, consistent worldview held by every member of the black community. Beliefs within black communities about beauty incorporated and resisted dominant standards, always included discourses of class and gender, and were renewed and rewritten by black social movements.

From their origins in the nineteenth century to the present day, African American beauty contests have reflected the ideological shifts and aspirations of racial politics. For most of that history, black beauty contests continued to disparage dark-skinned women by celebrating light-skinned women as the jewels of the race. These contests were in the tradition of constructing parallel institutions, simultaneously asserting independence from and accommodating a segregated world. The strategy of developing parallel institutions was one that brought some benefits to the black middle class, as they constructed an exclusive social world of relative comfort and distinguished themselves from their poorer brothers and sisters. With infrequent exceptions, darker-skinned women were excluded from that world. The contests that the Negro elite sponsored in the name of racial pride incorporated and promoted their rejection of the majority of the race.

The meaning of the black beauty queen shifted according to a changing racial climate, but the black woman in a beauty pageant was always in a contest for the definition of the race. Class and gender had been racialized by the dominant culture. Black beauty contests, as reported in the black press, demonstrated over and over and with much variation that African Americans did not believe that being middle class or being beautiful meant being white. They proclaimed that black women were beautiful, too. The black beauty queen was public proof of the beauty of black women. The producers of early black beauty contests and the sponsors of black beauty queens fought symbols with symbols by claiming conventional positions as their own. Until 1965, most all-black beauty contests challenged white supremacy but served to reinforce the privileged position of light-skinned women. In 1966, contests began to reflect a new aesthetic that had grown on college campuses and among civil rights activists. Chapter 5 traces the origins of that new vision of beauty.

Chapter Five

HOW BLACK BECAME POPULAR:

SOCIAL MOVEMENTS AND RACIAL

REARTICULATION

> When I was a kid coming up, if you wanted to fight you called
> a person "black." Black was not popular.
> —*An Oakland barber*

In 1952, a black woman proudly wearing "nappy" hair was unfathomable. In 1960, she was a curiosity, in 1965 a militant, and in 1968 stylish. In 1970, she might have been arrested for too closely resembling Angela Davis. By 1977, she was an anachronism.

In the 1960s, black pride, which for many years had been privately and idiosyncratically expressed, became public, visible, and performable through a shared repertoire of symbols. Beginning as a practice that had no name, the natural hairstyle developed into a defining symbol of racial pride on black college campuses and in Civil Rights Movement organizations. As television, magazines, newspapers, and posters transmitted the natural beyond these centers, it became possible for any African American to wear one and join the abstract community of proud black men and women.

The history of the natural begins with African American intellectuals, mothers, fathers, poets, and lovers who praised dark skin, tightly curled hair, and full lips long before 1960.[1] In 1914 black intellectual and political leader W. E. B. Du Bois wrote to his daughter, bracing her for the insults he feared she would encounter at school in England: "You will meet curious little annoyances. People will wonder at your dear brown and the sweet crinkley hair. You must know that brown is as pretty as white or prettier and crinkley hair as straight even though it is harder to comb."[2]

Du Bois himself was denounced for color prejudice by his contemporary Marcus Garvey, who charged that Du Bois aspired to maintain privileged positions for blacks who had white ancestry.[3] Garvey called upon black men and women to reject interracial unions in order to restore the race's purity. Odes to "Negritude" written during the Harlem Renaissance echoed Garvey's praise of the pure African type.[4] The refrain could be heard decades later in an April 1954 *Ebony* article, "African Beauties," which told readers that "black skin instead of white sets [the] standard of what is beauty on continent where darker shades predominate in pulchritude."[5] Noting that some African women straightened their hair, the authors included a full-page portrait of a South African young woman with unstraightened hair worn gathered above her head with a string of pearls.

At least ten years before "black is beautiful" emerged as a rallying cry in the late 1960s, the message that dark skin and tightly curled hair were beautiful was promoted by the Nation of Islam. Established in the 1930s in Detroit as an Islamic movement for black Americans, the Nation of Islam grew steadily under Elijah Muhammad's leadership after 1945.[6] Through newspaper columns published in the black press, radio shows, streetcorner orators, and Nation of Islam publications, Elijah Muhammad urged African Americans to reject the white man's standard of beauty. In 1957, the Black Muslims devoted a chapter of one of their standard texts to "Kinky Hair."[7] Many African Americans would not renounce Christianity for the Nation of Islam's theology but were inspired by its message of racial pride.

In 1958, in a column printed in the widely read black newspaper the *Pittsburgh Courier*, Nat B. Williams satirically proposed the formation of the "American Society for the Protection and Preservation of Cullud Folks' Hair." He urged readers to see straightened hair as a mark of racial shame: "What's being done about cullud women's hair goes all the way to the roots. . . . If Negro women are so convinced that they ought to look like 'something else' until they spend millions of dollars a week . . . then somebody ought to spread the word to abolish Negro History Week."[8]

Before 1960, a very small number of African American women put the critique of straightened hair into practice by wearing unstraightened hair. Black professional dancers, who could not avoid working up a sweat in performance or rehearsal and thus had a hard time keeping their straightened hair straight, were among the first to adopt unstraightened styles. Ruth Beckford, a modern dancer who had performed with Katherine Dunham, pioneered a short unstraightened style in 1952 in Oakland, California.[9] Beckford explained how practicality led her to stop straightening her hair and to have it cut short so that her tight curls would form a neat frame around her face: "I'd get my hair done then I'd go to dance class and sweat it out. And I said, there must be a better way. So I got it cut. I said [to the barber], 'Just give me the natural shape.' And he said, 'But you can't.' And I said, 'Do it.' People would stop and say, 'I can tell you who to go to help your hair to grow.' [Laugh.] I'd say, 'I don't want it to grow! I wish it wouldn't grow, then I wouldn't have to go get it cut.' "[10] The practical difficulty of maintaining straightened hair was what encouraged some black dancers to abandon the routine of continual hair pressing. As performers, dancers may have been able to ignore social conventions more easily than black women outside of the art world. Nonetheless, in the 1950s, each unstraightened hairstyle represented the brave choice of an independent woman.

In the 1950s, a black woman's straightened hair expressed conformity with African American community standards and as such was a dignified form of self-presentation. Unstraightened hair on a black woman who had the means to straighten it most probably would have been viewed by other black women as eccentricity at best, bad grooming at worst. In the 1960s, blacks began investing unstraightened hair with new meanings that developed in concert with a rejection of the deferential behavior that had been a social requirement for blacks who lived in the Jim Crow South. Gloria Jackson was born in 1950 in Mississippi, where, too often, blacks who violated the South's racial code of behavior paid with their lives. By the time she was a teenager, the Civil Rights Movement had won some measure of success in exposing and diminishing the reign of white terror in the South. Having grown up in the generation that would dismantle Mississippi's apartheid, she recalled her early awareness that she would not imitate her parent's deference to whites: "I don't know why I had these feelings growing up or what made me have this kind of feeling that something's wrong here. It bothered me greatly that my father would say 'yes, ma'am' and 'no, ma'am' to these people who were younger than he. I knew it wasn't right. My father said, 'You do certain things just to get along. It's not necessarily what you might want to do but you do these things because it may get you what you want or where you want to go.' "[11]

CENTERS OF CULTURAL PRODUCTION

The generation of young black men and women who came of age in the 1960s witnessed, and sometimes participated in, the rise of a social movement that met terror with courage, won the long overdue rights of citizenship for southern blacks, and allowed black youths the youthful privilege of being and looking defiant. This sense of defiance was both a youthful rejection of the values of their elders and a critical response to a somewhat weakened structure of racism. That generation was in its childhood when Ruth Beckford, wearing short, unstraightened hair, endured curious stares in Oakland. As girls of that generation grew into women, they would make choices in substantial numbers that women like Ruth Beckford had made nearly alone. Hair in its kinky, untamed state, whose coils had not been pressed into straight submission and whose texture was distinctively African, was readily transformed into a symbol of both pride and defiance.

One impetus for the transformation in the way young blacks saw themselves was the emergence of independent black nations throughout Africa. Jean Wiley, a black woman raised in Baltimore, recalled the experience of watching new African heads of state, like Ghanaian leader Kwame Nkrumah, appear on television: "You knew about Nkrumah because you'd watched him with your mom as he ascended the podium and heard your mom say, 'He is fantastic!' She'd never seen anybody like that. A head of a country, looking like her!"[12] Race, not gender, is salient in her comment. Nkrumah looked like her because they were both black. The impressions made by the decolonization of Africa and the strengthening Civil Rights Movement were particularly forceful at African American colleges and universities, which became centers of production of new cultural codes and practices that embodied the new spirit. Howard University was one center at which an African American culture of defiance took shape. A group of students who met there in the early 1960s proved to be exceptionally influential.

When he arrived at Howard in 1962, Cleveland Sellers recalled feeling disappointed by his fellow students, who seemed so obsessed with preserving the "Howard image" that they had no interest in joining the Civil Rights Movement.[13] Most of Howard's students were well groomed and tastefully dressed, and they maintained a decorum that they hoped would distinguish them as members of the next generation of African American elite. Black fraternities and sororities dominated campus social life. These organizations were examples of what Pierre Bourdieu calls "structuring structures," key institutions for reproducing the tastes, strategies, and dispositions that comprised the conventional bearing of the Negro middle class. Sellers described his first impressions of the campus where conformist students seemed to dominate: "When I was [at Howard] young ladies wore skirts and stockings and heels. And the young men wore slacks and shirts and ties. I thought that I was going to Howard University because it was going to be the hotbed of civil rights activities. When I got there it was the reverse."[14] Sellers soon learned that there were others at Howard and they rejected the conventional social life and conservative standards of the fraternities and sororities and were committed to ending racism. H. Rap Brown, Stokely Carmichael, Charlie Cobb, Bill Mahoney, Muriel Tillinghast, Jean Smith, Cynthia Washington, and Jean Wheeler were all members of the Nonviolent Action Group (NAG), an organization formed at Howard, and they would go on to become key participants in SNCC.[15] Sellers recalled how some of the NAG members flaunted their disregard for the "Howard image" by reappropriating a symbol of black debasement, the watermelon: "In the middle of the day, when all the students would come out and all the Greek letter organizations would be out there, we'd go down by the Fine Arts Building, and we'd get a watermelon and split it and start eating it. People would actually start down the walkway until they saw that watermelon and they'd stop and turn. They'd be, 'Oh my goodness. Right here on this campus! What if some whites came by and saw this?' "[16]

Mary Lovelace O'Neal may have been the first woman to wear a natural at Howard University, adopting one in 1961. O'Neal, who was considered a very attractive woman, arrived at Howard in 1960 with a chic wardrobe and was, from the beginning, popular. Soon after arriving on campus, she was elected to the "Kappa Court" in a popularity contest sponsored by a fraternity. Her inclusion in the Kappa Court signaled change even among the ranks of the conservative fraternities because all previous court members had been women with lighter skin.

O'Neal could have continued to rise within the Howard University social scene. She had heard rumors that she was a potential candidate to become the next Kappa Queen. However, two important changes took place that set her on a different path. She became a serious artist, spending the money that had previously gone into her wardrobe on oil paints and other art supplies. At the same time, she began to participate in civil rights demonstrations organized by NAG and ultimately landed in jail. O'Neal became friends with fellow NAG member Stokely Carmichael, who encouraged her to cut her hair, stop straightening it, and wear it like the South African singer Miriam Makeba: "I started wearing my hair natural because somebody said, 'You look really beautiful like this.' And it was more acceptable to me. Before that no one had said, 'You are a beautiful woman and you don't have to do all this.'"

Like many black women involved in the Civil Rights Movement, O'Neal went to her first demonstrations with straightened hair. Her activism preceded her decision to stop straightening her hair. When she did make the decision, it provoked a chorus of disapproval from her former friends: "The Kappas were so upset with me. As I walked across the campus with this natural, the guys used to say to me, 'Why don't you get your hair pressed?' I was kind of ditched and couldn't be the Kappa Queen." O'Neal's refusal to straighten her hair was incomprehensible to her former peers. Despite the sharp criticism of her former admirers, natural hair seemed reasonable to her because of the support she received from fellow NAG members and from the larger movement:

> We used to have something that was called Project Awareness, and we would invite people like [James] Baldwin, Sidney Poitier, Malcolm, Bayard [Rustin] down for these various panels. And that evening we went to Carmichael's house, and this discussion about beauty came up. I said that I had been made very unhappy and said, "What's wrong with me? They hate me [because] I'm wearing my hair natural." Sidney Poitier, James Baldwin, and Malcolm X said

to me, "You're beautiful." I questioned them because I was going across campus with my hair nappy as the day I was born and people were screaming at me.

So I got all of this petting. Well after that I couldn't think that I had ever worn my hair any other way. Because they talked about it in such wonderful and grand terms that this is the way you should look. Then Jean Smith started wearing her hair natural, she and I and her sister, who was a class younger. So then there were a few of us, and there was solidarity in that.[17]

Because she was at Howard, where NAG members constituted a new center of cultural production, O'Neal could ask, "What's wrong with me?," and receive reassurance from figures who had become much more important to her than her former Kappa friends.

O'Neal entreated Muriel Tillinghast to stop straightening her hair so that she would not feel so alone. Tillinghast recalled the day she got her first natural hairstyle:

I joined NAG in 1961, and less than a year later, there was a girl in SNCC at that time—Stokely's girlfriend, whose hair was natural. I never really paid much attention to it, but one day she came up to me and said, "Muriel, don't get your hair straightened anymore. I need somebody to be with me in this." And I said, "Well what are you in? What is the problem?" She explained it to me. So when I went to the hairdresser that day, after she washed my hair, I said, "Don't press my hair." And that just sent a boomerang around the hairdressing parlor.[18]

Jean Smith Young also remembers the political and intellectual fervor of Howard in the early 1960s. In that atmosphere, choosing to wear a natural seemed to her the obvious thing to do: "We arranged for Malcolm and Baldwin to come to campus and that was a high point of my intellectual life. I was among the early Afros. It was because of the logic of, 'Well, you don't need to straighten your hair to be beautiful.' I just woke up one day. I can't remember how I did it. I can't remember saying, 'OK, this is the day I'm going to cut my hair and stop straightening it.' It was just part of the whole atmosphere. It was just a sort of natural thing to do."[19]

Mary O'Neal, Jean Smith, and Muriel Tillinghast were among the first women to wear natural hair on Howard's campus. Though the style drew strong reactions from students concerned about the "Howard Image," O'Neal, Smith, and Tillinghast felt it was an inevitable expression of their political commitments. Once these women adopted the style, it was difficult for them to ever consider straightening their hair again. In that sense, their commitment to wearing natural hair was firm. Yet, when asked, few of these women will say that the hairstyle was important to them by itself. This apparent contradiction can be resolved if it is understood that these activists are saying that the hairstyle had little meaning when separated from the context of activism in which it developed. They remember the hostile reactions they received against what they saw as a small expression of their larger commitments, but, as activists facing jail in Washington, D.C., and preparing for worse in Mississippi, a hairstyle was a minor detail.

The new self-image that was expressed in women's unstraightened hairstyles was not celebrated for its own sake. Instead, it had emerged from political action and would lead to further action. The discussions and activism that were taking place at Howard University in the early 1960s had parallels on many black campuses. While social movements never have fixed beginning points, it is possible to identify certain decisive moments when an action taken by a small group inspires great numbers of others who feel the need for change but have not yet been mobilized. One of those galvanizing moments occurred in February 1960, when four well-dressed, black, male students from North Carolina Agricultural and Technical College sat down at a whites-only lunch counter in a Greensboro, North Carolina, Woolworth's and ordered coffee. The students, who remained in their seats at the counter until closing time, were never served. They returned the next day with more supporters and later in the week were back again with a still larger group. Word of the Greensboro sit-ins spread, and black students throughout the South went into segregated businesses, sat down, and demanded service. By April, tens of thousands of southern black students had participated in the sit-in movement.

Before that point, the Civil Rights Movement had not been a student movement. The largest activist organization was the minister-led Southern Christian Leadership Conference (SCLC). Ella Baker, an extraordinary SCLC organizer who was sympathetic to the youth movement, persuaded SCLC to call a meeting to bring college activists together. The meeting, held in the spring of 1960 at Shaw University in North Carolina, was called "Sacrifice for Dignity" and resulted in the formation of SNCC as a coalition of college activists who sought to work together to keep civil rights activism alive on their campuses.[20] Howard University's Nonviolent Action Group became a SNCC affiliate. From its origins as an attempt to draw together disparate pockets of student activism, SNCC grew into one of the most important and progressive organizations of the Civil Rights Movement. As it made the transformation from loose coalition to tightly-knit organization, SNCC shifted its activities to Mississippi. SNCC was central to the campaign to win black voting rights in Mississippi and became, inadvertently, a center of cultural production and a vital site for the rearticulation of race.

Cleveland Sellers noted that at the "Sacrifice for Dignity" meeting members of the newly formed SNCC dismissed a call by a Black Muslim minister to "develop a greater sense of racial pride."[21] At that point in the development of the Civil Rights Movement, SNCC members viewed self-esteem and displays of racial identification as secondary to the task of fighting discrimination and ending racial terror in the South. Yet student activists were inadvertently reshaping black identity. In 1963, black students who wanted to commit their lives to the movement went to Mississippi to work with SNCC. SNCC offices became "structuring structures" that fostered a new black "common sense," vision of dignity, and image of beauty that was utterly different from that promoted by the fraternities and sororities of the black elite. In the South, one by one, activists began to adopt a similar style of self-presentation that began to be recognizable as the look of a person involved in the movement.

Unita Blackwell was a young woman in Lula, Mississippi, when she saw her first Afro. SNCC volunteer Muriel Tillinghast came to Lula to organize a voter registration drive. Blackwell noticed Tillinghast's unstraightened hair and asked her if she would like to know where to get her hair "fixed." To her surprise, Tillinghast rebuffed the offer. As Blackwell became more involved in the Civil Rights Movement, she learned that Tillinghast's hairstyle was more than one woman's eccentricity: "We went up to Greenville . . . and there were about five or six other women in there like that and then I discovered that this was a style. We were used to having our hair pressed. . . . Muriel Tillinghast was the first black woman I saw with a nappy head smiling."[22] Blackwell remembers being struck by the way these women wore their hair, the way they spoke, and their knowledge of black people she had never heard of. The look these women had, their confidence, and their knowledge drew her into the movement and transformed her life and her world.

Juadine Henderson, a black woman from Batesville, Mississippi, similarly described her powerful first impressions of meeting young SNCC members and the beginnings of her personal transformation:

> I was fifteen [when] I went to Greenwood [Mississippi] in 1963 to participate in a voter registration workshop. I wasn't sure what the workshop was going to be about. But I knew it was the movement and I wanted to do it. The first thing that struck me when I went to Greenwood was everybody in the office was young and they all seemed very serious, and I thought, who are these people?
>
> So we sat around and we talked about the Kennedy administration. It was kind of surprising that they weren't all overjoyed with Kennedy. Because all the black people had said before he was elected that he was the best thing since baked bread. And here were these people saying he's not really that great. So they had a different way of looking at the world. And it made you think about what you were

doing and what you were saying and why you believed what you were believing. So it had a lot more to do with life than just voter registration and voter education.

The second day, when we went to the SNCC office, all of these people had a different emotion going. One of the young kids from Greenwood said Medgar Evers got killed. That was the problem and people were organizing a mass meeting. About eleven o'clock in the morning we went to this church and there were more black people there than I had ever seen in my whole life. It was the biggest church I'd ever seen, too. The church was full and people were on the sidewalk. They had loudspeakers where people who couldn't get inside could hear. And it was a tremendous feeling of being together with other people. It was like what I imagine Christian people talk about when they talk about being converted. All of a sudden you really did understand what the movement was about, what unity was about. What believing in yourself and other people was about.[23]

Standing outside of the church, Henderson felt the emotional culmination of her growing commitment to the movement. Her interest in the Civil Rights Movement began at home, as she listened to her stepfather read newspaper reports of the activities of the "Freedom Riders." It grew when Frank Smith, a SNCC member and friend of her cousin, spoke to her when he visited her town. But her "conversion" occurred while she stood as a member of the largest group of black people she had ever seen, gathered together in mourning and anger over the murder of Evers. She likened her experience to a conversion because the new commitment she felt marked a turning point in her life.

Henderson's narrative expresses the feelings of membership in a larger collectivity, of new purpose, and of greater strength that can be evoked by participation in collective action. Gradually, as a part of the personal transformation that resulted from her involvement with the movement, she developed a new aesthetic. In 1966, after three years of active participation in the Civil Rights Movement, Henderson stopped straightening her hair. Henderson did not adopt the style to look like an activist; she *was* an activist. The culture of the Civil Rights Movement gave her a new way of seeing herself. She described her feeling of wonder at the appearance of a new way to be beautiful:

I stopped straightening my hair as soon as I graduated from high school. It was like, "I'm never straightening it again!" It was not the politics that it became later on. No, what happened is I had seen an album cover of Odetta. And it was amazing to me that her hair was really pretty. And I thought, that's interesting. She doesn't straighten her hair. Then somebody else came to Batesville with an Afro and I thought her hair looks really pretty. Just think, you can get it cut and you don't have to do anything. You don't have to get tortured by cousin Maude.[24]

When Henderson adopted the natural style, she was simply enjoying being beautiful according to the standards of the movement culture. Others may have worn naturals to express political commitments, but Henderson wore hers to be beautiful.

Politically active, black, female folk singers, jazz musicians, and actresses were important figures who helped expand beauty standards to include the tight curls of African American hair. It was the image of the folk singer Odetta that helped Henderson see the beauty of natural hair, and Mary O'Neal remembered that Stokely Carmichael suggested that she emulate the short natural of singer Miriam Makeba. The first female public figures to wear styled, unstraightened hair were entertainers who had strong political commitments and whose performances gave support to the Civil Rights Movement. Jazz singer and actress Abbey Lincoln was, in 1961, one of the first black women shown by the black press wearing natural hair. At that time, she had just finished recording *Freedom Now Suites* with her husband, Max Roach, and soon would record *Straight Ahead*, an album whose message of black pride so threatened white jazz critics that they denounced her for allegedly abandoning jazz in favor of propaganda.[25]

In 1961, the mainstream black press first noted the appearance of black women in the jazz world wearing unstraightened hair. Lincoln, Odetta, and jazz trombonist Melba Liston appeared several times that year in *Jet* and *Ebony* wearing a style that was described as "*au naturel*," "*au naturelle*," the "natural state," or the "natural look." Readers were introduced to the "natural" as a phenomenon emerging from the intersection of entertainment and politics. In their reports, the style was always viewed as a political expression that was neither pretty nor sexy. The following quotes from *Ebony* and *Jet,* the two most popular black periodicals of the 1960s, were typical of the way unstraightened female hairstyles were viewed by the black press.

> Abbey Lincoln, a singing star, abandoned the sex-siren role and adopted an *au naturelle* hair style.[26]
>
> Collins George, Detroit Free Press music writer, using an old adage to describe folk singer Odetta: "The most beautiful women are seldom the prettiest."[27]
>
> Melba Liston had her own unique way of dramatizing the aims of the confab (resolve problems concerning jobs, race bias and the Negro image). Her gimmick: She allowed her hair to revert to its natural state to express her "nationalistic" views.[28]

In Harlem in 1962, a group of models and entertainers, including Lincoln, demonstrated its belief in the importance of the natural by forming Grandassa, an organization that presented quasi-political fashion shows promoting naturals.[29] Throughout 1962, more entertainers with unstraightened hair were seen in *Jet,* including actress Cicely Tyson and singers Miriam Makeba and Nina Simone.

A natural hairstyle appeared on the cover of *Ebony* in December 1962. Considering the tumult that would surround Afros in subsequent years, the nonchalance with which *Ebony* treated the Afro's unassuming front cover debut is remarkable. Ironically, *Ebony*'s readers were introduced to natural hair in a cover story about the advantages of wigs. A photograph of Cicely Tyson wearing a straight, teased, and set wig dominated the cover. Beneath the larger picture was a smaller image, a "before" picture, showing Tyson in a short natural. Inside the front cover, *Ebony* explained: "While Cicely usually wears her hair cropped short, there are times when she, a model as well as an actress, finds a wig necessary. Wigs are becoming tremendously popular today among all women—from the society matron to the budget conscious housewife."[30] The article featured Tyson in seven wigs, including the blonde "Queen Nefertiti" style. With a fashion writer's talent for hyperbole, the author wrote, "For the Negro woman whose hair has been her biggest problem, the return of the wig as a fashion staple has been a Godsend." In 1963, Nina Simone, Lorraine Hansberry, Abbey Lincoln, Miriam Makeba, Cicely Tyson, Odetta, and SNCC member Dorie Ladner appeared in *Ebony* or *Jet* with unstraightened hair. The style was not deemed controversial by the writers whom *Ebony* employed. Scant attention was paid to the yet nameless hairstyle. Under a photograph of Makeba, a writer noted in a caption that she wore "her hair cropped close."

Before the natural was treated as a controversial practice by the two leading black magazines, it was debated and defended in black periodicals that straddled the border between social movement literature and the black popular press.[31] These included *Negro History Bulletin,* a publication of the venerable Association for the Study of Negro Life and History, and the *Liberator*, the most prominent black nationalist literary and political magazine of the 1960s. Both of these publications had close ties to the black movement community yet attracted a broad readership. Natural hair was also discussed in *Negro Digest*, which, patterned after *Reader's Digest*, presented condensed articles from other publications but had a more political focus than its white counterpart. After a brief closure, *Negro Digest* transformed itself in 1961 into a literary and political magazine with an increasingly black nationalist focus. The topic also arose in *The Urbanite,* a short-lived black literary magazine that attracted many of the best-known prointegration writers, and in *Muhammad Speaks*, the official publication of the Nation of Islam, which in addition to promoting Elijah Muhammad's doctrine carried numerous general interest features. Articles about natural hair began to appear in this kind of publication as early as 1961. In one way or another, each was more directly involved in African American social movements than *Ebony* and *Jet.* The articles published about the rejection of hair straightening by *Negro History Bulletin, Liberator, Negro Digest, The Urbanite,* and *Muhammad Speaks* took varied forms, from droll confession to impassioned tributes, but they shared a common emphasis on the importance of black psychological redemption. Wearing "natural" hair was seen as a practice that was both individually healing and collectively transforming. In 1961, *The Urbanite* published an essay by black artist and author Margaret Burroughs in which she expressed her belief in the psychological importance of learning to appreciate unstraightened hair. She said, "Mine was a determination to become aware of myself, and to aid other Negroes to become aware of themselves as a beautiful contribution to the human race."[32] The themes of self-awareness, self-love, and self-esteem as political projects were present early in the literature inspired by the Civil Rights Movement, and their influence would continue to grow.

The civil rights activism of the 1950s laid the groundwork for SNCC to challenge the intensely repressive racism of Mississippi. Participants in the Civil Rights Movement before the advent of SNCC incorporated a stance of propriety into the discourse and strategy of the movement, striving to maintain outward respectability while fighting racism. The young people who built SNCC were of a generation who questioned the deferential respectability of their parents. When they went to Mississippi, they did not set out to develop an oppositional culture, to replace respectability with self-respect, or to remake themselves. Regardless of their early intentions, a new sense of defiant racial identity grew out of their political engagement. In the spring of 1964, John Lewis noted a change in the way southern blacks saw themselves:

> Something is happening in the Southern Negro Community. They're identifying with people because of color. . . . They're conscious of things that happen in Cuba, in Latin America, and in Africa. Even in SNCC, we talk about integration, about the beloved community, but there have been great changes going on. There's been a radical change in our people since 1960; the way they dress, the music they listen to, their natural hair dos—all of them want to go to Africa. . . . I think people are searching for a sense of identity, and they're finding it.[33]

Like Juadine Henderson, described previously, who experienced a tremendous feeling of solidarity while attending her first mass meeting in Greenwood, Mississippi, many African Americans developed a new sense of self as they joined others in protest. Sociologist Rick Fantasia argues that "militant action creates a context in which ideas may emerge, change, and be subjected to scrutiny and renegotiation."[34] Marches, rallies, strikes, sit-ins, and other forms of collective defiance to domination create the conditions for rethinking what had been accepted in the past about the self and others. No early civil rights activist joined the movement to change her sense of self, but in the heat of struggle many found that a change had occurred behind their backs. SNCC veteran Jean Smith wrote: "When I left Washington, D.C., in 1963 to go South with SNCC you knew me. Now four years later I am a different person. Essentially the difference is that I became consciously black."[35] In the process of becoming different people, SNCC activists inadvertently created symbolic material for others to adopt as their own. For activists, changes in consciousness that often found expression through personal style stemmed from political action. African Americans outside of the movement could adopt elements of that consciousness without ever participating in any action. Achieving that kind of borrowed transformation increasingly became the goal of spokespersons for black pride. A belief in the power of symbols of black consciousness grew.

In late 1963 and early 1964, the conviction that personal transformation was more important than organized protest gained ground. The trend can be seen in the words of Don Warden, leader of the California-based Afro-American Association, who placed the development of racial pride ahead of picketing for integration. Calling integration "irrelevant," he exhorted African Americans to "throw away your bleaching creams. Throw away your hair straighteners. Quit dropping out of school, quit flunking. Get off welfare."[36] Linking personal accomplishment to racial pride, he argued that personal transformation as an expression of group identity was more effective than protest.

Activists found support for their growing belief that personal transformation was a requirement for political change in Frantz Fanon's *Wretched of the Earth*. Mary King, a former SNCC volunteer, recalled that people in that organization were passing around an advance English language translation of Fanon's book in 1963, two years before its official English publication. Fanon's descriptions of the devastating psychological consequences of colonialism had a profound impact on her and on many other SNCC members, who saw parallels between racism in the United States and colonialism in Africa.[37] In *Freedom Song*, a memoir of her years in SNCC, Mary King wrote that "there was one inescapable conclusion from exposure to Fanon. The most important innovations were not necessarily external but had to take place internally—in the self-concept of black people. Reading Fanon, I saw that barriers lay within as well as without and began to believe that our energies would have to be directed at attitudes, especially the self-contempt and assumptions of inferiority produced by centuries of oppression."[38] Spokesmen within the Civil Rights Movement increasingly addressed psychological issues of shame. In 1965, both *Wretched of the Earth* and *The Autobiography of Malcolm X* became widely available, fueling the growing emphasis on personal transformation. Telling the story of his personal journey from hoodlum to leader, Malcolm X's autobiography incorporated the Nation of Islam's emphasis on cleansing the body and mind of an attraction to whiteness.

If in 1965 many saw indications of black self-contempt, there was also ample evidence of black anger. In the summer of 1964, blacks rioted in cities throughout the Northeast, vandalizing and looting white-owned businesses in black neighborhoods. On August 11, 1965, the streets of Watts, a Los Angeles neighborhood, exploded in an undeniable demonstration of African American rage. Around the nexus of rage against the white man's power and assertions of black self-love, everyday practices were invested with new meaning. In the wake of the riots in Watts, the natural became a recognizable symbol that communicated both anger and beauty. For youths who had access to no other medium, the body was the primary canvas for the expression of pride. Armed with "natural" and "authentic" styles that expressed rejection of white beauty standards, one could feel engaged in resistance merely by "being oneself." "Black is beautiful," an inadvertent product of the Civil Rights Movement that was disseminated by the media, was available as a cultural resource in the late 1960s for use by anyone who wanted or needed it. Many black women felt it was just the thing they had needed all of their lives. There were new, increasingly accepted ways of being beautiful that had simply not existed in earlier years. Women who had needed to feel beautiful in order to be women at all but who had been categorically described as ugly because of their blackness were finally given a new mirror.

By 1965, women who wore naturals still endured derision but also enjoyed membership in a sisterhood, a family of women who resembled each other because of the choices they had made. Wearing a natural became a very public act of self-acceptance that was both personal and a way of being part of what felt like a solidifying community. Margot Dashiell, a black woman in Oakland, saw the natural as a "badge of this person's resistance. This is a brother or this is a sister because they have this natural."[39] Jean Wiley described the experience of wearing a natural in 1965 as the feeling of being a member of a certain club: "It was inconceivable to walk by a total stranger [wearing a natural] and not smile and say 'hi.' You might keep on going, you might never know their name, but you were in a certain club and you knew it."[40] In both of these statements, the Afro signifies membership. Wiley calls it a "certain club"; Dashiell saw natural hair as a "badge." The club was not a closed fraternity or sorority: It was open to any black person who would wear the symbol. Two conditions supported the badge's meaning. The first was the sustained vitality of a black movement community. It was possible for a hairstyle to convey an authentic commitment because the Civil Rights Movement was organizing massive protests and the Black Power Movement was beginning to emerge. The second condition that invested the style with a sense of consequence was the personal risk involved in wearing one. Though no one would encounter the confusion, shock, or ridicule met by women who wore unstraightened styles before the mid-1960s, Afros were still quite unacceptable in many workplaces, schools, and even at home. Young blacks often had to defend their hairstyles to their elders who read the Afro as a symbol of disrespectful and dangerous militancy.

For black men and women, the Afro represented a willingness to be publicly identified with the Civil Rights or Black Power movements, but for black women it meant something more. It was proof that the Eurocentric beauty standard had been overturned, and as a result, the brown skin and tightly curled hair that had been black women's "problems" were suddenly their joys. A black woman activist who described being treated as a walking curiosity when she wore a natural in 1962 recalled the pleasure of wearing natural hair a few years later: "We were like flowers, blossoming. We were finally coming into our own beauty. It was a common experience. In that sense it brought us together. It didn't mean that we would sit around in groups and talk about the experience. We just did it."[41]

The burden of disparagement had been lifted from all black women, creating a sense of relief that was widely shared. For a moment, vanity, the individual pleasure of self-acceptance, and a moral stance vis-à-vis the race converged. Another activist described the way in which the Afro created an exhilarating feeling of community among black women: "There was a part of it that felt so magical and so true and honest. The realization that we could be who we were and be beautiful. It provided me with a level of confidence that I'd never known in my life before. There was community in the beauty standard. It wasn't like it was one person who was doing this. It was a whole community of people who were embracing these standards. You could look around a room and see fifteen, twenty other women with an Afro."[42] She used the words "magic" and "truth." The speed with which the old standard seemed to lose all of its power felt magical. It was the kind of magic that removes a curse or a lie to reveal a form of goodness and truth that was both personal and political. Brenda Travis, who was born and raised in Mississippi, joined the Civil Rights Movement as a young teenager, and was punished for her activism by being sent to a reformatory, felt that her natural hair helped her feel more pride in her race and more pride in herself: "The Afro meant everything to me politically. Because it was like identifying. I was identifying with who I was. I was identifying with my culture. I was identifying with my background as a black person. Even though I didn't need an Afro to identify as black. I think what it did was it made me just feel more proud that I was black."[43] Travis expressed a sense of the recovery of a truth and birthright that was also present in the words "coming into our own beauty" and "we could be who we were and be beautiful," which were used in the previous quotations. Travis had always known she was black, but the meaning of black had been thoroughly transformed by the revelation that black was beautiful.

As the sisterhood of women with naturals grew, the natural became the strategic choice for advertisers seeking to reach young African American women. Norforms douche, Simplicity patterns, and Emko birth control began to use models with natural hair in advertisements in *Ebony* in 1965. Advertising copywriters for skin bleachers and hair straighteners scrambled to save a diminishing market by incorporating words of progress, racial pride, and nature into their advertisements. In 1965, after years of promising "lighter, brighter skin," Bleach and Glow's new campaign simply showed a light-skinned woman being kissed by a man, a rose, and the words "natural beauties." The Posner company Africanized its hot comb grease by claiming that "Cleopatra's hair secret is yours" and offered men "that natural look" with Posner's So-Mild hair straightener. In a textbook example of the construction of hegemonic discourse, the manufacturers of Lustrasilk hair straightening pomade fought the natural by excluding it from the realm of reasonable possibility. Underneath a photograph of a hot comb, their pitch read: "Curse it all you want but until there's a safe way to straighten hair without it, use it, and use it, and use it, and use it." Trying desperately to keep unstraightened hair out of the picture, their implication was that black women were limited to two alternatives, hot combs or the newly developed chemical hair relaxers. Though substantial numbers of black women were wearing naturals, the advertisement's text recreated a pre-1960s world in which all black women were obligated to straighten their hair.

As the natural became more popular, it was rediscovered by *Ebony*. In June 1966, *Ebony* heralded the arrival of "The Natural Look" with a cover photo of a dark-complexioned, dignified beauty wearing her hair in a short natural. Four years after *Ebony* readers first saw the small "before" picture of unstraightened hair in the cover story about the advantages of wigs, the style returned to *Ebony*'s cover as the startling and controversial new Afro. In an article that intermingled the words "coiffure" and "bouffant" with "rebellion" and "crusade," women attested to the political, aesthetic, and practical reasons for wearing naturals. The following month, eight readers, including actor Ossie Davis, wrote to *Ebony*, praising the editors for presenting the proud and beautiful new style. Nine defenders of the hot comb inveighed against displays of "nappy," "bad," "kinky," or "woolly" hair, which they saw variously as laziness, an affectation, a retrogressive return to "grass huts" and "nose rings," and a style for "soul brothers only."

By 1966, "militant" blacks, defiant, proud, and often wearing naturals, could be seen regularly on the evening news. "Black is beautiful" imagery increasingly appeared in mainstream black publications as well as in the proliferating magazines, newspapers, and posters of the Civil Rights and the emerging Black Power movements. Whether explicitly or implicitly, these words and pictures called for the self to be constructed in a new way. They provided new symbols and practices that were adopted by African Americans who wished to stand in opposition to an oppressive culture.

In June 1966, Stokely Carmichael gave a speech in Mississippi during which he led the assembled crowd in a chant of "black power." The speech became a defining moment that marked the decline of demonstrations to achieve integration and the beginning of something ill defined but somehow angrier and more black.[44] In the ensuing weeks, both established and rising leaders vied to define, claim, or distance themselves from black power. In a speech given in Watts later in the year, Carmichael prioritized the development of racial pride: "The most important thing that black people have to do is to begin to come together, and to be able to do that we must stop being ashamed of being black. We are black and beautiful."[45]

In 1967, the natural was so powerful a symbol that it provoked debate in the popular black press, was treated as an icon in the Black Panther Party newspaper, and represented a provocation to college administrators. In December of that year, *Ebony* featured its second cover story on the style, "Natural Hair, New Symbol of Race Pride." In the Black Panther Party's newspaper, cameos of black women with naturals captioned "Black and Beautiful" were regular features. In Baltimore, the administrators of the historically black Coppin College, expelled Jean Wiley's sister for wearing a natural: "They told her to come back when she could do something with her hair. It got to the newspapers. By the time she was expelled the Afro was being seen as a statement of real defiance. The school was reacting to a firebrand on campus. If she dared to wear her hair like that she was dangerous."[46] Coppin's administration feared the ability of the style to communicate a spirit of unified defiance. Neither defiance nor racial pride was new in 1967, but the widespread belief in the importance of their bodily expression was unprecedented.

Televised coverage of the movement heightened the importance of an embodied image of black militancy. Emory Douglas, who became minister of culture of the Black Panther Party, described how his thinking was shaped by this medium: "I was very inspired by Stokely and Rap [H. Rap Brown]. I used to see them on TV all the time. And they were fearless in that time. I identified with them. [Stokely] was talking about black pride and black power."[47] Pearl Marsh, who at the time was a student at a historically black college, decided to stop straightening her hair after seeing militants on television. In these militants she saw something that seemed to be her authentic self:

> It was in Alabama when I was at Huntsville, and this was a really strict school. We got to watch television every now and then, and I remember seeing militant students being interviewed and seeing naturals. So one day I washed my hair and stole a fork from the dining commons. I mean literally a kitchen fork and did my hair up and went to class. I felt so relieved.
>
> [I asked her why she felt relieved.]
> Black is beautiful didn't overcome everything. The one thing it did

overcome was shame. That we were ashamed that our hair was kinky. I mean the thought that a white person would ever see your hair not straightened was just inconceivable. And so it was relief. That this was me.

My father died when he saw it. He just died. I came home with this hair out there looking like this globe. "You look like an African!" That was pejorative. I said, "Yeah. So I look like an African. I am an African."[48]

When Marsh began to view her hair in a new way, her transformation was immediate, lone, and without reservation. The "militants" on television gave her a new way to be herself. Kinky hair, a feature she had worn with shame, was recast into a glorious symbol of membership in a proud and beautiful race.

A second medium flourished in the late 1960s that shared television's visual appeal: the poster. In neighborhoods bereft of museums, parks, or humane architecture, billboards were among the few sources of external visual material. Billboard images were imposed on communities from the outside, but posters were permanent, portable, accessible art that came from within the community. As minister of culture of the Black Panther Party, Emory Douglas was the creator of most of the party's posters. Beginning in 1967 and continuing through the early 1970s, these posters received wide circulation because they were included as part of the Black Panther Party newspaper. Their popularity helped to sell the paper. Douglas deliberately sought to create images that reflected the people of the community around him or their southern roots. Through his posters Douglas hoped to facilitate "people identifying with themselves." He said: "When they see themselves, they identify with that. When people [see] the images, they can identify with their uncles, their brothers, their sisters, their aunt. Somebody that they knew."[49] By depicting black residents of Oakland and Berkeley as beautiful, worthy subjects of art, he was teaching them to value themselves, to find their identity in their own community. He portrayed white police and politicians as pigs, thus drawing a world in which figures of white authority were debased creatures.

The leaders of the Black Panther Party were keenly aware of the power of imagery, yet they very deliberately distinguished themselves from cultural nationalists, typified by Ron Karenga. For the Black Panthers, culture was a means —not an end. Cultural nationalists saw black cultural revitalization as an important end to be achieved in the struggle against racial domination. In their analysis, the core of racism was the suppression of African culture by European culture. According to Karenga, the devastating result of racist cultural domination was a black population weakened by the loss of its own African forms of expression and value systems. Cultural nationalists embraced African culture as the source of a renewed black nation in America. The Black Panthers mocked cultural nationalists for their embrace of a generalized African culture. Black Panthers generally did not adopt African names or African clothing. The material for their posters, the music they sponsored, and even their somewhat uniform style of dress were primarily derived from black urban America and less frequently incorporated African imagery. Though they defined themselves in opposition to cultural nationalists, they were certainly cultural activists who effectively used graphic arts, created media events, recorded music, and developed a distinct style of dress as a means of building a movement. Posters were one way that the Black Panther Party communicated with its own community. One of the enduring images of the era was a poster, which was advertised for sale each week in the party's newspaper, of Black Panther leader Huey Newton seated in a throne-like wicker chair, gun in one hand and spear in the other. The Black Panthers made themselves visible on a national scale by staging startling media events. In May 1967, they silently toured the California state assembly carrying loaded rifles, pistols, and shotguns, stunning Governor Ronald Reagan, the press, and visitors to the capitol. The press and the old guard of civil rights leadership had barely finished responding to what seemed an earth-shattering new phrase—"black power"—when the Panthers brandished weapons and increased the stakes. The Black Panthers personified militant blackness, chanting "black is beautiful" in a context that fused beauty and anger, self-love and defiance. Though their armed militancy was well beyond the extent of activism personally acceptable to most African Americans, many youths identified with their stance from a safe distance.

POPULAR BLACK

Whenever, at the beginning of a social movement, a particular slogan seems to be on everyone's lips and to capture the mood, its power is likely to come from the fact that it condenses some of the most deeply felt sentiments of the hidden transcript.
—*James C. Scott*

In 1968, the slogan on everyone's lips was "black is beautiful."[50] The black consciousness movement took long-standing sentiments and gave them expression and validation. Black men and women who had not been directly engaged in political activity began to adopt the cultural material produced by the Civil Rights and Black Power movements. Choosing to express identification with the movement required relatively little effort because the cultural material was easily accessible. The message embedded in the styles and practices was throw off the old and love yourself. Self-love became understood as a political act.

A former member of the Black Panther Party described the joy of discovering black culture. She remembers being captivated by black men who could "get up on stage and talk" and decided to be like them: "I loved my husband, but I was in love with Stokely Carmichael, Rap Brown, and wished I knew Malcolm X! And every black man that got up on stage I fell in love with. He could have looked like doo doo if he was up on stage. And Jesse Jackson. I loved me some Jesse Jackson. Any black man that could get up on stage and talk. I guess that was when I saw [Afros]. I just remember my husband said, 'Why don't you get a natural?' "[51] She stopped straightening her hair and got it cut into the Afro shape. At the same time in her life she decided to return to school, enrolling in a community college where she found a culture that she felt belonged to her even though she had never known it.

> These folks was talking about doing stuff! They were political! I wanted to go over there where that action was. I wanted to go see what was going on over there. And classes were radical. They were reading poetry! And books! And stuff about, by, and for black people! And it was like, "Oh! Black is really beautiful!" I mean golly! How could you think otherwise? Black was truly beautiful! It was arrogant, too! People were wearing bubas [African styled shirts] and colors and jewelry. I felt like I had to identify with the African thing. I was so happy to have something that went beyond slavery. I was just here. And then when the culture came along I was here and I was somebody. I was a person that counted. Before that I was just existing.

She became a political activist, but the natural hairstyle, black pride, and a militant stance became part of a symbolic repertoire that could be claimed by African Americans who had no direct involvement in any movement. Seventh graders formed Black Student Unions in which they had telescoped versions of discussions that emerged out of years of political struggle. Sheila Head recalled becoming an "instantaneous radical" as a preteen attending junior high school in Oakland.

> I remember being in seventh grade and I was twelve and I went to the first Black Student Union meeting. And the whole conversation was whether we were going to be Negroes, colored, or black. Me and my best friend went to the meeting and were like, "Oh, what are we going to do? Negro? No. Black? I don't know." Colored was definitely out. "OK, well, we'll be black!" That afternoon I decided I was black. I would not respond to Negro. I would definitely not respond to colored. I was black and black was beautiful, and power to the people! So I became an instantaneous radical.
>
> By eighth grade I wanted a natural. I thought it was just necessary for my cause. And my mother said "No way." . . . My mother eventually started wearing a natural about six months after I did.[52]

It was not uncommon for women to first reject their daughters' naturals but soon after adopt the same hairstyle. Many women described having arguments with their mothers about naturals. These arguments were often resolved through compromise, when the daughters would agree to have their hair straightened for special events, particularly those in which the daughter achieved status and especially if the new status was to be recorded in a formal photograph. Many daughters conceded to straighten their hair again for graduation or a wedding. But, as time progressed, unstraightened hair became more conventional, less politically meaningful, less threatening, and more stylish. Mothers who initially were dismayed by the style began to wear naturals themselves or helped their daughters pin graduation caps and wedding veils to Afros.

When Sheila Head came of age, the symbolic repertoire of militant blackness included a belief in the appropriateness of anger. From the time that Africans were brought to America in chains, African Americans have had to be invisible, silent, servile, and amusing. The new stance was conspicuous, loud, demanding, and humorless when dealing with whites, which was sometimes stylized into a mode of behavior that became identified as "militant." In the late 1960s and early 1970s, "beautiful" was often synonymous with good, but it was also a time when "bad," pronounced with a particular relish, meant emphatically good.[53] The Afro was part of the look of an angry, black militant. Pearl Marsh gave an explanation for the deliberate use of bad manners during the late 1960s:

> We meant it to be threatening. That it was a statement that "I'm here." That "I'm not to be mistreated. I'm not second class." It was meant to be threatening in that way. That I have to be respected. That I'm not trying to be you. I'm not trying to cover who I am. This is who I am. So I'm sure it intimidated people. We were intimidating.
>
> I'll never forget going to white people's houses. I would never misbehave, but friends misbehaved. People would have these parties for us because they wanted to invite the militants out. First of all, you'd never show up on time. Work up a hunger and thirst. And then go to their party and they always had cheese and crackers. So then you'd whine that there was no meat. The brothers always said, "Where's the meat?" And so then they went scurrying into the kitchen to find some meat. We were rude. And so part of the Afro was to intimidate. And we misbehaved. I hate to say it. We acted badly. . . . It was part of the performance. What did we get out of it? To be generous to it, we were taking a message to the suburbs in a way. Our generation, for better or for worse, shifted the white stereotype of black people from Steppin Fetchit and docile to militant and angry and violent. And we worked that. We may have misbehaved, but we really changed the stereotype. . . . They were scared of us.[54]

The performative and stylistic repertoire of the new black identity had many roots. Natural hairstyles began to be adopted by African Americans outside of the Civil Rights or Black Power movements who admired the courageous young activists wearing Afros. Afros expressed black racial pride. However, in the mid-1960s, natural hairstyles, African clothing, the raised fist black power salute, and other symbols and practices of black identity conveyed more than self-love; they expressed defiance against the dominance of white culture. Though there had been numerous civil rights victories by the mid-1960s, activists continued to face violence at the hands of intransigent racists, and many blacks continued to live in poverty. Racial riots erupted in American cities every year throughout the mid-1960s, making visible the rage of black youths who were not engaged in organized social movements. The heroically polite decorum in the face of racist danger that had characterized early Civil Rights Movement protests for integration was interpreted as foolish patience and pointless risk a few years later. Jean Wiley recalled that blacks had ceased seeking white approval by the mid-1960s. She associated that change with the level of repression faced by activists:

> At some point by 1965 nobody's agonizing over [natural hair] anymore, nobody's, "Well, should I or shouldn't I?" and "What do the white people want?" We loved it when the white people hated it! Oh they hate that. [Snaps her fingers.] Let's do it. But by then there'd been a great deal of repression. Guys were in jail or out of the country because of trying to get out of the Vietnam War. There's a movement and there's a very repressive arm happening at the same time. So you love it when somebody doesn't like the way you look.[55]

Phil Gardiner, a tall, hefty black man, was always aware of his intimidating physical appearance. He recalled that the styles he wore in the 1960s exaggerated those qualities: "I'm six foot five, two hundred and forty pounds. I'm a big guy. That's the type to be. That's the Mandingo slave. I've always been aware that people are very intimidated by my size, and in the sixties you used to use that. But in the sixties when your hair is even longer and you haven't shaved and you've got boots on, shit, you're six seven, you're walking down the street, it's like, no one even fucks with you."[56]

In 1968, James Brown, "Soul Brother No. 1," took the anger and pride that was widespread in black communities, set it to a funky beat, and turned it into gold:

> Some people say we got a lot of malice.
> Some say it's a lot of nerve.
> But I say we won't quit moving,
> Until we get what we deserve.

Say it loud: "I'm Black and I'm proud."
Say it loud: "I'm Black and I'm proud."[57]

Brown was one of the last black male entertainers to abandon the chemically straightened "conk" hairstyle. *Jet* noted the demise of his anachronistic hairdo in a two-page article that included "before" and "after" pictures.[58] His haircut was followed one month later by the release of the song that was to become the popular anthem of black pride, "Say It Loud, I'm Black and I'm Proud." As an Oakland barber recalled, "When 'I'm Black and I'm Proud' came along, you was allowed then to call your fellow man black. At that time black was in real heavy."[59] The song, which was performed by someone so far outside of the movement that he would play at Richard Nixon's inaugural ball, carried the message to others who had never walked picket lines. Brown, known as the "Godfather of Soul," stood for the common black man. His fans knew that he had picked cotton and shined shoes for a living before attaining success. He carried the message of black pride to all who had grown up tuned in to soul music. Imshi Atkins, an Oakland cosmetologist, quoted the song when she recalled the prevalence of strong feelings of black identity during the late 1960s: "I think everybody was more black. More into their culture. It was saying that 'hey, I'm black and I'm proud, like James Brown said.'"[60]

Teenagers who would never hear of Fanon could quote James Brown and celebrate black identity as a vague combination of soul, funk, hard work, dance, success, southern roots, anger, and joy. The recording was supported by strategically placed advertisements in *Jet* and *Muhammad Speaks* to reach the common black man. The advertisements printed the song's full lyrics alongside the following rearticulation of the meanings of "Negro," "colored," and "black."

We know the Negro deejay won't play this record.
We know the colored deejay won't play this record.
But every black deejay will play this record.

The song raced to the top of black popular music charts. Although he was one of the last to adopt the new black style, Brown was nonetheless the quintessential soul performer. In the song, the theme "black and proud" was severed from every political project except personal achievement.

By 1968, black was "in" so heavily that African Americans adopted for mere convenience the style that had formerly represented militancy. Like Imshi Atkins, Michelle Bailey quoted James Brown when describing the period during which she wore an Afro. She remembered it as a time when she was free, but primarily free from the need to spend time on her hair: "An Afro? Sure. I went through that period, remember? 'Say It Loud. You're Black and You're Proud.' I loved it. It gave me total freedom. I didn't have to put much energy into my hair and I felt good about it."[61] Bailey began wearing an Afro sixteen years after the dancer Ruth Beckford overcame a barber's objections and had her unstraightened hair cut short. Their reasons for wearing the style appear similar. They both found the style easier to maintain than straightened hair. But the context surrounding the hairstyle had changed dramatically by the time Bailey discovered its freedom. Social ease conditions what is considered practically easy. Afros, wigs, chemically straightened hair, braids, and dreadlocks have each, at various times, been experienced by black women as the easiest among culturally available alternatives. In 1952, an Afro provoked ridicule and confusion; in 1968, it was a style that had lingering associations with black pride; and so, by 1968, the style had become both practically and socially easy.

In 1970, the natural was transformed from a style of increasing popularity into an internationally recognizable symbol through portraits of Angela Davis. Davis caught the public's attention as a black woman intellectual when in 1969 she was fired from her teaching position at UCLA because of her Communist Party membership. Her fame grew when she was charged with kidnapping, conspiracy, and murder in connection with Jonathan Jackson's unsuccessful attempt to take hostages at the Marin County Courthouse in order to bargain for his brother's freedom. She became a fugitive and was imprisoned, supported by an international campaign to "Free Angela," and ultimately was acquitted. Her image was disseminated on Federal Bureau of Investigation "wanted" posters, reprinted constantly by the media, and sold on countless posters produced by her defenders and by independent artists.

An early poster of Davis showed her in an office in front of a poster of W. E. B. Du Bois, placing her (for those schooled enough to recognize Du Bois) in the context of black participation in the Communist Party (see figure 5.1). At the beginning of the campaign to gain her release, new posters were produced that included no visual reference to the party, but instead coupled her with prison activist and writer George Jackson. As the campaign grew, posters presented only the beautiful and defiant face of a hounded black woman. Her regal head, crowned by a halo-like Afro, was an ideal image of black womanhood for an era of black consciousness (see figure 5.2). Like the natural hairstyle, posters from the "Free Angela" campaign were banned at certain workplaces as challenges to authority.[62]

The dimensions of Davis's Afro were by no means unique in 1969. Davis commented that the nation's fascination with her hair surprised her. In a reflection on the nationalism of the 1960s, she wrote, "I had no idea my own 'natural' would achieve its somewhat legendary status; I was simply emulating other sisters."[63] Black Panther Party spokeswoman Kathleen Cleaver and actress Gloria Foster were shown many times in the black press with similarly grand natural hairstyles, but the large Afro became so identified with Angela Davis that beauticians, wig makers, and people on the street referred to it as the "Angela Davis look." More women let their Afros grow long to achieve the look that,

Figure 5.1. Poster of Angela Davis with W. E. B. Du Bois in the background. Courtesy of the Bancroft Library, University of California, Berkeley (86/157c., carton 3, folder 3:90).

Figure 5.2. Free Angela button. Courtesy of the
Bancroft Library, University of California, Berkeley
(86/157c., carton 3, folder 3:10).

to some, represented defiance and, to others, simply beauty (see figure 5.3). As the number of large Afros increased, reports spread of black women with large Afros being mistaken for the fugitive Davis.[64] Some of these reports were accurate but unfortunate accounts of innocent women suffering indignities as a result of the wide search for her, and some were bolstered by rumors stemming from the history of unjustified arrests of African Americans by police operating on the basis of racial profiling. The repeated accounts also reflect identification with the beautiful fugitive and black heroine and a common desire to have some small connection to her flight.

I have been tracing the evolution of the meaning of the Afro within black communities. African Americans perceived that their ways of reading the meaning of an Afro were, in a sense, local knowledge that was inaccessible to whites. By 1970, when Barbara Williams, an Oakland hairdresser, adopted a highly styled, "curly" version of the style, the Afro had become widely accepted by black women as fashionable. Williams contrasted the way she felt her Afro was understood by other blacks with how the same style was viewed by whites. She enjoyed staying current and said that her Afro "was just another style" and that in her community stylish was all that it meant. She explained that "the people that I was around knew me. If I had a 'Curly Natural' and I was in white corporate America, they would think of me as . . . what's that lady's name that was in so much trouble years ago?" I was interviewing her in her beauty shop and asked her if she meant Angela Davis. She agreed that Davis was the name she was looking for and continued with an account of racial profiling as part of her explanation of what the Afro meant to the whites, who appeared in her account as dominating outsiders she referred to as "they." She said, "My girlfriend had a natural and they stopped her in downtown Oakland. I was around my own, so people [thought], 'Oh, you sure look nice in a natural.' "[65]

As the natural traveled ever farther from its origins among dedicated activists, an oxymoron was born: the natural wig. The Afro wig was the basis of a booming industry in the 1970s. Black hairstylist Lee Gilliam recalled that popular identification with Davis increased his wig sales: "Lots of women wanted their hair to look like Angela Davis. I sold a lot of wigs and that was the main cut. I think it had to do with the bigger the natural the more the pride."[66] Despite his recollection that the wigs were worn to express pride, many women I interviewed who adopted Afros in the 1970s recall instead the whimsy of a new style. Gloria Jackson wanted the Afro look. She had long wavy hair that she would not consider cutting for what she knew was just a style: "I wanted a natural during the days when everybody was wearing the big 'fros. So I thought, "I'll buy it!" [Laughs.] I bought this humongous Angela-look wig. So that was my Angela Davis period. Because I always thought she was beautiful. It was just that I wanted a new look. [My friends] just thought it was more funny than anything else."[67] As unstraightened hair gained wide acceptance as a style in black

Figure 5.3. Althea Buckner, the author's cousin,
wearing a large Afro, circa 1974.
Author's personal collection.

communities, blacks increasingly overcame sanctions against the style that had been in place in institutions controlled by whites. By 1970, three bastions of conformity, TWA, the U.S. Army, and the Marines, permitted flight attendants and soldiers to wear Afros.[68] In the early 1970s, struggles over Afros continued only in the most repressive institutions. In 1972, the Black Panther Party newspaper reported that a maximum security men's prison in North Carolina had issued a ban on Afro haircuts. According to the article, prison officials justified the ban with the argument that prisoners with Afros could conceal guns in their hair![69] Prisoners and their supporters on the outside felt that the Afro was worth fighting for. A North Carolina conference challenging brutality in prisons included in its demands for prison reform an end to the ban on Afros. Whether or not prison officials actually believed the "guns in their hair" rationale, the Afro became an issue in the struggle over the balance of control.

Outside of prison walls, a robust capitalist economy sold thousands of synthetically authentic wigs. But after it achieved peak popularity in the early 1970s, the Afro rapidly lost its appeal. By 1970, men and women wore Afros for a variety of reasons. For a relatively small group of current and former political activists, the style was one they had adopted while immersed in social movement cultures. Most African Americans, however, had never participated in protest activity. The majority of African Americans encountered the Civil Rights and Black Power movements through televised images, which represented political movements as styles and postures. Many African Americans adopted these styles to express affiliation with positions of black militancy. Rather than transforming themselves in the context of political action, many men and women transformed their style. They became "militants" by adopting the look. The widespread belief in theories of black self-hatred and the related belief that certain cultural practices (hair straightening being the essential one) embodied self-hatred gave credence to the idea that one became a "militant" by looking like one.

A second reason to wear a natural had little to do with political convictions. Beauty had changed. In 1970, an Afro was beautiful. Women who had been unable to see the tight curls of their hair as beautiful before the birth of the Afro could, by 1970, view their hair in new ways. Quite apart from any political stance, many women wore Afros in the early 1970s to feel attractive.

A third and closely related reason to wear a natural was that it was stylish. The Afro had quickly been modified into a variety of styles, including "mushrooms," "Afro puffs," the "Angela look," and the "curly Afro" or "curly natural." Each variation was more an expression of creativity than of racial pride. The "curly Afro" was obtained by first straightening and then recurling the hair to achieve the look of ringlets of curled hair. After an initial period during which the natural was unacceptable to an older generation of African Americans, school administrators, and white employers, the natural gained currency as a stylish way of wearing one's hair. *Ebony* parodied the change of the Afro from threat to style in a 1970 cartoon in which a balding, white, older businessman wearing a conventional suit enters a black barbershop saying, "Give me an Afro."[70]

By 1970, all of these reasons for wearing natural hair were in circulation. Even those who may have adopted natural hairstyles in order to express political convictions felt the diminution of the meaning conveyed by the accouterments of militancy. By the turn of the decade the Afro was dismissed by many as merely a style. H. Rap Brown complained that too many blacks had "natural hairstyles, but processed minds."[71] The hairstyle had suddenly been drained of its meaning. It could not remain for very long a way of expressing rebellion when it was also a popular commodity.

When and where there is repression, what a woman does when she gets dressed in the morning may be considered political. Wearing or not wearing a veil, disobeying laws that prohibit transgender dressing, or wearing a large Afro in an institution that seeks to diminish the formation of racial alliances are all actions that can serve as challenges to domination. When the context shifts to accommodate forbidden expressions, powerful symbols can return to being pieces of cloth. The natural, once it had become acceptable, became a mere style. As the social activism out of which the style was born fractured in disarray and defeat, the style referred to an increasingly distant historical period of activism.

It is unlikely that oppositional definitions generated within local communities will be sustained intact in a culture in which the mass media has such an overwhelming presence. Styles that originated outside of fashion circles as expressions of opposition to normative orders historically have provided fresh material for the novelty-hungry commercial fashion industry. Women in the Civil Rights Movement stopped straightening their hair to express racial solidarity and self-love. Their creation became the Afro. By 1977, the large Afro, rarely seen on the streets, remained for most African Americans only in snapshots that were viewed as reminders of a laughable, youthful time. An inadvertent product of the Civil Rights Movement, the Afro had become an exhausted commodity.

The rapid dissipation of the meaning of the practice of wearing unstraightened hair and its subsequent incorporation into the market as a mere style might be interpreted as an example of the futility of making gestures of resistance through everyday practices. Yet, in another way, it represents an astounding victory. Historians have demonstrated that beauty, rather than being transcultural and eternal, is a culturally and historically specific set of attributes. The Civil Rights Movement set in motion changes in consciousness and practices that overturned and exposed the fallacy of a national beauty standard which found no place for black women. Nappy hair was no longer unconditionally shameful. Public perceptions of unstraightened African American hair went far beyond mere acceptance to recognition of its beauty. A shift had taken place in popular images of beauty. When kinky hair became stylish, African American women could see new beauty in their bodies. "Black is beautiful" expanded idealized media images of beauty to include some black women. On television and in posters and magazines, black women with tightly curled hair, dark skin, and full lips were portrayed as beauties. These images expanded hegemonic beauty to include black women. In the interviews I conducted, African American women described how they learned to see beauty where they had not seen it before. One woman recalled that "it took me a long time to recognize beauty in people who are really dark. And I think that the ability to do that did have a lot to do with the 'black is beautiful' promotion."[72] Another explained that "you could look at a black person and see that they were beautiful in their own way. In an African way. And this was facilitated by black women themselves where they would accentuate what they had previously tried to obscure."[73]

The Civil Rights Movement set in motion a vast change in the racial picture of the United States, altering the social meaning of black female bodies and, as a result, the way black women could perceive themselves. One of the first challenges faced by many social protest movements is the need to forge a group identity, to get people to think of themselves as workers or as environmentalists.[74] Black social movements in the United States have been unique in that respect. In a country divided by racial inequality, the salience of racial identity persists even in the absence of a movement. And black pride remains, even in the absence of what was for a decade its most distinctive symbol: the natural. Although the natural lost its communicative power, the hairstyle, and other 1960s accouterments of black militancy, were merely the decade's shorthand for racial pride. They were replaced by an ever-changing repertoire of black language, performance, and style that continue to be vehicles for a racial solidarity that transcends fixed expressions.

Chapter Six

YVONNE'S WIG: GENDER

AND THE RACIALIZED BODY

In 1971, I was a student at a junior high school in a predominantly black area of Brooklyn, New York. By then, most of the young female students had persuaded their mothers to let them stop straightening their hair. My schoolmate Yvonne had naturally short, tightly curled hair, the kind that the first critics of Eurocentric beauty standards wanted people to appreciate when they urged African Americans to see black as beautiful.[1] By 1971, however, the natural had been transformed from a symbolic commentary on Eurocentric beauty standards to a new "look" that had itself become the standard of beauty. In a perverse reversal of its origins, the natural had evolved into the Afro, a style that many black women desired but could not have. The Afro look that was considered beautiful was a large round style that required longer hair. The only way for Yvonne to have one was to buy an Afro wig. Students traveled to the school by subway from several Brooklyn neighborhoods, and the ride home was often the most social, playful part of the day. One afternoon, as we stood on the platform, a young man in our group snatched the wig off of Yvonne's head and hurled it onto the subway track. Yvonne stood stunned and humiliated, her short nappy hair exposed and ridiculed by one of her African American classmates.

Why, in 1971, after all of the celebrations of black as beautiful, was her short, tightly curled hair still unacceptable? Was it simply that "black is beautiful," as a racial project, had failed? An analysis based on race alone cannot adequately explain why she wore the wig, why a male schoolmate would grab it from her head, or why the exposure of her own hair was so emotionally devastating.

A generation of black activists and intellectuals had attempted to revise the meaning of "black" in the popular imagination. Their rearticulation of its meaning was embraced widely in black communities. "Black is beautiful" meant that black skin was beautiful, black culture was valuable, black history was worth knowing, and African ancestry was a source of pride. For many blacks, accepting that black is beautiful meant discarding any practices that could be construed as an imitation of whites. In the minds of its proponents during the 1960s and 1970s and in many retrospective accounts of the period, "black is beautiful" was entirely about race. Yet so much of the celebration and critique that stood behind the words was precisely about the meaning and value of the body, and bodies are gendered. As sociologist Paul Gilroy wrote, "Gender is the modality in which race is lived."[2] The practices and social meanings challenged by African Americans in the 1960s were not only racial, but they also signified gender. Although black men and black women shared considerable experiences, the opportunities, dangers, and forms of racism that they faced had never been identical. These differences were often masked by a discourse of racial unity that ignored the specifically gendered ways racial domination expressed itself in the lives of men and women. Identical practices had dissimilar social meanings for black men and black women because anyone evaluating the meaning of their actions would have viewed them through the lens of gender. An examination of the transformation of the meaning of straightened hair for black men and black women reveals these differences. Though the rhetoric of black consciousness exhorted both men and women to wear naturals, straightening hair had different meanings, different consequences, and different chronologies for different sexes. This chapter begins by tracing the transformation in the meaning of straightened hair for black men from the 1940s through the 1960s and then returns to the very different meanings associated with hair straightening for black women. It is a narrative about race but equally one about gender and class, about the allure of dangerous men and the appearance of proper women.

MEN WITH CONKS

In the mid-1960s and early 1970s, straightened hair was the symbol of an imprisoned, self-hating frame of mind. I argue, however, that when black men in the 1940s, 1950s, and early 1960s used lye-based creams to straighten their hair, they were not imitating white men. Rather, they were adopting a black, male style that within some segments of black communities communicated prosperity, sophistication, and an alluring danger. By combing their straightened hair into a pile of loose curls at the top of their foreheads, black men created a style called the "conk," whose variations ranged from the elegance of Nat King Cole's smooth and impeccable peak to James Brown's swirling untidiness. The conk had great visibility because it was the hairstyle of choice for many black male entertainers who popularized it on nightclub stages and in the pages of magazines. Through analysis of oral history interviews and African American publications, I will attempt to recover what conks meant to black men and women in the era before the Civil Rights Movement. Different groups of black men wore conks: entertainers, men who had recently found a way out of poverty, and men who were outside of the boundaries of conventional black norms of respectability. My concern is with what the conk meant to average black men and to the women with whom they associated rather than its meaning for celebrities, who operated under different demands in a public sphere.

Mainstream black men never wore conks. From the 1940s to the early 1960s, the majority of black men did not alter the texture of their hair and wore simple short haircuts that conformed to nationwide expectations of masculinity. Men with conks stood out. Most famously, entertainers wore conks, but the hairstyle was part of the flamboyance that was acceptable for and even expected of people in show business. Among noncelebrities, the style divided men by class and spoke volumes about their socioeconomic location, class aspirations, and heroes within black social worlds. From the perspective of a man who was poor or newly emerging from poverty, a conk conveyed prosperity. For a rural to urban migrant, it displayed an urban look. Members of the black middle class or those who accepted middle-class values generally granted that the style was appropriate for celebrities but assumed that ordinary men who wore conks were either of a lower class or criminals.

When viewed in hindsight, from the perspective of a post–black power era, the conk is associated with racial shame and with the pathos and absurdity of the painful technique of straightening hair with lye, an interpretation that is epitomized in *The Autobiography of Malcolm X*, which contains literature's most familiar account of a man with a conk. Malcolm X's recollection of processing his hair and burning his scalp begins his classic account of his journey from degradation to self-love. The association the autobiography, published in 1965, made between hair straightening and black shame resonated with the growing belief that black self-hatred was a formidable obstacle to black power. The text nonetheless reveals not only Malcolm's mid-1960s interpretation of the conk but also the meaning of a conk in 1941. Before 1965, within black communities, black hair practices signified as much about class and gender as they did about race.

The painful straightening of Malcolm's hair was a rite of passage that marked his transformation from hick to hipster, from rural adolescence to a distinctively black style of manhood. When Malcolm arrived in Boston in 1941, he was a provincial bumpkin. In his words, "I looked like Li'l Abner. Mason, Michigan, was written all over me. My kinky reddish hair was cut hick style, and I didn't even use grease in it."[3] In time, he befriended Shorty, who helped transform Malcolm from Li'l Abner to Detroit Red, from a rustic who was self-described as a white cartoon character to an urban, black hipster. Shorty taught Malcolm how to mix lye, potatoes, eggs, Vaseline, and soap to create a straightening agent. The lye mixture was notoriously harsh, routinely burning the scalps of the men who used it. Pain was central to Malcolm's description, as it was crucial to the appeal of the conk during its heyday. Pain rendered narcissism masculine. As Malcolm shouted to his friend to be careful, Shorty reassured him and praised him for his endurance: "The first time's always worst. You get used to it better before long. You took it real good homeboy. You got a good conk."[4] The scene ends, and Malcolm X shifts the narrator's perspective forward to the mid-1960s when he writes, "This was my first really big step toward self-degradation: when I endured all of that pain, literally burning my flesh to have it look like a white man's hair." Indeed, that was the meaning of the conk in the mid-1960s but not earlier.[5] In the 1940s, 1950s, and early 1960s, he and the other men with conks fashioned themselves after black celebrities and other cool, black, urban men. Former Black Panther Emory Douglas recalled: "I used to process my hair when I was younger. That was the thing, process and put the conk in your hair. You used to want to be like Jackie Wilson and Marvin Gaye and them during that time. Blacks used to identify with the black entertainers. And they used to want to have that pressed hair that had that look. You used to see B. B. King and all those and James Brown. All of them had the 'dos' at that time."[6]

When Douglas wore a conk, he was not attempting to look like Elvis Presley or any other white man. His models were black entertainers. In order to achieve the sophisticated look of an R&B star, ordinary men went to processing shops where they paid to have their hair straightened and styled into conks that were far more elegant than those that were produced at home (see figure 6.1). As a migrant from rural Arkansas to urban Oakland, California, Lee Gilliam was typical of those men for whom the conk symbolized upward mobility. Finding employment in a factory as an adolescent, he suddenly had more cash than ever before. Gilliam's conk was a way of exhibiting the prosperity that was the product of his hard work and of defining his new urban status. As he recalled, "When I was sixteen, I went to a cannery in Hayward, California, and got a job, and so I was making 170 dollars every two weeks, and it was more money than I had ever had in my life. So, therefore, the first thing I did was went and bought clothes and started going to a processing shop. So I went there once a week and sometimes twice a week. A process showed that I had money and prestige. I could afford to do anything I wanted. I was showing that I wasn't poor."[7] For Gilliam, the professional look of his hairstyle was an important element of its distinction. The polished look demonstrated that he had sufficient disposable income to have his hair straightened and styled by an expert. The significance of the cost of a professionally straightened and styled

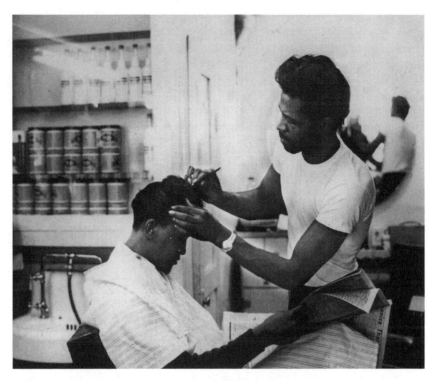

Figure 6.1. Processing shop. Red Powell/Reggie Pettis Archive,
photographer unknown, Fillmore District, San Francisco, circa 1950s.

conk registered with poor women. One woman who came of age in the 1950s
described her unease around men who had conks. She noted that those men
would have been middle class, "because they could afford to get their hair
processed and at that time it wasn't cheap."[8] Describing her view of the middle class from the distance of her poverty, she said she "would feel uncomfortable with [men with conks] because you feel like they are . . .," and then she
paused before finishing, "well they had." The price of a visit to a hair stylist
seemed well out of her reach and beyond the grasp of the men with whom she
felt comfortable. Men who wore conks knew that their swirling hairstyles could
impress others as status symbols, which is at least part of the reason that they
wore them. However, that is not how conks were always perceived. From the
perspective of some impoverished blacks, men with conks were middle class.
Many other blacks had entirely different views.

In order to learn how conks were perceived, I asked the women I interviewed
whose contemporaries wore conks if they would have dated a man with a conk.
The answers I received revealed how central class was to the meaning of the

conk and how issues of class were associated with prevailing notions of desirability and danger. Barbara Williams, who was from a working-class family, was categorical when she insisted that she would have never dated a man with a conk.

> No. No. No. Because when I was a little girl it was a different day! There were hardworking men. But you would see the pimps with the conk on their hair. That's the kind of man that did it. When you see men with a conk on their hair you stayed away from them.
>
> *Author*: So you wouldn't date a man with a "conk"?
>
> *Williams*: No! Oh no! That was terrible! Because you know they were a player. They didn't have the right attitude. They weren't educated. They were hustlers. "Hustlers" is the word I want. You stayed away from those kinds.
>
> *Author*: Okay, so in your neighborhood it would be a hustler. But what about Nat King Cole and Hank Ballard?
>
> *Williams*: It was the thing to do. That's what all the entertainers did. I guess if all the men did it, it would have been okay too. But they didn't! It was just that specific group that did it.[9]

According to Williams, it was acceptable for an entertainer to have his hair straightened, since he was not expected to be conventional. But in her view any other man with a conk lacked education, had a bad attitude, and must have been surviving through some illegal hustle. In her eyes, the conk divided black men by class, and she stayed away from men with conks.

"Never, never, never, never, never, never!" was Mary O'Neal's answer when I asked her if she ever dated a man who wore his hair in a conk. Her response was as emphatic as Williams's, but she conceded that the very danger that those men represented made them appealing. "I'm not suggesting that this was some kind of righteous thing. Because I liked men with 'conks.' They were grand. They were the nightlife. They were the other side. They were dangerous. I never dated a man [with a conk] because I was too timid."[10]

Given her respectable, middle-class background, Mary O'Neal lived on one side of the class divide, while men with conks represented "the other side"— the world of the street, the night, and the various forms of survival by one's wits known as hustles. It was a male realm par excellence for men who eschewed conventional achievement and domesticity. There were many names for these flamboyant, stylish, dangerous men: players, hustlers, slick dudes, and pimps. Their style presented a host of contradictions. The femininity of their attention to appearance was countered by their hypermasculine association with violence, the ostentation of their clothing countered by the precariousness of their finances. Former Black Panther Eldridge Cleaver called them "slick dudes" when he remembered the highly styled, "croquinole" conk, manicured nails, and eye-catching clothes he wore as a young man, when he was getting into trouble on the streets of Los Angeles. "They used to do what you'd call the croquinole. That's what all the slick dudes wanted. We let our fingernails grow, and we'd wear pretty clothes, and go down and let Pat Moore do our hair."[11]

The "slick dudes" lived on the margins of black society. These were men whose masculinity and blackness were not generally questioned within their communities despite the flamboyance of their tailoring or the length of their curls. In the general, as opposed to the specifically African American, culture in the United States, long hair and elaborate hair care routines have been considered feminine since 1840.[12] Though one can easily think of exceptions, from the short "bobs" of female flappers in 1920s to the long hair worn by male hippies, the exceptions actually confirm the rule. Rebels defy gender norms.[13] Because it constituted part of the look of a slick dude, the conk was masculine, but it was always a marginalized masculinity. Sociologist Robert Connell describes hegemonic masculinity as the dominant but not the only way of being masculine in a culture.[14] The dominance of hegemonic masculinity is reinforced by the marginalization of alternative ways of being male. Some black men who were marginalized because they were black and who were further marginalized by their exclusion from conventional employment, proudly and intentionally created distinct black and masculine forms of self-presentation. Part of the look was the conk. Processed hair on men was a peculiar symbol that conveyed male toughness through what were generally considered feminine symbols: long hair with soft waves, hair that moved. Through the "conk," marginalized heterosexual males created a form of maleness that transcended the narrow boundaries of hegemonic male styles. The conk—like the flamboyant tailoring of a zoot suit or a hippie's long hair—was unquestionably masculine within certain subcultures precisely because it represented rebellion. Hence, the importance of pain in descriptions of "conking."

However, irrespective of the pain, many black men and women did not consider the conk masculine. In the 1940s, 1950s, and early 1960s, there was never a single, universally accepted meaning of the conk within black communities. From the perspective of different social locations within black communities the conk meant different things. Likewise, there was never a single black community view of what constituted masculinity. For some, the polished nails and elaborately styled straightened hair of a player were expressions of hip masculinity. For others, who defined manhood as the polar opposite of femininity, such forms of primping could only diminish a man's masculinity. These differences may have been regional. The conk was an urban look that ostentatiously displayed an identity with an urban base. Brenda Travis, who grew up poor in McComb, Mississippi, did not recall seeing many conks during her years in rural Mississippi. She knew the style from the photographs of entertainers that appeared weekly in *Jet*. Bo Diddley's mother was a neighbor, and when her famous son would return to Mississippi for a visit, Travis would see the conk-wearing rock and roll star in person. Beyond Bo Diddley, she could not recall any conks and was highly amused when I asked her if she would have dated a man with a conk: "Nn nn. I don't think I would have dated a man with . . . [big laugh], no [still laughing]. No. Because to me it almost looked like the processed hair was too feminine, you know? To me it looked feminine. I felt that it was okay for me to do it because it would add something to me. But then what was it supposed to be doing for him? Make him look as good and pretty as me?"[15]

Before the emergence of the black consciousness movement, the conk had a variety of meanings. To poor, urban, black men and women, it often represented sophistication and prosperity. Wearing a conk, one could be like the entertainers, who were virtually the only African Americans who received national recognition. To others, it bore the stigma (or appeal) of its association with dangerous men. Many accepted it as a masculine style, but others could not reconcile its fussiness with a masculine ideal. And, to some, it represented a desire to imitate whites. Before the mid-1960s, the belief that straightening one's hair was an attempt to look white was not the dominant interpretation of the practice, but it was one of the meanings in circulation. In 1953, a reporter from *Jet* asked men and women on the street the question, "Should Negro men marcel their hair?"[16] The responses he received indicated the variety of ways blacks understood the conk in the 1950s. One black New Yorker who thought black men should not straighten their hair voiced the argument that would, by 1965, become the prevailing view of the meaning of a process. In his opinion, men who put chemicals in their hair to straighten it were vainly trying to look like white men. Another, however, rejected hair processing on grounds of aesthetics and gender norms. "Nobody," he said, "has found a way to make a man's hair look 'good' when it is not. Conks are obviously 'conked.' They are either very greasy (what woman would want to run her fingers through one?) or very shiny (which makes a man look like he is Simonized)." Furthermore, they were "impossibly sissy." References to race or to racial self-hatred are absent from the respondent's list of objections. His concern was gender. What kind of man would wear greasy, shiny, sissified hair? (See figure 6.2.) *Jet* was closely attuned to trends in black communities. By asking passers-by about the appropriateness of the conk, they called attention to the prevalence of objections to the style. These interpretations became more common and eventually led to the conk's demise. Four years later, black New Yorkers were still divided about the meaning of the conk when the *Amsterdam News* asked the same question. Though a few respondents considered the style attractive, others objected to conking on medical grounds, warning of dangers ranging from baldness to brain damage. Two respondents criticized men who wore conks for wishing to look like whites.[17] Although the style still had many adherents, it was losing its appeal even among its former social base. The conk's dwindling appeal may have been

Figure 6.2. High school class picture, circa 1956, San Francisco. Clean-cut young black men did not process their hair. Their black female classmates all had straightened hair. San Francisco History Center, San Francisco Public Library.

hastened by the increasing number of middle-class blacks who did their best to stigmatize what they considered a dirty and lower-class style.

A 1960 headline in the *Baltimore Afro-American* announced JUDGE "DE-CLARES WAR" ON "PROCESSES": "NATURAL" HAIR-DOS ORDERED.[18] Philadelphia judge Juanita Stout had ordered twenty-five conk-wearing male defendants to cut their hair. Stout viewed conks as "badge[s] of delinquency" that were furthermore unsanitary and injurious to the scalp. Beyond that, a "conk," she said, "makes boys look like girls." Nowhere in the article, which appeared in a black newspaper, was any reference made to race. For Stout, the conk was a disreputable form of lower-class rebellion that transgressed social standards by violating gendered norms of appearance. Stout criticized the conk because she felt the style was both lower class and feminine. She did not expel these men from her courtroom for trying to emulate white men; rather, she expelled them for wearing a style that was strangely hypermasculine—a dirty, injurious, "hoodlum" style—and too feminine. Respectable men wore short, untreated hair. The gendered meaning of straightened hair is evident in the coverage the case received in *Jet*, which quoted a critic of Stout's decision: "Does this mean she's going to stop women from attending beauty shops and getting their hair straightened?"[19] His question was telling, since Stout wore her hair as the vast majority of black women did in 1960—straightened. Though straightened hair on men was considered part of a hoodlum's look, women were expected to straighten their hair to maintain a conventional appearance.

Stout's order reflected the growing perception that conks were a lower class and effeminate style, a view that threatened the livelihoods of the legions of men who ran processing shops. Duke Price, the barber who put the conk in Nat King Cole's hair whenever the singer visited Philadelphia, tried to create a distinction to rescue the perception of conks when he commented that only nonprofessionally processed conks constituted the "hoodlum look."[20] The distinction he drew was meaningless to members of the black middle class who continued to attack the image of the men who wore conks and the shops that styled them. An item in the November 4, 1965, health column in *Jet* citing Veteran's Administration findings echoed Stout's 1960 charge that conks were unhealthy. Further attacks came from licensed barbers. Commercial processing had been a distinct occupation that, unlike barbering, required no formal training and was unlicensed. The January 13, 1966, issue of *Jet* reported that the Pennsylvania Barber Licensing Board had shut down more than two hundred unlicensed processors in Philadelphia. The same year, a news photograph in the August 4 *Jet* from the "long hot summer" contrasted trim respectability to conked criminality as a shorn black policeman frisked a conked rioter. The caption under what the magazine called one of the week's best photos read: "A hard-driving policeman in Cleveland gives a young 'du-rag brother' a thorough search during the raging violence. As in [the] Watts, Harlem, Chicago riots, Negro policemen and national guardsmen were used prominently in curbing the violence and looting."[21] Men who had felt stylish wearing conks began to feel out of date or foolish. The conking ritual or the trip to the processing shop lost its former aura and was simply a painful nuisance. Hip young men began to wear an unstraightened style cut in an angular shape called the "Quo Vadis." The number of entertainers who wore conks declined, and the style's remaining association was with lower-class men.

In the thousands of images of black men that appeared in the ninety-six issues of *Ebony* published between 1960 and 1967, a period during which the overwhelming number of black women straightened their hair, only thirty-five showed men with straightened hair in feature stories. Of this group, twenty-four were popular musicians, seven were other types of entertainers (e.g., stunt performers), one was a boxer, another a billiard hall owner, and the remaining two had entertainment industry ties: James Brown's barber and the cotillion escort of Nat King Cole's daughter.

Excluded from this count were the models who appeared in advertisements for men's hair straighteners. During these years, Posner's So-mild, Johnson's Ultra Wave, Perma-Strate, Super Crown, Duke, and Glossine continued to promise black men gleaming straight or wavy hair. The regular advertisements for male hair straightening products in *Ebony* during those years are evidence of the presence of a market for the products. Black men bought hair straighteners, but those men were too far outside of *Ebony*'s normative vision of black America to be shown in *Ebony*'s pages except as entertainers. Poorer men, not the middle class, were buying these products. Because the conk represented a form of marginalized black masculinity, it was spurned in the 1960s by an emerging young, black middle class.

Masculinity is closely associated with economic power, and up until 1960 all but a small fraction of African American men were excluded from everything but the most menial work. In the 1960s, as a result of the push to end discrimination and the expansion of the public sector, more conventional middle-class occupations became increasingly available to black men.[22] As professions and professional organizations opened up to African Americans and African American concerns, conks, the men who wore them, and the establishments that produced them were increasingly pushed aside. As opportunities for achieving hegemonic masculinity grew, the style increasingly represented nothing but poverty. No longer the mark of a hip urbanite, the conk was worn by those left behind.

Shortly after the conk lost its position as a symbol of urbane masculinity, a new form of rebelliousness appeared—the natural look, a new form of boldness that was more than a rejection of middle-class norms. The new style represented identification with the emerging Black Power Movement and carried with it the dignity of racial pride. As historian Robin D. G. Kelley has shown, the style known as the Afro began as a female style but transformed into a symbol of black male militancy.[23]

As low-income men were abandoning the conk, versions of black power ideology were forming that would reinterpret the style in racial terms. The ideology had roots in black college campuses, social movement organizations, and in the journals produced by those in the early black consciousness scene, a milieu with a disproportionately middle-class leadership that may have always looked askance at "du-rag brothers." After the publication of *The Autobiography of Malcolm X*, which carried the message that those who wore conks had all along been ashamed of their race, countless writers repeated the formulation that processed hair was a repudiation of black identity. In 1967, Ron Karenga attacked processing in *The Quotable Karenga*: "We say 'Negroes' are suffering from 'mass insanity.' Any man who burns his hair, bites his lips, or bleaches his skin, has got to be insane."[24] That same year, Julia Fields published a short story in *Negro Digest*, "Not Your Singing, Dancing Spade," about a self-hating black man who straightens his hair and is married to a white woman. His dark-skinned, short-haired black maid tries to teach the man's daughter black consciousness.[25]

By the time straightened hair became a symbol of racial shame, most African American men who had processed their hair had already stopped. In giving up processing his hair, a man moved from a marginalized toward a more conventional form of black masculinity. Hair, formerly a marker of gender identity and class position, became a marker of race. New codes, riding the crest of a powerful social movement, obliterated previous meanings of the conk. For men, these new codes of racialized practices easily articulated with already existing gender and class codes. To be black and proud was also to be, unambiguously, a man.

Emory Douglas grew up in the Fillmore and Hunter's Point sections of San Francisco. As a youth, he identified with men who wore conks and wore one himself for many years. I asked him when he stopped straightening his hair. His answer interested me, precisely because it was so vague. He could not pin down when he stopped processing his hair: "I think I got away from that during the mid '60s, just prior to the Panthers. I think about three, four years before the Panthers, about '63 I started getting away from that because it used to burn my head so much. I used to do it myself with the lye. I mean it was just painful. You could go to the barber, but I never could afford that. So you used to do it yourself. But I think it was somewhere around then because at the same time flat hairstyles used to be the styles from that time too."[26] Douglas could not remember when he stopped processing his hair. Perhaps it was 1963 or perhaps not. After all, the process was only a hairstyle. His account of the change from straightened hair to a natural contrasts strikingly to the detailed accounts black women give of their transition from straightened hair to naturals. Women I interviewed about the switch remembered details such as the name of the shop they went to, how a stranger on the street reacted to it, or the first glimpse of themselves in the mirror. They remembered their experiences because of the intensity of their feelings about the transition. By contrast, men remembered little. The transitions men made from wearing conks to non-straightened hairstyles were steps toward more conventional masculinity. Processed hair on women carried quite a different set of meanings, and as a result the transition from straightened hair to naturals was more difficult, more memorable, and often more temporary for black women than for black men. The next section traces these very different set of meanings that circulated in black communities regarding black women's straightened hair.

"BALD-HEADED" WOMEN

Within black communities, women with long and wavy hair were prized for their "femininity." As soon as an infant girl's hair began to reveal texture, adults would begin speculating about whether the girl would have "good" hair. This norm cut across class and region, and all black women, regardless of the natural length or texture of their hair, were judged by the standard. This standard of beauty was constant from the nineteenth century up until the emergence of the Black Power Movement when, for a very brief period, women with short, tightly curled hairstyles won broad approval. In a few years' time, the old norms of beauty and femininity crept back into acceptance, Afro styles were worn longer, the curls of Afros were looser, and finally women returned to a variety of styles that either flaunted or emulated longer and wavier hair. Women with hair that would not grow long were subject to ridicule. Some wore wigs and when exposed were subject to even greater scorn. Henry Byrd, a black Louisianan who recorded as Roy Byrd and more frequently as Professor Longhair, released in 1950 "Bald Head," the only chart hit in his long career as a rhythm and blues musician. The lyrics refer not to an absolutely bald woman but to an African American woman whose tightly curled hair has broken from combing and has never grown long. The words capture the derision directed toward women who lacked the essential feminine attribute of long enough hair.

> Looky there. She ain't got no hair.
> Bald head!
> Hiding over there. Bald head!
> Where that girl hair? Bald Head!
> Oh looky here. Bald head!
> She ain't got no hair.
> Bald head! Aah looky there. Bald head!
> Where that girl hair? Bald head![27]

The song's popularity attests to the acceptability of ridiculing women who lacked sufficient hair. Twenty years after Professor Longhair recorded "Bald Head," at a time when "black is beautiful" was on the verge of becoming a cliché, Yvonne stood humiliated on a subway platform because her schoolmate knew he could raise laughter among his friends by exposing her "bald head." In the previous pages, I have traced the changing meanings associated with longish, straightened hair and short, kinky hair when worn by men in black communities. Short, unstraightened hair was the norm for conventional masculinity. Rebellious men flouted these standards by transgressing the gender norm and wearing longer, straightened hair in the 1940s and 1950s and then by wearing longer, unstraightened hair in the mid- to late 1960s. Since short, unstraightened hair represented conventional masculinity for men, women with short, unstraightened hair were pressured to hide or transform it or be subject to scorn.

While black social norms barred conventional men from lavishing too much attention on their hair, women's hair was only presentable when it was elaborately groomed. Young girls' hair was braided. Adult women wore their hair straightened or, at a minimum, greased and pulled back. First widely adopted in the 1920s, the practice of hair straightening gained greater and greater acceptance until it was essentially mandatory for any black woman, rural or urban. If there was no time or money to have it straightened, kinky hair was hidden under a scarf. The only women who did not cover, control through braiding, or straighten their hair in some way were those whose hair was naturally straight, although even these women frequently straightened their hair to achieve the conventional look. Hair straightening was one of the most basic elements of a young woman's grooming. Civil rights activist Juadine Henderson, who grew up in rural Mississippi in the 1950s, recalled:

> I always knew once you washed your hair until it was straightened you put a scarf on it. You always knew that it was not a good thing to have nappy hair. One of the first things you learned about taking care of your own hair was how to straighten it. Nobody ever said why you couldn't go outside with your hair washed. But you learned very early on that you couldn't. I remember being very happy because my mother didn't want my hair straightened when I was really little because she thought it would ruin it. It would take the natural straightness out. But when they were trying to make you pretty, your hair was straightened.[28]

The customs that defined acceptable appearance for women were about gender and dignity. Short hair was considered masculine, and naturally kinky hair on women was considered shamefully unkempt. Just as the Civil Rights and ensuing Black Power movements led to a reexamination of male norms of self-presentation, it also led to a questioning of the conventions that women followed. Recognizing the part that racism played in constructing norms of long and straightened hair, advocates for a new racial pride defined kinky hair as beautiful and dignified.

Men who gave up conking their hair abandoned a style that was not widely accepted as either dignified or appropriate in terms of gender. Women who stopped straightening their hair refused to follow a practice that was still viewed by most African Americans as essential to a dignified and appropriately feminine appearance. Black women who wore naturals earlier than 1966 did so before the style was widely recognizable as a symbol of militancy or beauty. Ruth Beckford wore a natural in 1952, years before the style even had a name. She taught dance to little children, and when she walked into her familiar dance studio with a short natural for the first time, one of her perplexed young students asked her, "Are you a man?"[29] When the first women, motivated by racial pride, started wearing natural hairstyles, they felt opposing tugs between feminine ideals and racial pride. Unlike men who moved toward more conventional gender identities by ceasing to straighten their hair, women who wore their hair in naturals broke with dominant norms of femininity. A common theme in the recollections of women I interviewed about their early natural hairstyles was mistaken gender identity. Linda Burnham recalled being yelled at as she approached the women's bathroom: "They would do double takes, a lot of double takes. I remember once I was driving across the country. And I got out of the car at a gas station and was headed toward the bathroom. And the gas station attendant yelled at me from behind that I was going to the wrong bathroom. He thought I was a man. Because of the hair. And it wasn't malicious. It was just sort of out of his experience. I had on earrings and everything, but he had a hard time putting it together."[30] Pearl Marsh remembered being called "sir": "The thing that [women with Afros] all complained about was white people. When you went to stores or you were at the gas station or something, they would always refer to you as "sir." But it felt like we were invisible anyway. And somehow having Afros meant that we couldn't even be distinguished sexually. Whether we were women or men."[31]

Many men stopped straightening their hair in the early 1960s, but when these men returned their hair to its untreated state they did not create a new style. When women moved from straightened conventionality to unstraightened transgression of racialized gender norms, they created a style so startling someone had to name it. Men had masculinity to gain and nothing to lose by wearing unstraightened hair. By contrast, many women who chose to express proud black identity by wearing a natural felt that they diminished their identity as women by doing so.

When men received conks, it was in a masculine context. Recall the way Shorty initiated Malcolm X into his hip new identity by training him in the home chemistry of conking. If men could afford to have their hair professionally transformed, they went to processing shops run by and for men. In the early 1960s, women had to go to an all-male institution, the barber shop, to obtain a natural style. A woman who adopted the style ahead of others explained that she felt that asking for an Afro in a women's beauty shop would have been tantamount to insulting the beautician: "If I go in a beauty shop and ask for that [style], they would be offended. Because the purpose of black beauty shops was to make you look as European as possible. That was their mission! So you can't go to them. I mean they would be offended. They'd be pissed off. And your hair would probably look terrible. It was clear that going into a beauty shop to ask for an Afro was an act of suicide."[32] She enjoyed stepping into the cool, male world of the barbershop. In an era when acts of rebellion were becoming acceptable, she felt welcomed there.

When and where women have been able to transgress gender boundaries, they often experienced the thrill of being included in a higher status realm. "It was like, 'Hey, I'm one of the fellows,' " she recalled. "I can tell my brothers I've been to the barber shop. It just felt like the place to be." Black women were not always welcome in the male public space of the barbershop, and when they appeared some barbers, trained to think of black male and female hair care in distinctly different terms, did not know what to do with them. In the early 1960s, near Washington, D.C., Juadine Henderson had been covering her unstraightened hair for a year and decided to go to a barbershop to have it cut into an Afro shape: "The man said 'If you need your hair done . . .' because it was fairly long by then. It hadn't been straightened in a year, and I had worn it covered most of that time. Comb it back and put a scarf on it. He said 'I'll give you money to get your hair done.' And I said, 'No, thank you. I came to get it cut. Now are you going to cut it or not?'" Against his better judgment, the barber cut Henderson's hair, and she delighted in her new look. When she visited her relatives in Mississippi, she recalled, "The older people who would say 'Hey little boy,' and stuff like that to try and tease you because you had short hair. It didn't make any difference. I loved it."[33]

"Black is beautiful" promised to satisfy femininity and black identity, and for many women it did. Generally, these were women who found support for the yet unconventional act of wearing a natural through their membership in black movement communities in which others shared in a growing sense of black consciousness. These circles of activists provided a buffer against the conservative judgments of their families and the wider community. Zoharah Simmons, a SNCC member who attended classes at the historically black, male Morehouse College in Atlanta in 1963, recalled that when she first adopted the natural style, she only found acceptance when among other SNCC members: "Walking down the street in the black community, people thought nothing of insulting you about it. It was definitely difficult to face the world every day and go over to my classes at Morehouse. It was an act of defiance. You were fighting yourself to keep up your sense of self. But it was difficult. Because, you see, the only place where you were even hearing this notion of " 'black is beautiful' and all of that was in the SNCC office."[34]

In the early 1960s, short, natural hair on women was viewed by most black men and women not as natural but as "nappy," unattractive, and masculine. Within the black movement community, however, alternative standards prevailed. These standards spread beyond the confines of civil rights organizations to black neighborhoods and college campuses so that by 1966 the natural became a recognizable symbol of racial pride or political or generational defiance. Women with naturals were greeted with warm recognition rather than shocked stares, and for a few years black women wearing naturals could feel beautiful and know that the beauty of their unstraightened hair was recognized by others.

In the late 1960s and early 1970s, the Afro became masculinized.[35] Whereas any unstraightened hairstyle when worn by a woman constituted a radical new look, a man's unstraightened hair was only distinguished as an Afro when it was grown longer than a conventional man's short, unstraightened hair. The large Afro became a hallmark of the popular image of black "militants," male or female. As men adopted the style, a space was opened for hegemonic gender norms to be reasserted. As the size of the Afro became the focus of its appeal, the original critique of Eurocentric constructions of femininity that had been central to radical black women's rejection of hair straightening was lost. Historian Robin D. G. Kelley notes that the masculinization of the Afro ushered in the return of Eurocentric beauty standards for women.[36] When black men claimed the Afro as their own, it ceased to be a style black women could describe as feminine. Few within black movement communities questioned whether women needed to be feminine. In the late 1960s and early 1970s, analyses of race seemed crystal clear, but analyses of gender within black communities were awkward and tenuous and their proponents vulnerable to accusations of race betrayal. The rhetoric of black consciousness had so often framed discussions of natural hair versus straightened hair in terms of race alone that the specifically gendered way that Eurocentric standards had made black women's hair a source of shame was obscured. The sure acceptance black women had felt when wearing naturals during the brief period in which black movement standards had disseminated into broader communities slipped away as conventional Eurocentric constructions of femininity were reasserted. The femininity of natural hair was questioned in a 1967 article in *Jet* when Maria Cole, the widow of singer Nat King Cole, commented that wearing natural hair was "a form of defiance. Beauty should always come first . . . femininity is the most attractive thing a woman could have."[37] In 1969, a black woman expressed similar sentiments in a letter to *Ebony*: "I go along with being black, thinking black and living black, but I don't go along with the new 'Afro' hairstyle on our women. . . . Disagree all you want, but think. The men look great and masculine in their Afro hair styles—our women look great and masculine too."[38] She noted that black men were dating white women with long, "silky" hair. In her view, women who wore unstraightened hair completely relinquished their femininity. Her understanding of black pride did not require her to critically examine a racialized standard of female beauty that demanded long, silky hair.

The next year, the image of Angela Davis was reproduced in untold numbers of posters as a symbol of defiance. Though she stood for unwavering commitment to freedom and justice, in the age of mass reproduction her face and especially her hairstyle were rapidly transformed into widely recognized images of beauty and further into a mere style. The halo-like Afro's stylishness made it an acceptable expression of femininity, but like all hairstyles, the large, round Afro's stylishness was eventually supplanted by fresher trends. Women who had adopted it merely as a style could easily abandon it when fashions changed. The Afro, in its iconic large round form, also disappeared in the late 1970s as a male style. Its demise was the result of the reassertion of hegemonic gender norms. The end of the grand Afro as a style for black men was, in part, like the earlier rejection of conked hairstyles, a male retreat from the image of the dandy and a move toward a more conventionally masculine appearance.

Likewise, when women returned to straightening their hair, they returned to conformity with longstanding racialized gender norms. The old standard that considered longer, wavier hair "good" hair reemerged. Many women, under pressure to be conservative at work and feminine at all times, resumed straightening their hair. Black and white manufacturers in the hair care industry had, in the meantime, awakened to the expanding potential of selling hair care products to an upwardly mobile black population. Industrial chemists created permanent straighteners that were somewhat milder than their home-brewed precursors. Cosmetic companies then euphemistically promoted these products as "relaxers." Black women in the 1970s flocked to drugstores to purchase the newly available chemical "relaxers," which produced the miracle of straightened hair that moved and could be washed. Straightened hair resumed its position as the dominant hair care practice for African American women, a status it has largely retained to this day.[39]

In the early and mid-1960s, it was much more difficult for a black woman to wear a natural than it was for a black man. The normative style for black women had been straightened hair, and as a result wearing unstraightened hair required greater courage for women than for men. Hair had for generations been a difficult and painful issue for many black women. Short hair was the subject of ridicule, and the need to straighten hair was taken for granted. Black women who had long hair were prized especially if their hair had a straighter, wavier texture. Zoharah Simmons recalled that her older relatives were incredulous when she cut her hair to wear it in a short Afro during the 1960s: "All the years that I had had my hair done, straightened and curled and all, people admired my hair because I had a full head of hair. So it was almost as if people would say, 'I mean the one thing you had going! You cut that off. My God!' "[40]

One of the initial surprises of my research was the number of black women who first decided to stop straightening their hair while attending predominantly white colleges. Though natural hairstyles were symbols of heightened racial consciousness, they were, ironically, easier to adopt when isolated from black communities. Away from home, women were free of the particular demands of conventional African American standards. Among whites, who were less sensitive to differences among blacks, African American women escaped standards that made important distinctions between black women based on hair texture. One black woman who stopped straightening her hair while she was a student at a predominantly white university explained the difference between the way she was perceived at home in a black community and at college in a white environment: "When I was growing up in Chicago, there was the whole thing about light-skinned, straight hair, black girls. I was definitely of the skinny legged, brown-skinned, nappy-haired grouping. What I realized was that the white men didn't care about that. If they wanted that they could be with somebody blond haired and blue eyed. And so I feel like that's what allowed me to cut my hair [to wear an Afro] more than anything that was happening with blacks."[41] Black women on predominantly white campuses encountered a beauty standard that had traveled a circuitous route. Black activism in the early 1960s partly inspired white student counterculture. Whites in the counterculture, naive about black differences, exoticized blacks and glorified "soul." Black women who attended predominantly white colleges found, among some white students, more accepting beauty standards than the standards they learned at home. While black activism provided inspiration for the white counterculture, white counterculture's refusal of conventions had its influence on African American youths.

Chinosole, who stopped straightening her hair and cut it into a natural while at a predominantly white college, was quite uneasy with the style long after she adopted it. The standards of the women who raised her remained with her even after she rejected the grooming practices they required. Her mother and aunts taught her that good grooming represented black dignity. Even away from home, while attending a white college, where in some circles rebellion was respected, cutting her hair felt like committing a sin against the race:

> I can remember feeling very embarrassed and self-conscious and like I had committed one of the gravest wrongs to all black women by not straightening my hair. And I was in a predominantly white environment. I'm not sure I could have done the same thing in a predominantly black environment. . . . By that time I wasn't the type of person to be wondering what people thought about my Afro. But it was more like my sense of responsibility to black women and how they had reared me. To keep myself, so the break was with my aunts and guardian mother. And all the trouble they went to get a certain length of hair. And then I cut it off! That's where the turmoil was.[42]

Black women whose hair had never grown long had been subject to disparagement when they were judged by a standard that expected women to have a full head of hair. Those whose hair had grown long were aware of how much their families valued that length. To see themselves as beauties when they had short, unstraightened hair, black women had to rid themselves of any memory of the ridicule of "nappy-headed," "bald-headed" women. A black woman's first natural hairstyle was a major, memorable step that combined trepidation and joy. In the brief span of years when the words "black is beautiful" were widely accepted, black women may have felt greater pleasure in the celebration of the beauty of black skin and in the acceptance of African hair texture than men. For women with short hair and for all of the women with tightly curled hair who had felt compelled to straighten it just to appear normal, the moment of acceptance of natural hair was euphoric. By the end of the decade, however, dominant gender norms, which were infused with ideals of European beauty, reemerged, and many black women wanted straightened hair.

For the majority of black women to continue to feel comfortable, beautiful, and proud wearing short, unstraightened hair, it would have been necessary for there to have been wide discussion of gender and how sexism and racism interacted in various ways to place different demands on black men and women. Instead, what remained in the aftermath of the peak years of "black is beautiful" was a strong sense of black pride but a confusing set of social expectations for black women. Women returned to straightening their hair to conform with what they knew were prevailing standards of feminine beauty, but they did so with guilty consciences, looking for ways to see the styles they adopted as authentic, African, or natural.

Black women's hair had been politicized. The politicization was an extension of the way black women generally had served as symbols in the process of racial rearticulation. As artists, intellectuals, and community spokespersons fought racism by rearticulating the meaning of race, they relied on symbols that carried with them a host of meaning about gender differences and class distinctions. The next two chapters look at the difficulties of being a living representation of the race. Pre–civil rights era discourse of racial uplift placed particular emphasis on the role of women as upstanding representatives of the race. According to this logic, women would stand as living refutations of racist characterizations of blacks by their embodiment and display of middle-class propriety. When young African Americans, in tune with youths nationwide, turned against the middle class, women became easy targets for scorn. Chapter 7 is about black women as symbols of the middle class. Women continued to function as symbols in the proliferating discourses of the black power era. Chapter 8 traces the ways in which black activists strove to find a basis for unity grounded in the body and symbolized by the beautiful black woman.

Chapter Seven

PRIDE AND SHAME:

BLACK WOMEN AS SYMBOLS

OF THE "MIDDLE CLASS"

> More Negro girls are rising to the middle class and
> they are therefore more beautiful.
> —N. L. Barnett, M.D., *letter to the editor*, Ebony, *March 1966*

> The bourgeois female, young, whorish, working, extremely well
> dressed . . . as near in simulated looks and make-up, stance, and blandness
> as possible to the Glamour-Mademoiselle-Vogue image . . . uses (and
> emasculates) her man as a social coat-hanger, a bill payer, a dude,
> a vehicle to further her own confused self-image.
> — Black Panther, *July 20, 1967*

Black leaders attempting to rearticulate the meaning of black in American society have time after time used the black woman as symbolic material. For turn-
of-the-century Negro clubwomen, for the middle-class leadership of the Baptist
Women's Convention, and for the convention's mainly working-class membership, the black woman was the chaste pillar of society.[1] For race men of the
1890s, for Marcus Garvey in the 1920s, and for black nationalists in the 1960s,
she was a queen whose beauty was evidence of the glory of the race. When leaders sought an object of blame for black failures, she could epitomize the race's
problems. Moral crusaders of the 1920s faulted sexually active, single, black
women for disparaging the reputation of the race.[2] When black intellectuals
of the 1960s criticized the middle class, women were portrayed as responsible
for the worst excesses of the black bourgeoisie. Black women were not mere
subjects of these representations, but they actively participated in the process

of reinventing the image of the race through their words and conduct. In speeches and writing, female leaders chose from and reshaped the culturally available images of womanhood. Ordinary black women participated in racial rearticulation in their day-to-day lives by positioning themselves in relation to an ever-changing world of representation.

Each of the racial projects advanced by black leaders incorporated a particular stance toward socioeconomic class. Some leaders asserted their own middle-class status in order to demand that whites give them the respect and privileges that American society granted to the middle class. Others distanced themselves from middle-class positions to defend the rights of the masses of black people. In every decade of black activism, conflicts arose over the question of which class could legitimately lead a movement for all black people. The debate over class surfaced with great intensity in the late 1960s, and women were symbols in the verbal slinging matches that ensued.

The continuous process of racial rearticulation works from above and below, at the institutional and symbolic level, and in day-to-day life. When black leaders framed already existing popular sentiments about class in particular ways, they reshaped the world of meaning in which women lived. In this chapter I outline a small part of the history of African American class conflicts by tracing how a narrow and strategic critique of middle-class leadership that surfaced within the Civil Rights Movement expanded on college campuses and beyond into a war of words in which "middle class" became synonymous with "white" and "effeminate." I look at how the middle class became demonized in the 1960s and how that judgment affected black women.

The classic expression of the critique of the black middle class appeared at the end of the 1950s. Black sociologist E. Franklin Frazier's scathing *Black Bourgeoisie* remains a reference point for all subsequent analysis of the black middle class. In it, Frazier draws on the themes of black self-hatred that were taken for granted in the scholarship of race in the 1950s, as he argues that the class of black elites was ashamed of its black, folk cultural heritage and had adopted the most superficial imitation of white culture to fill its cultural void. Some of the most stinging words of the book were its descriptions of the "idle, overfed women among the black bourgeoisie."[3] More recent scholarship that documents the middle-class origins of so many civil rights activists and the serious contributions of middle-class black clubwomen has undermined Frazier's argument.[4] Yet his work was influential and found broad resonance among black intellectuals because it accurately exposed the bitterness caused by class fissures within black communities.

Conflicts about the legitimacy of middle-class leadership emerged early in the Civil Rights Movement. In 1960, black, middle-class ministers, lawyers, and other professionals stood at the head of the established civil rights organizations and had, up to that point, shaped the goals and tactics of the movement. That year, the pace and militancy of the Civil Rights Movement suddenly accelerated as black students staged sit-ins at lunch counters throughout the South. College students, frustrated with the rate of change given the continued magnitude of injustice, began to question the old guard leadership, often characterizing their elders and the tactics they used as "middle class." Their critique of middle-class leadership was initially an argument in favor of using new, more defiant tactics to achieve long-standing civil rights goals. The old strategists of the Civil Rights Movement were the leaders of the NAACP, who, with the support of their dues-paying members, pursued civil rights for blacks through the courts. The new strategists were the young members of CORE and SNCC who felt that progress required taking greater risks through civil disobedience.

Though young civil rights activists opposed what they called middle-class strategies, respectability, in the form of stoic civil disobedience, was the hallmark of the youths' protests. Among the memorable images of the era is that of well-groomed black college students sitting at lunch counters braving the hoodlum-like abuse of segregationists. In the 1950s and early 1960s, social conformity was completely compatible with racial pride. In the early days of the Civil Rights Movement, attention to the appearance of propriety figured into organizational decisions about whom to select and support as challengers to segregation laws.[5]

In comparison to the stances taken by black power advocates after 1965, the participants in early civil rights protests, dressing well for demonstrations and maintaining a non-violent stance despite degradation and assault, were the most stalwart adherents to the tradition of defying the system by insisting on one's respectability. That was not, however, how young civil rights workers saw themselves or how their elders saw them. At SNCC's founding conference in Raleigh, North Carolina, in 1960, James Lawson described the students' new sit-in tactics as "a judgment upon middle-class conventional, half-way efforts to deal with radical social evil. It is specifically a judgment upon contemporary civil rights attempts."[6]

Echoing Lawson's comments a few years later, SNCC member Chuck McDew told an *Ebony* reporter that he was "in open revolt with the middle class ethic."[7] In their statements moral and strategic arguments were interconnected and inseparable. When Lawson criticized the middle class at the Raleigh conference, he was referring to the NAACP's legacy of fighting racial injustice through the courts, a strategy that required a degree of patience that the new activists viewed as complacency. By the time Lawson spoke at the meeting in Raleigh, he had already paid dearly for his commitment to activism. As a result of his participation in Nashville's sit-ins, he was expelled from Vanderbilt University's Divinity School three months before he completed his degree.[8]

"Middle class" represented an attitude of shameful guardedness given the enormity of racial injustice. Activists employing the new tactics took the highest moral ground by wedding dignified presentation-of-self to dangerous civil disobedience. Lawson highlighted this strategy in his speech at the Raleigh conference when he contrasted Nashville's civil rights activists to their white opponents: "Law enforcement agents accustomed to viewing crime, were able to mark well-dressed students waiting to make purchases, as loitering on the lunch-counter stools, but they were unable to even suspect and certainly not to see assault and battery. Thus potential customers, quietly asking for service, are disorderly, breaching the peace, inciting riots, while swaggering, vilifying, violent, defiant white young teenagers are law-abiding."[9] When youthful participants in the Civil Rights Movement criticized the middle class, their charges were directed precisely at the limited tactics used by the NAACP. Young civil rights activists were willing to take greater risks to pursue similar goals, which were referred to as "first-class citizenship": the right to make purchases, the right to service, the right to vote, the right to be educated at the best state-supported institutions. They demanded access to the privileges of service, consumption, and opportunity that were available to white, middle-class citizens.

Though the critique of the middle class began as a rejection of legal tactics used by the NAACP, in short time the young activists' rejection of these methods developed into a renunciation of integrationist goals themselves. As this expanded critique of political tactics and integrationist goals diffused among activists and intellectuals, it stretched again into a wholesale rejection of a vaguely defined middle class. The "middle class" label was used loosely to describe a style of life and a set of values as well as an economic position. The vagueness in the meaning of a term that was so sharply divisive had roots in the social and economic history of the middle class in black communities. Because residential segregation had restricted all blacks to the same sections of cities and job discrimination confined blacks, regardless of their educational attainment, to a narrow range of menial and service occupations, "class" within the black community was commonly used to differentiate among groups adhering to different values and lifestyles. It could also refer to income. Some of those who were referred to as middle class were black men whose ownership of businesses serving blacks, such as funeral parlors or insurance agencies, provided them with comfortable incomes. Just as often, the term "middle class" was associated with attendance at particular churches, levels of education, and modes of appearance rather than substantial income. Financially struggling elevator operators, waiters, and school teachers could be included in the middle class.[10] The black middle class functioned as a Weberian status group distinguishing itself from "lower-class" blacks not by income but by behavior. When black youths of the 1960s began to reject the middle class, they inverted these distinctions as they distanced themselves from the pretensions of a striving status group.

Criticism of the black middle class may have increased during the 1960s because of the transformation that was occurring in black class structure. The successes of the civil rights activism of the 1950s and early 1960s set in motion the end of legal segregation in the South and ushered in a decade of expanded opportunities for African Americans. The 1960s were pivotal years in the history of the black middle class. Between 1960 and 1970, as a result of an expanding economy and the lowering of racial barriers, unprecedented numbers of African Americans reached the lower rungs of the middle class. Analysts of black class structure, each using somewhat different economic measures of class position, arrive at varying figures about the size of the black middle class during those years. Nonetheless, all report that the victories of the Civil Rights Movement led to an extraordinary growth in the numbers of those who could be included in a black middle class defined by some occupational measure. In 1940, fewer than 10 percent of black, male workers were employed in "white-collar" professional, managerial, or sales occupations.[11] Estimates for the percentage of black men in middle-class jobs in 1960 range from 13 to 24 percent of the black workforce. By 1970, between 25 and 35 percent of African Americans were in middle-class jobs.[12] Despite these important gains, disproportionate numbers of blacks remained poor. As late as 1968, 29 percent of black families lived below the poverty line, compared to 8 percent of white families.[13] Although the black middle class had grown substantially, nearly a third of African Americans remained in dire poverty. As the black middle class took advantage of recently won opportunities in housing, education, and employment, divisions between the black middle class and the black poor sharpened.

The critique of the black middle class that surfaced in the 1960s might at first appear to be a direct reflection of the divergent interests of different socioeconomic segments of the black population, but it was more complicated than that. Critiques of the black middle class were often voiced with fervor by young members of that group. Young activists from diverse socioeconomic backgrounds employed a common language when they condemned what they saw as the individualistic achievements of members of the black middle class. Many of the early civil rights activists made their commitments to activism while attending elite black colleges that had traditionally prepared young men and women to enter the middle class. College campuses became arenas in which the contests over socioeconomic class orientation were highly visible. As bastions of social conservatism, elite, historically black college campuses were settings in which small acts of self-expression provoked sharp reactions. In 1965, civil rights activist Jean Wiley was employed as a teacher at historically black Tuskegee Institute when she decided to start wearing an Afro. Her students quickly demonstrated their disapproval of her new look: "I can't forget the first time I wore an Afro. I walked into the classroom with a natural. I was so proud. That was a Monday and for the rest of that week there was not a single woman in any of my classes. The women boycotted the classes. They felt that it wasn't appropriate for a professional woman. There's a certain way you're supposed to look if you're a professional."[14] Wiley's students, whose sense of personal dignity came from their attachment to symbols of conventional achievement, could not see her unstraightened hair as a symbol of racial pride. They felt that their escape from the stifling racial order of the South into upward mobility in the North was dependent on their social conformity and the prestige of their education. "Everything in their lives was pointing them out of there to a better life in the North," she explained. Wiley's Afro posed a threat to the carefully guarded image that had been nurtured at Tuskegee and other southern black campuses. The female students in Wiley's class, who valued that image, were appalled that a professor would so casually discard the professional look. SNCC member Zoharah Simmons encountered similar reactions when she stopped straightening her hair while a student at Spelman College:

> I began wearing an Afro my second year at Spelman, and it caused a big furor. I was actually called into the dean's office, and she asked me, "What happened to your hair?" I said, "I'm wearing an Afro." And she [said], "Well that's not how a Spelman young woman is supposed to look. You have to be well groomed." I said, "I am well groomed. I just happen not to have my hair straightened." . . . [Students] wouldn't say it right out but somebody would say something so you could hear it behind your back like "Isn't that a disgrace? She ought to be ashamed of herself. What is wrong with her?"[15]

When they wore Afros, Simmons and Wiley transgressed norms of femininity as well as expectations about the appearance of middle-class black women. In the conservative context sustained on their campuses, femininity and middle-class status together produced the professional look that was associated with racial pride. Students and administrators at these historically black colleges felt that the hard-won middle-class status of their institutions was threatened by the presence of unseemly female rebels.

Hardy Frye, a black southerner who became involved in the Civil Rights Movement, tried to get other black college students to join the movement but was frustrated by their unwillingness to take the necessary risks. Thirty years later, he reflected on the reasons for their reluctance: "I didn't know enough about the situation. I didn't put together the fact that they were maybe the first generation going to college in these black schools. They were paying a tremendous amount to go compared to the income they had. I tended to look at these kids and say 'Oh, how can you be so conservative?' We were rejecting what they were striving so hard to get to, which was to be dressed in a certain way, representing a certain class position."[16] SNCC member Martha Norman understood that perspective because her parents, who were unambiguously proud of being black, conveyed to her the importance of middle-class achievement. Over their objections, she committed herself to civil rights organizing, knowing that a rejection of middle-class aspirations was built into her participation in SNCC:

> My parents were fairly political people. . . . They loved black life. There's always been a kind of a black pride in the middle class. If it was nothing but defensive and cultural. . . . They sacrificed a lot for me to have a good education. . . . I think the first decision that people made when people made a decision to become full-time field secretaries for SNCC [was] to leave school. That was a rejection of the middle-class camp. To become a full-time community organizer. I mean is this a career? What happened to lawyer, doctor, engineer? And I was saying I was going to do this for my life work. And they're like, "Yeah right." . . . There was a certain rejection of a middle-class path. [Many] never got right back on that path either. I think that it was a tremendous thing that they gave up in terms of economic security [and] potential power in the system. It was built in from the beginning. Our partners in activism were poor people. We weren't trying to organize the middle class. We ourselves took a nontraditional role. Then we joined with a nontraditional part of the community to do our activism.[17]

Her parents' aspirations and political commitments had been formed in the context of both de jure and de facto segregation in education and severely limited occupational opportunities even for educated blacks. Norman's generation faced a very different world. Once middle-class status had become a possibility for substantial numbers of African Americans, some talented, young, black college students chose to renounce or postpone careers in order to join the Civil Rights Movement.

The experiences the young SNCC organizers had in the South were transformational. Working with the disenfranchised rural, black poor, witnessing and surviving the violence of white racist responses to demands for basic rights, and realizing by 1965 how distant goals of equality and justice remained, the civil rights veterans returned from the front lines of the movement with unwavering commitments to social justice but without a unified vision for the possibilities of change. Some activists shifted their energies to attempts to politically organize blacks in poverty-stricken urban neighborhoods in the North. In 1964, CORE, having had some success with organizing in northern cities, attempted to expand its efforts. SNCC repeated the pattern in 1965, opening offices in northern black ghettos but failing to organize substantial numbers of the "grass roots" people who lived in these communities. The Black Panthers, which organized in 1966 in Oakland, California, did find their base among the poor and built an organization that had two thousand members at its height. However, activism in general stalled, failing to develop effective strategies to address the confluence of race and class inequality that strangled urban ghettoes. In this time of bitterness and relative hopelessness, a discourse of racialized class morality in which class and race were fused proliferated. Without strategies for action or the presence of a clear and successful movement, black consciousness devolved into a matter of personal stance, a terrain in which symbols had exaggerated importance.

The rhetoric inside SNCC's urban organizing forays, the Black Panther Party, and black student organizations contained a broad critique of the middle class that was not present in the early Civil Rights Movement. African Americans both inside and outside of black political organizations used symbols of middle-class hypocrisy and of anti–middle-class authenticity to make personal claims about who they were, where they stood, and where they were going. The content of these clashes formed the culture within which African Americans inside and outside of the movement defined themselves—as beautiful or ugly, proud or ashamed, in sync or in conflict with their mothers. A new image of black dignity, grounded in black urban and African culture, was ascendant.

The contests between new and old formulations of black dignity can be seen in an incident that sprang from what *Ebony*'s editors probably imagined would be an innocuous cover story about "pretty Negro girls." The pairing of class and skin tone had been the rule in black popular magazines. *Ebony*, the long-time chronicler of black progress and the champion of individual achievement as racial advance, routinely represented prettiness with light skin. The February 1966 *Ebony* cover story asked, "Are Negro Girls Getting Prettier?"[18] In answer to the headline's question, *Ebony*'s cover showcased several light-brown women with straightened hair as representatives of the new Negro prettiness. Explaining that "she is the delightful product of a better way of life," *Ebony* noted that the new prettiness manifested itself in bodies that more closely met conventional standards: "Gone are the spindly legs, sagging bosoms, unruly rumps and ill-groomed heads of yesteryear." Thus, *Ebony* touted attractiveness as an indicator of social progress. Like houses in white suburbs and black professionals in supervisory jobs, the new prettiness was one more achievement of the expanding African American middle class.

Black polarization regarding the interlaced issues of class and color was clearly expressed in the range of letters *Ebony* received from its readers. Some correspondents, like Dr. N. L. Barnett, concurred that better times produced prettier women. He argued that professional women were prettier than women who labored in menial jobs. In his view, career women could afford to "groom themselves well and are not masculinized by strenuous physical labor. More Negro girls are rising to the middle class and they are therefore more beautiful. Did you ever see a beautiful cotton picker? In seven and one half years in Mississippi cotton fields I never did."[19]

Ebony's selection of light-skinned, "pretty" women maintained the old standard, a pigmentocracy that reinforced the link between color and class while it disparaged dark-skinned African American women. Barnett unquestioningly appreciated the images, but other readers did not. One correspondent suggested retitling the article, "Are Negro Girls Getting Whiter?" A group called Concerned Black Women voiced its protest by picketing *Ebony*'s offices. Carrying signs that asked, "Has *Ebony* murdered the Black Woman?" and placards advertising an upcoming Grandassa show of Afro-coiffed models, the women protested what they considered *Ebony*'s Eurocentric beauty standards. Evelyn Rodgers, who covered the demonstration for *The Liberator*, one of the most influential journals of the black consciousness movement, charged that "*Ebony* magazine stands today as a classic illustration of middle class negro attempts to assimilate themselves into the mainstream of white american life."[20] The fair ladies celebrated as beauty queens in the past were deprecated by Rodgers as the ugly middle class. Perhaps she and other critics had some effect. Just a few months after its feature on the new prettiness, *Ebony* announced on its cover the arrival of the "Natural Look" with a photograph of a woman with deep brown skin wearing a short natural.[21]

By 1967, a more sizable black middle class had become a bigger target for black intellectuals who hoped to redirect the stalled black movement. While earlier critiques faulted middle-class leaders for the timidity of their racial projects, later critiques accused the entire middle class for altogether abandoning their poorer brothers and sisters. Being black and middle class had come to stand for indifference, individualism, and a way of behaving described as "acting white," which gave legitimacy to the system that held blacks down. In their 1967 explanation of black power, Stokely Carmichael and Charles Hamilton wrote: "The goals of integrationists are middle class goals, articulated primarily by a small group of Negroes with middle-class aspirations or status. Their kind of integration has meant that a few blacks 'make it,' leaving the black community, sapping it of leadership potential and know-how . . . those token Negroes—absorbed into a white mass—are of no value to the remaining black masses. They become meaningless show-pieces for a conscience-soothed white society."[22] Among spokesmen for a new black consciousness, black and middle class were contradictory positions that could only result in loss of self.

The black power critique of the black middle class was grounded in a mix of fact and myth. The central myth was the extent to which members of the black middle class left the black community to live in a white world. Although the weakening of residential segregation allowed African Americans to leave traditionally black neighborhoods and move to formerly white areas, black flight to white enclaves was limited.[23] Most members of the black middle class continued to live in predominantly black neighborhoods, though many found ways to leave areas of concentrated poverty. When upwardly mobile blacks moved out of inner cities, they often moved to predominantly black suburban enclaves.

In leisure activities, middle-class blacks sought venues that provided the comfort of socializing with other blacks.[24] Part of why it was possible for black power spokesmen to describe the middle class as fleeing the black community was the way in which they denied black diversity by making "the black community" synonymous with the experience of the urban, black poor. Framed in this way, middle-class blacks disappeared into a "white mass."

Although the members of the black middle class did not assimilate into invisible nothingness, there were sharp differences between their lives and the lives of unemployed or underemployed blacks living in the most impoverished sections of inner cities. Many middle-class blacks fled from the greatest problems faced by black communities and additionally were able to pass considerable advantages to their children.[25] The most important way that advantage was conveyed was through the cultural and economic capital that secured access to higher education. The percentage of black adult college graduates grew from 3.1 percent in 1960, to 4.5 percent in 1970, and to 6 percent by 1973. To place these statistics in perspective, the comparative figures for whites during the same years were 8.1, 11.6, and 13.1 percent, respectively.[26] Although the percentage of black adults who were college educated almost doubled between 1960 and 1973, black educational attainment did not reach parity with whites. The new black college students at four-year colleges and universities were disproportionately children of the middle class.[27] The elite, historically black colleges continued to attract middle-class black students, but by the late 1960s, the majority of black college students attended predominantly white colleges or universities. Black students in the late 1960s and early 1970s entered college at a time of heightened political awareness. Once there, they questioned what they were doing with their lives and what that said about their relationships to other African Americans who lived less privileged lives. Their rejection of a model that equated individual achievement with racial advancement placed African American college students in a bind. In the absence of a viable movement, in a country geared toward individual achievement, the useful alternatives to striving for individual success were limited. Black students focused their political energies on issues located on their own campuses, demanding that the universities establish black studies departments, accommodate the needs of black students, and in numerous other ways end white cultural supremacy within institutions. Black student protests swept through universities in the second half of the 1960s.[28]

The demand for black studies departments fit well with the cultural turn that had taken place in black power rhetoric. Encouraged by a political discourse that had broadened its focus from tactics to lifestyles, from action to essence, students focused on personal expression to vigorously display where they stood, and college campuses became frequent arenas for clashes of symbols. A student could assert her rejection of the easy path to assimilation by being a righteously angry "militant." Black youths from upper-middle-class backgrounds downplayed their origins. Brenda Payton described the climate among black students at Claremont College: "I went through a period of trying to deny or diminish the privileged background that I had come from. It wasn't cool to be a doctor's daughter in 1969. You know everybody was supposed to be the lumpen proletariat. And, of course, the kids at Claremont College were hardly lumpen proletariat. Everybody was trying to be blacker than or downer than and poorer than because that was how we at the time defined authentically black."[29] At the same time, whites on college campuses were voicing similar critiques of "middle-class values." White and black youths shared a generational perspective that cut across racial lines but was inflected by the experience of race. White youths rejected "middle-class values" for their vacuous materialism. Black youths rejected middle-class materialism from the perspective of the group whose members lived at the bottom of the social hierarchy. Because of the racial imbalance in the distribution of America's wealth, black students' critiques of the system placed race in the foreground. Nonetheless, black denunciations of "bourgeois" blacks shared a common cultural root with the antiestablishment expressions of white youths and drew upon the same available political frames. The potential transracial affiliation of the black and white countercultures was not lost on the leadership of the Black Panther Party. A *Black Panther* editorial urged the brothers to "stop vamping on the hippies. They are not your enemy. You [*sic*] enemy, right now is the white racist pigs who support this corrupt system. Your enemy is the Tom nigger who reports to his white slavemaster every day."[30] Black Panther Party calls for countercultural unity against "the system" did not carry the day. Though the words "middle class" and "bourgeois" were in almost constant use in political diatribe, they were rarely linked to a developed class analysis or to a political strategy. Their arguments were moral arguments that criticized selfish quests for individual advancement. When critical attention shifted to lifestyles, the earlier critique of political tactics was lost, and it was unclear what a movement for black power should do. The words "middle class" and "bourgeois" became signposts that allowed individuals to position themselves along a spectrum in which white, middle class, effeminate, and conventional were on one end and black, poor, masculine, and fearless were on the other. This formulation did not bode well for black women. Within black communities, women were central figures in these class-coded conflicts about presentation-of-self. Structurally located as the keepers of traditions as mothers, grandmothers, teachers, and hairdressers, women were often the most resistant to change. In the ways that they presented themselves and the values that they held dear, one can see the presence of embedded agency. Their choices were embedded in the constraints of their social locations as black women and formed in relation to culturally available representations of black female dignity. Socialized to maintain appearances in the name of femininity, dignity, and race, conventional black women became central targets in attacks against conformity. Many black women had responded to calls from within their own communities to be upstanding representatives of the race by conforming to middle-class standards of behavior and appearance. Others who paid attention to fashion were simply conforming to norms of female behavior. Both groups of women, and the daughters they had reared to deport themselves in similar ways, became the very women who were ridiculed as bourgeois race traitors.

The late 1960s were characterized by decentralized political action, bitter sectarian disputes, and a class moralism that heaped scorn on members of the black middle class who were, at most, vulnerable minor beneficiaries of the capitalist system. As strategic action outside of college campuses stalled, the rhetoric of black power elaborated a politics of essence. What began as a rejection of individualism transformed into a belief in the importance of presentation-of-self and a politics of divisive posturing.

"Middle class" became a term that had less and less to do with occupation or income and more to do with presentation-of-self. This was illustrated in 1970, when *Black World*, a popular publication owned by the publisher of *Jet* and *Ebony*, ran a series of advertisements that highlighted the perceived differences between militants and the black middle class. One advertisement portrayed a man wearing an Afro, combat boots, a dashiki, and a big gun. It read, "Would he look better in a sweater and chinos with a science book under his arm?" The ad's copy contrasted militants with black "moderates," "that ever diminishing breed of success oriented, middle class straining blacks, [who] will follow white liberals' lead."

The figure of the black militant had two forms: the cultural nationalist typified by Ron Karenga and the Black Panther. Karenga and his influential Black Arts Movement follower Amiri Baraka had abandoned critiques of class in favor of visions of a restoration of lost traditions of patriarchal black aristocracy.[31] Creating ceremonies and poetry that celebrated past and future kings and queens, they rejected any semblance of class analysis and sang praises to an imagined monarchy in a return to a recreated "African" past that was unabashedly male supremacist.

In sharp contrast to cultural nationalists, the Black Panther Party took an explicit stand in favor of sexual equality as it continued to denounce "bourgeois" blacks. Black women were expected to be at least as tough as men in their confrontations with police, landlords, and store owners. The party vigorously called upon women to give up "bourgeois" modes of femininity. In a poem attributed to "Marsha," the party newspaper instructed black women on how to be revolutionaries:

TO THE WOMEN OF BABYLON
You are not here as powder puff bitches
The pig is oppressing you too!
So don't think you can Georgia your way out!
The amount of suffering we have all been subjected to
Does not separate we females
The hog don't care who he beats on the head
so remove your false eyelashes
So you can see that they will suppress you too.
If you cannot remove your disguise
then young hoe you don't belong here!
cause a fat ass and silk stockings don't create a bullet proof shield
And if a silk stud Daddy is your goal
then you might as well watch a rat run in his hole
cause a punk decorated in diamonds
and gators will leave you on your fat ass.
You better get real slick, hop into some big bens
and become a worker for the people
Become a revolutionary woman and have a revolutionary man.
To be the other half, you must be
strong and carry the love of your people
instead of mascara. Because I
know for a fact, mascara
runs when you cry.[32]

Writers and cartoonists in the Black Panther Party's newspaper ridiculed and disparaged women for clinging to old modes of femininity and called upon them to exchange false eyelashes and straightening combs for the odd package of babies, guns, miniskirts, and sex with a revolutionary man. Despite its egalitarian claims, the Black Panther Party employed conventionally formulated symbols of gender to express its denunciations of the middle class. Though the *Black Panther*'s news accounts effaced gender differences, its graphic depictions of women highlighted sexual difference and reinforced male domination. In some typical illustrations, a voluptuous woman shoots at the police, another carries a baby in one arm and a gun in the other, still another guards her home and young son with a gun, and a pregnant woman in a miniskirt holds a gun. In a rule-bound, dogma-driven organization, the one reference to women among the party's 10–10–10 point program, which includes twenty-six additional rules, three main rules, and eight points of attention, was the seventh point of attention: "Do not take liberties with women." The rule constructs the Black Panther as a man, just as the newspaper's is drawings constructed the Black Panther woman as his fantasy mate.

Whenever African Americans have debated the role of class in their communities, women's behavior, sexuality, and appearance have been focal points of the disputes. When middle class became a pejorative description, women frequently represented the despised bourgeoisie. The image can be traced from the "idle, overfed women" of Frazier's *Black Bourgeoisie* to Marsha's "powder puff bitch." In a movement culture that valorized masculinity, women were at a disadvantage. Constructions of the middle class as weak, effeminate, and deserving of scorn made women the particular targets of anti–middle-class rhetoric. Women's adherence to female norms of appearance and the roles they had been asked to play as guardians of social conventions made them easy targets for writers seeking bourgeois culprits.

As black power advocates challenged old models of black progress, they presented anti–middle-class alternatives for women, yet these revisions of womanhood were frequently anchored in conventional gender constructions. Rebellion has typically been socially constructed as a masculine trait, while dominant constructions of femininity stressed conformity. The *Black Panther* challenged images of female frailty by arming women but reinscribed conventions of femininity onto "revolutionary" modes of womanhood by depicting armed sex kittens and mothers. Women were valued primarily as companions to men and bearers of sons. The portrayals of women in black power rhetoric and imagery fused the contradictory elements of militarism and maternalism or created romanticized versions of the patriarchal family. Against these idealized images stood the image of race traitor, the bourgeois woman on her futile and selfish quest to assimilate into whiteness. None of these representations was an accurate characterization of or a reasonable model for actual black women. Yet they were powerful images for intellectuals trying to direct the course of black social movements. The next chapter looks at the ways in which the image of the beautiful black woman helped black organizations to build unified political identities.

Chapter Eight

THE APPEARANCE OF UNITY

The historical record presents a puzzle. On the one hand, there is the continuous presence of alternative beauty standards within black communities that were autonomous from dominant Eurocentric values. On the other there is a clear sense of the profound impact of the emergence of "black is beautiful" in the mid-1960s. "Black is beautiful" was news in 1965, but the sentiments that the phrase expressed were not new. In the 1920s, Marcus Garvey urged black people to "take down the pictures of white women from your walls" and honor the greater beauty of black women.[1] On the basis of racial pride, Garvey mobilized more than a million blacks into a movement that drew upon and reinforced widespread feelings of racial pride.[2] Garvey's Harlem-based United Negro Improvement Association had hundreds of chapters throughout the United States. Ruth Beckford, the dancer who stopped straightening her hair a decade before the Afro became a style, learned racial pride as a child in the 1930s from her Garveyite father. He raised his dark-complexioned daughter to be proud of her skin color. Traditional fashion advice for color phobic Negro women was to avoid bright shades of clothing, especially red, because such colors made dark skin appear darker. Beckford loved the way red highlighted the color of her skin: "I can hear my father say, 'You are a proud black woman.' I was very secure with dark skin, and I always wore bright colors. I always wore white and red. Daddy would always tell me how beautiful I was. So I never had any insecurity about being a dark-skinned young black girl who pressed her hair in those days."[3] She ends her recollection of being raised to be proud with the reminder that in those days even a girl proud of being black straightened her hair. Like the vast majority of black women, Beckford straightened her hair, but her hairstyle did not cloud her understanding that she was a beautiful black woman.

As a child growing up in the Pacific Northwest of the 1950s, Pearl Marsh recognized the beauty of smooth black complexions, the color of her own skin: "There were always people in the community who had that beautiful black skin. Not brown skin, but that smooth black skin that you just have to be awed by if you see it. And there was this woman in the next town, Aunt Ruby, who had that skin. And I just loved her. And they would say that I looked like her and I looked like Ethel and these were dark black women. And they looked beautiful to me as a child."[4]

Long before the emergence of "black is beautiful" in the mid-1960s, some within black communities held and transmitted a tradition of counterhegemonic beauty standards. They appreciated dark skin and African facial features. A few criticized the practice of straightening hair. Their standards of beauty were not reflected in the early beauty contests sponsored by middle-class race men. Nor were they documented in the black popular press, which unquestioningly associated beauty with light skin. Nonetheless, the beauty of black women, including and especially dark-skinned women, was a recurrent theme in early black literature and political writing. In day-to-day life, many black girls were taught to love themselves by black adults who refused to accept dominant beauty standards. Appreciation of dark skin, tightly curled hair, broad noses, and full lips constituted an exceptional but constant part of the spectrum of African American standards of beauty.

Still, in the mid-1960s, the words "black is beautiful" felt new and important. The words appear to have announced a never-before-spoken break from a hierarchy of attractiveness that had been a highly personal manifestation of racist culture. Even African American women and men who knew the tradition of autonomous black beauty standards experienced "black is beautiful" as a complete rupture from the past. The personal joy and relief black women felt when their beauty was praised in poems, speeches, and in the values that were generated by the Black Power Movement need little explanation. What does call for an explanation is how and why in the late 1960s personal relief became synonymous with political project. What was new in the late 1960s was the magnitude of political importance given to the formulation of beauty. Self-love was no longer a private matter between mother and child. Self-love and erotic love were experienced as political actions. Why did young African Americans, in the late 1960s, feel that the defense of the natural body was both new and extremely important? Part of the explanation is that "black is beautiful" served members of a fractured black political movement in their efforts to build a unified community.

The previous chapters have shown how the question of identity emerged as an issue within civil rights organizations. The students who initially joined

SNCC and CORE did not set out to reshape black identity, but in the practice of activism their identities changed and helped to initiate a broad generational questioning of the meaning of black. "Identity" became a necessary new word and a problem to be solved. In 1962, for example, the San Francisco chapter of CORE launched "Operation Identity" with talks by Sam Wiah, a Nigerian, on "Who Am I?" Films of ancient and modern Africa were shown to accompany his talk.[5] In this construction, the answer to the question of black identity was to be found outside of the United States in Africa. Though the San Francisco CORE chapter was a predominantly white organization in 1962, when "Operation Identity" asked, "Who Am I?," the subject in the question was black. The announcement proclaimed, "All are welcome," belying a tension that would, within a few years, shatter the fragile interracial union within that organization and in the larger Civil Rights Movement.

The question of identity that arose among black participants in the Civil Rights Movement was a product of the ordeals and triumphs of the movement. By experiencing the power of collective action, black civil rights workers felt a greater sense of personal efficacy as well as deepened bonds to other African Americans. Along with the development of greater racial identification, fear of whites was replaced by anger and a demand for black power. When an integrationist movement gave way to the nationalist's call for black power, black activists were compelled to perform a new kind of cultural work. As the vision of transformation changed from "black and white together" to "black power," the meanings of black and white had to change. Efforts to establish black political and cultural autonomy and to build separate black political organizations fostered an exploration and elaboration of black identity. By the mid-1960s, however, locating and defining black culture had become very difficult: black culture was diverse and intertwined with the dominant American culture.

A singular black collective identity that could serve as the basis for political unity would at any conjuncture have been an achievement, an overcoming of black differences. It would have been the result of an organization's ability to sidestep, bridge, or overcome, among other things, the bitterness of class divisions within black communities, the divergence between generational aspirations, and the differences in the experiences of black men and black women. I am distinguishing between racial category and collective identity. For African Americans, racial category is a fact of life, imposed by a society structured, in numerous ways, on the basis of race. With or without a social movement, African Americans rarely have the luxury of forgetting race. Nonetheless, in 1966, though black appeared to be a fixed racial category, there was no consensus among African Americans about what black meant and no consensus about what celebrating black would mean.

In the attempt to develop a collective black identity, nationalists drew upon and developed a reservoir of racialized symbols, stances, and practices that articulated with wider familiar narratives. A beginning point for the establishment of an autonomous black culture was the rejection of what was understood as white culture. Throughout most of the history of the United States, a white supremacist society refused to acknowledge the contributions of black people to American culture and enforced rigid racial boundaries through a classification system that denied creolization. Black nationalists, in their efforts to recover and recognize uniquely black achievements, mirrored that process. In their most extreme expressions, black nationalists built black identity in strict opposition to white identity. By rearticulating whiteness as the source of all harmful characteristics, nationalists created a utopian vision of black culture that was cleansed of individualism and decadence. Cultural nationalist Ron Karenga sought to build communal values among blacks and so asserted, "Individualism is a white desire."[6] In Black Muslim theology, whites were literally the devil incarnate.

Much of the effort to define black identity proceeded by looking within black life for sources of authenticity. Some African Americans located authenticity in the lives of contemporary and historic African Americans of the South. Harriet Tubman, Nat Turner, Denmark Vesey, and others were resurrected as heroes and heroines in the fight against slavery. A black woman who was born and raised in a black neighborhood in Oakland felt that, as a non-southerner, she had to prove that she was black. Southern blacks, she explained, didn't have to "be into black things" to know they were black: "[My friend] wasn't into African stuff and neither was her boyfriend. And they weren't into black things, like we were culturally. But they were very, hey, they were from the South. From Oklahoma, so they knew what time it was. They didn't need to wear this to prove that they were black."[7] Constructing an image of authenticity grounded in the experience of southern blacks was problematic. By 1966, the base of black social movement activity had shifted from the South to the North.[8] By 1970, almost half of the American black population lived in the North.[9] Many members of an increasingly urban movement, who did not share the pastoral leanings of the white counterculture, saw in the South only the remnants of slavery. For many of the urban and mostly northern spokespersons for black nationalism, southern black traditions of spirituality, cooking, styles of dress, speech, and naming were tainted by their origins in the South. Many northern blacks were only one generation away from living in the South, which to them represented backwardness. There were problems not only with what the South represented but also in the representation of southern blacks. The potential dignity in a portrait of a motherly southern black woman had been preempted by the countless derogatory images that had been produced of comical, subservient, and asexual "mammies."

The force of demographics and the shift in the geographic focus of the movement contributed to an emerging black identity that defined the authentic black person as a poor resident of an urban ghetto. However, the image of the ghetto militant did not satisfy African Americans who sought black traditions that were ancient, noble, and untainted by white culture. For Karenga and other cultural nationalists, an imagined and relatively unknown Africa offered a pure source of the collective self. "We don't borrow from Africa," he said. "We utilize what was ours to start with."[10] Africa was a powerful symbol for black men and women. Myesha Jenkins's natural was a way of feeling closer to Africa: "It was like, once I did get into the style and got really political, it was like I couldn't understand why anybody would ever straighten their hair. I mean it just seemed such, like the most obvious contradiction. And in that sense that's the kind of an authenticity that I felt the hairstyle meant. And it's like we have this alternative. We can create this new way of being that's closer to Africa and farther away from Europe."[11] In Jenkins's words, "Getting away from imitating white" meant that African Americans would have to "create this new way of being." Yet locating black identity in Africa was difficult: too remote for some who knew little of Africa and a preposterous notion for others who knew Africa well. A black, female musician who had read extensively about African culture complained to me about cultural nationalists: "They always had to be from Egypt. They were the Queens of the Nile. They were King Farouk's descendants and what have you. Nobody was a descendent of somebody who might have come from the bush."[12]

Unlike a distant continent or a defined region, the body was a proximate and personal racialized symbol. It had the potential to be an unambiguous sign of unity. In the late 1960s and early 1970s, the glorified black woman's body became a powerful symbol. By 1970, sentimental drawings of black women's faces, puerile love poems, or even mildly pornographic images were construed as political expressions and published in magazines entirely devoted to politics. A drawing entitled "Black Is Beautiful" appeared in the January/February 1970 issue of *Black Scholar*. Bust portraits of a young man and woman with full lips, rounded noses, and huge eyes stare at the reader. He has a mustache. Her eyes are heavily made up. They are both brown-skinned, but he is darker. She is smaller than he but strangely rises above him as if she is standing on a step stool. His Afro is big, but hers is bigger and rounder. He wears a dashiki. Her shoulders and neck are bare. This was the archetypical expression of "black is beautiful."

The Black Panther Party rearticulated black to mean urban and anticapitalist. A real black man was a fearless revolutionary, a woman his beautiful mate fighting by his side. The faces of beautiful black women, shown under headlines that read, "Black and Beautiful," were regular features of the party newspaper. Blackness and its beauty were represented by physical embodiment, augmented by adornments, with images that reinforced traditional gender hierarchies, placed in a context that suggested a political message. The message was that blacks were a race apart and that self-love and the love between black men and black women were political commitments. Images of "natural" and "beautiful" black men and women became part of the reservoir of racial symbols.

Ron Karenga contributed to the feeling of newness and significance surrounding "black is beautiful" by making awareness of black beauty a test of a man's black consciousness. A black man's duty was to be responsible to black women and to recognize their beauty. Black male desire for white women was seen as a sickness, a self-hatred to be overcome. A follower of Karenga wrote the following confession in his introduction to *The Quotable Karenga*: "I can remember myself before Maulana showed me the 'Path of Blackness.' I was so sick no one but Maulana could have saved me. . . . I no longer have to want those stringy haired, colorless, white women. Now I can look at them and say, 'Get back devil.' Every time I see a beautiful black sister with a natural, and can appreciate her beauty, I say, 'All praises due to Maulana.'"[13]

The image of the purity of the black woman's body, as opposed to the white woman's filth, was also central to Black Muslim ideology. This message was expressed graphically in a 1965 *Muhammad Speaks* cartoon in which a white woman displaying cleavage and wearing a minidress gives a black man a "death wink." "Stay Away!" is spelled out on a dotted line from his eyeball to her thigh, which bears the message "doom of the black man."[14] Similar cartoons in which the black man is caught in a struggle between white temptresses and salvation were regular features in *Muhammad Speaks*. In contrast to the evil white woman's body, the pure black woman was a symbol that helped the Nation of Islam perform the cultural work required by nationalist movements. The leaders of the emergent Black Power Movement had to perform three types of cultural work: racial rearticulation, formation of a collective political identity, and organizational distinction.[15] They had to change the meaning of black in American life, simultaneously build a unified black identity, and finally distinguish their organizations from others that might also claim to represent the best hope for black liberation. Black power organizations operated in a crowded social movement field. One of the ways organizations distinguished themselves was by elaborating the meaning of black in distinctive ways. Together, black nationalist organizations added to the reservoir of symbols and stances with which African Americans created racialized and gendered selves. Each contributed to the feeling of revolutionary newness and significance surrounding the assertion that black was beautiful. The Nation of Islam provides one example of the cultural work of nationalism at the organizational level. The following discussion traces the development of Black Muslim ideology through the pages of the organization's newspaper, *Muhammad Speaks*, from 1960 to 1968. The theme of the goodness of the black woman's body was a constant, yet it shifted as it was articulated with other elements of Black Muslim ideology. Hair, that potent symbol in black discursive battles about racial pride, has a surprising and changing role in this narrative of racial rearticulaton.

Formed in the early 1930s from the vestiges of Noble Drew Ali's Moorish-American Science Temple, the Nation of Islam, also known as the Black Muslims, predated and outlived all other black nationalist organizations of the 1960s.[16] If measured by ability to build a sustainable organization, the Nation of Islam was the most successful organization of the Black Power Movement. It rearticulated the meanings of race in America by defining whites as devils and blacks as an Islamic people. By elaborating a distinctive way of life for Black Muslims, the organization fostered a strong collective identity among its followers. The Nation of Islam may appear, at first glance, to have formulated an unchanging ideology based on the teachings of Elijah Muhammad, which are consistently followed by its highly disciplined members. A closer analysis of the organization's ideology as articulated in *Muhammad Speaks* reveals an organization closely attuned to broadly held sentiments in black communities, actively engaged in cultural work, and responsive to the field of social movements in which it operated.

The Nation of Islam's overarching message was one of racial pride founded in a sense of kinship and self-love. The message of racial pride was bolstered by its alignment with the familiar and dominant cultural themes of financial independence and a rejection of artifices. The wide influence of *The Autobiography of Malcolm X* means that the Nation of Islam is strongly associated with the rejection of hair straightening, yet the positions the organization took regarding the practice were as varied and subject to change as the black community from which it drew its membership. The image of the inherent beauty of the black woman remained central to the Nation of Islam's message of racial pride, but the themes of financial independence and rejection of artifices led in contradictory directions that complicated the stands the newspaper took.

After several attempts to establish a newspaper, the Nation of Islam began regularly publishing *Mr. Muhammad Speaks* in 1960.[17] In its first year of publication, the newspaper established the importance of women in the project of solidifying racial unity. The September 1960 issue displayed a photomontage of black women with the caption, "We love, respect, and marry our own kind." Female followers of the Nation of Islam were distinctive within black communities because they adhered to the traditional Islamic practice of covering their hair. Their head coverings, which were symbols of faith, shielded their hair from the public scrutiny that has read so much meaning about class and black identity into black women's hair practices. Head coverings were indicative of Black Muslim identity and its concomitant black pride and dignity. All but one of the women shown in the photomontage covered their hair and thus were recognizable as Nation of Islam followers. The lone woman whose hair was visible had the look of a conventional attractive black woman of her day. In other words, she had straightened hair.

Shortly after the publication of the photomontage, a special edition appeared that focused on women and the Nation of Islam's rejection of artifice. The author of one article urged black women to give up cosmetics for the sake of racial pride and physical well-being: "Mr. Muhammad says that Black Women are the Mothers of Civilization and by nature are the most beautiful women on earth. Although Islam does not forbid cosmetics, most enlightened Muslim women shun the poison-laden cosmetics for health reasons."[18] Black Muslim rejection of cosmetics resonates with long-standing cultural mores that associated make-up with immorality and particularly with the purported immorality of lower-class women.[19] In its first two years of publication, *Mohammad Speaks* urged black women to eschew cosmetics but did not ask them to stop straightening their hair. On the contrary, they featured photographs of women with straightened hair. The inclusion of these photographs without criticism implicitly suggested that hair straightening remained a necessary part of good grooming. Within black communities, however, the feelings about straightened hair were rapidly changing, and the newspaper would quickly respond to the change.

The issue of artifice did not arise again in *Muhammad Speaks* for a year. When it did return, it was cast in significant new ways that had been shaped by an essential piece of the Nation of Islam's doctrine: the importance of black financial achievement. The Nation of Islam succeeded where many other black organizations failed in building a base among poor, urban blacks.[20] The organization's endorsement of middle-class strivings may in part account for its success among impoverished blacks. Elijah Muhammad once explained why he drove an ostentatious car: "The reason I drive a Cadillac is obvious. Negroes place a high value on things like this. Personally, I would prefer any little old car that would take me places. But if I did so, Negroes would begin to say 'Islam made him poor.'"[21]

Articulated with the theme of the importance of sound household financial management, the topic of artifices reappeared in the pages of *Muhammad Speaks* with a headline that read, "So-Called Negroes Waste Billions of Dollars Yearly in Hair Preparations." The author described hair straightening as a senseless drain of resources for both men and women. "To get that well-groomed, shiny head of hair, Negro men and women annually spend more than a billion dollars." The thrust of his argument, however, was a warning to black men that they would not advance into middle-class jobs if they persisted in conking their hair: "One rarely finds Negroes . . . holding down good paying jobs that require intelligence, ability and dependability who have conked hair. . . . [W]hite employers are turning them down by the thousands simply because they are afraid to take a chance with people who persist in putting acid on their heads."[22] Out of tune with Nation of Islam rhetoric, the author uncritically encourages black men to abandon a black style in order to become more acceptable to white employers. In the article, black economic achievement takes precedence over a strictly racial ideology, and there was little emphasis on the evils or dangers of artifice, arguments reserved for articles aimed at women. The *Muhammad Speaks* article reflected the changes in African American values as it gave voice to a perception, which at the time was becoming dominant in black communities, that the conk was a hairstyle for lower-class men. A small headline in the body of the article, probably added by editors hoping to bridge the text back to Black Muslim ideology, read, "So-called Negro Told Be Satisfied with Self." Though not present in the text of this article, the association between straightened hair and racial shame was growing, and that sentiment would be the focus of the newspaper's next article on the problem of straightened hair. In San Quentin prison, a prisoner named Eldridge Cleaver wrote "As Crinkly as Yours," an essay on hair straightening, and succeeded in having it published in *Negro History Bulletin*. Several months later, *Muhammad Speaks* reprinted his article with a slightly altered title, "As Crinkly as Yours, Brother," that framed it as a discussion between men.[23] The article effectively joined two elements of Black Muslim ideology, racial pride and the rejection of artifices. *Muhammad Speaks* editors illustrated it with a portrait of a beautiful black woman, noting, "Beauty such as this needs no artificial props. . . . Kinky hair and an unpainted face are the true marks of beauty." Its position appeared clear. Hair straightening was wasteful and shameful. But there was a problem with maintaining an anti–hair-straightening position. The Black Muslims encouraged entrepreneurship as a key component of their belief in the importance of economic independence from whites. Beauty parlors whose financial mainstay was hair straightening were among the most numerous black-owned businesses.

The contradiction was visible in the newspaper's "Natural Beauty" feature, which regularly displayed photographs of black women as evidence of the race's glory. Often the women had straightened hair.[24] *Muhammad Speaks* was supported in part by its advertisers, including manufacturers of hair straightening creams and beauty shops such as the Feminine Woman, which specialized in "relaxers," the hair industry's euphemism for hair straightening chemicals. One of the newspaper's readers noticed the inconsistency inherent in the presentation of a woman with straightened hair as a natural beauty and wrote to express his concern: "I notice that most of the sisters represented in your paper straighten their hair. . . . This leaves me, and quite a few others, somewhat confused as to what your position is on this matter." He recalled Cleaver's article and asked other readers to think again about the meaning of hair straightening and to stop straightening their hair.[25] The correspondent sought to stem an anticipated argument that "natural" hair would rob black beauticians of their livelihood. He suggested that enterprising beauticians create new services by developing skilled methods of grooming especially for the new unstraightened styles. His letter, which focused on women, was indicative of the changes in perceptions of straightened hair that were sweeping through black communities. Fewer and fewer men straightened their hair, and as a result there was little reason to continue denouncing black, male hair straightening. The spotlight had turned to black women's hair as the most important signifier of racial pride.

One of the ways that natural hairstyles were promoted outside of social movement communities was through fashion shows. Sophisticated, young, black cultural elites used fashion shows, a form of self-promotion and self-definition popular with previous generations of middle-class blacks, to disseminate their vision of the look of racial pride as embodied in elegant women flaunting styled "natural" hair.[26] The Nation of Islam, which organized poor African Americans on the basis of racial pride and middle-class aspirations, initially endorsed the new look and included favorable coverage of the natural hair fashion shows. The February 1963 *Muhammad Speaks* featured a photo of Abbey Lincoln under the headline, "Women Who Dare Wear Their Hair Natural." An article described the touring "Naturally '63" fashion show in which models wore different "au naturelle" hairstyles that were said to represent the varied regions of Africa. The natural was touted as "part of the process of building, of emerging from the shadowy world of self contempt, of overpowering the destructive psychological impact of a standard of beauty worshiped by the majority in American society."[27] Elegant women, formerly symbols of black, middle-class achievement, when presented in garb and hairstyles evocative of Africa, stood for more than class position and the implicit racial pride of an earlier generation of race men. They, and particularly their unstraightened hair, embodied a new form of black pride that embraced and celebrated African origins.

A few months later, the same touring fashion show was covered in a *Muhammad Speaks* article that was drawn primarily from a black wire service report. Here, the fusion of middle-class aspirations, symbols of Africa, and black pride as embodied by fashionable and "natural" black women was more explicit. The article stated that most African women wore natural coiffures. The director of the show was quoted as saying that "Naturally '63" was "destined to dignify the Negro image and present racial standards which promote dignity, class, and pride."[28] With these articles, it seemed that the Nation of Islam gave its full support to the belief in the importance of unstraightened hair as an expression of racial pride.

The Nation of Islam had been extremely effective in building a collective identity by using images of black beauty, autonomy, and superiority. It rearticulated the meaning of blackness grounded in the African tradition of Islam. In the 1940s, 1950s, and early 1960s, the organization occupied a unique position in its advocacy of black separatism. In the latter half of the 1960s, black nationalism surged. The field of organizations promoting black nationalism became crowded, and the need for each organization to perform the cultural work of organizational distinction grew. One of the ways that the Nation of Islam sought to maintain its position among competing black nationalist groups was to stress the links between itself and the figure of Marcus Garvey. In order to claim Garvey's legacy, *Muhammad Speaks* printed a supportive letter from his widow and published articles such as "Route of Ace Salesman from Marcus Garvey to the Messenger" and "Marcus Garvey Said a Messenger Will Follow Me."[29] By establishing links between the organization and Marcus Garvey, the Nation of Islam distinguished itself from more recent entrants into the black nationalist field.

Another of the Nation of Islam's strategies of organizational distinction revolved around the new style or symbol of natural hair. Between 1962 and 1968, the Afro emerged among committed civil rights activists, grew into a widely recognized and accepted symbol that represented racial pride, and then became a popular style. As it became a style, blacks questioned its significance as a representation of pride or commitment. The tensions surrounding the questions of whether the natural was a style or a symbol and, if it was a symbol, who or what it represented were exhibited on the pages of *Muhammad Speaks* and created a space for the work of organizational distinction. But the tasks of distinguishing itself from other black organizations, building a black collectivity, and rearticulating the meaning of black racial identity often led the Nation of Islam in divergent directions and added further complications to the public positions Black Muslims took on black beauty. In articles in which the main cultural work performed was that of racial rearticulation by creating images of racial pride, the newspaper celebrated the symbol of the elegant woman with natural hair.[30] Where the emphasis was more focused on building a collective black political identity, followers were encouraged to reject hair straightening and skin bleaching because the practices represented attempts to imitate whites.[31] But as the Nation of Islam worked to distinguish itself among black nationalist organizations, it performed ideological somersaults as the natural transformed in the popular mind from an authentic symbol into a trivialized style.

Through the end of 1967, the newspaper continued to publish articles that praised natural hairstyles. A new, competing, and contradictory theme appeared in 1965, however. In an article titled "The Revolution in Hair Grooming: Is the Black Beautician Losing Fight for Life?," the author argued that black beauticians were endangered by the triple threat of white salons using "secret" formulas, the popularity of wigs, and the growing number of women who wore their hair natural and avoided beauty parlors altogether.[32] The author was entirely sympathetic toward the threatened black beautician entrepreneurs and made no mention of self-hatred or imitation of whites in relation to hair straightening.

The next month, two articles stood side by side, on a single page, each expressing an opposing half of the newspaper's split position.[33] One performed the work of collective identity powered by racial pride as it argued that black women should shun cosmetics because they were the most beautiful women on earth. "Why spend millions, possibly billions, of our hard earned dollars on beauty aids when the Honorable Elijah Muhammad has taught us we are the most beautiful people on earth?" The other article rearticulated the meaning of black as financially secure as it celebrated the financial achievement of the five stockholders of a black cosmetics firm, "Miracle Products, Inc." On the following page, the newspaper reproduced a photograph of Mrs. Lillie Mae Cobb, a mother and beautician who was described as a "dedicated practitioner of beauty culture, with a burning desire to make every woman's hair a crown of glory."[34] Her hair was straightened, and presumably her business was hair straightening. Racism shut black entrepreneurs out of most business lines. Products and services designed for blacks, especially cosmetics that profited from black women's insecurities about their looks, were among the few business niches in which black men and women had an advantage over whites. Widespread black rejection of artifices might crush countless numbers of small black businesses. The contradictions surrounding hair straightening as a black business and a black social practice were unresolved as black beauticians and cosmetics manufacturers were praised as business leaders while straighteners and other beauty products were condemned as shameful wastes.

As the year progressed, the newspaper's support for the practitioners of hair straightening continued and a new analysis emerged that reframed natural hairstyles as styles for elites who stood apart from the more authentic readership of *Muhammad Speaks*. The author of a 1965 article played on class divisions that conceptualized middle class as white and effeminate and black as masculine and working class. Straightened hair was ideologically recovered as the more authentically black practice. The article profiled a successful, manly beautician named Paul. He was "100 per cent man. There's not a fairy bone in his body."[35] It reversed the prevailing racialization of hair care practices by describing the natural as a passing style for distant Negro elites: "The 'Natural' Look, which seems popular in some *Negro intellectual circles*, may be a beauty fad for a short time . . . it will not last long. It is too difficult to style and manage" (emphasis added). In the context of an article about a hardworking man, the natural was just a style popular among the intellectuals. The writer predicted that the style would soon be abandoned when capricious women moved on to the next fad. Distancing himself from elite "Negro intellectual circles," the author reinforced the position of *Muhammad Speaks* and its parent organization, the Nation of Islam, as the movement of the common black man. The article prefigured a change that would, within a few years, resolve the contradictions surrounding hair straightening that had emerged in the newspaper.

In the late 1960s, black organizing surged in many forms. The Black Panther

Party developed vibrant chapters throughout the United States, Ron Karenga established Kwanzaa and other expressions of cultural nationalism that became enduring parts of African American life, and black student protests paralyzed and then reshaped universities. In 1968, amid this proliferation of black organizing, the Nation of Islam took steps to assert its primacy among nationalist groups. Under the headline, "Finds 'Black Is Beautiful' Inherent in the Messenger's Teachings," the writer claimed that Elijah Muhammad had been the first to present proof that black was beautiful—unlike the numerous recent converts to black consciousness who had only lately awakened to black beauty.[36] By establishing Muhammad's position as the discoverer of black beauty, the Nation of Islam claimed preeminence among organizations promoting black pride. The organization's long history of declaring the superiority of the race substantiated its claim. Though its first move in 1968 was to distinguish itself from the others by claiming precedence, later in the year the Nation of Islam took a more drastic step and distanced itself from the styles that had come to popularly represent black beauty. On June 28, 1968, Elijah Muhammad issued a warning to the members of the Nation of Islam: "This is a warning to the M.G.T. (Muslim Girl's Training) and G.C.C. (General Civilization Class) against adopting the African dress and hair styles (this applies to the Brothers of the F.O.I. also) and . . . against accepting African tribal styles and garments with gay colors."[37]

In 1968, black nationalism took many forms. Of all of the manifestations of black power sentiments, cultural expressions had the widest acceptance.[38] Working class and middle class, young and old delighted in the beauty and symbolism of clothing sewn of African fabric. Men wore dashiki shirts with recognizable African designs, women wrapped their heads in elegant "geles." These boldly appealing styles threatened to undermine the position of the Nation of Islam, whose adherents were identifiable by their conservative appearance. Abdul Basit Naeem, a regular *Muhammad Speaks* writer whose area of expertise was explication of Nation of Islam social dogma, followed Muhammad's June 28 warning with a column clarifying Muhammad's reasoning. He reminded readers that "for reasons of identity, unity and discipline, my Muslim brothers and sisters in the wilderness of North America must forever and fully carry out the Honorable Elijah Muhammad's injunctions and instructions on such matters. . . . In DUE time, they would all be emulating YOU!"[39] The directive was a maneuver to hold the members' loyalty through the visible symbols of appearance. By suggesting that "they" will be imitating "you," he exhorted members to hold on to their visible identity, which would endure beyond the passing styles of newcomers to black nationalism. Wearing bright African garb, the Nation of Islam's followers would disappear into the crowd of advocates of racial pride. Maintaining their conventions—simple head coverings and dark, long dresses for women and conservative suits, bowties, and short haircuts for men—Black Muslims remained a visible presence in their communities. Though *Muhammad Speaks* had previously wavered between praising the Afro and calling it a threat to the black small business economy, in 1968 its position was firm. The Afro was a mere style, an affectation not permitted for Black Muslims. An article that appeared several weeks after Muhammad's anti-Afro directive invalidated the Afro as a sign of black pride. It declared, "Whites Buying 'African Hair' Wigs as 'Natural' Hair Style Gains Popularity."[40] The natural was no longer black. Between 1962 and 1968, the Nation of Islam went from celebrating the natural to viewing it as a threat to small black businesses, to trying to claim ownership of "black is beautiful," to banning the most popular symbols of black pride. This trajectory reflects the contradictory demands of building a movement based on a singular black identity when, in fact, black identity was complex and changing.

In the late 1960s, many African Americans were ardently committed to celebrating blackness, but little agreement existed about what "black" meant. In a racial field in which there were competing ways to be authentic, the way to invalidate someone was to charge him with being "a Negro" as opposed to a black man, to accuse a woman of "acting white" or pandering to whites, or to question the seriousness of a person's commitment to nationalism by calling him a "pork chop nationalist." These were serious charges in times of great racial polarization. Differentiation proceeded in the name of unification. Political actors in a fragmented social movement used distinctions to build a movement and to distinguish their positions within it.

The body, bodily practices, and representations of the body became sites for the construction of community and thus placed specific demands on women, whose bodies are generally more subject to symbolic usage and public scrutiny and who followed general cultural norms that required them to wear makeup and style their hair. Women were called upon, more frequently than men, to be "naturally black." Honor was used as the device to demand the conformity that unity required. The desire to build a unified community in the midst of another culture and the belief in the goodness of nature produced urgent calls for women to be black by being natural and beautiful and for men to be black by acting like men. To be black and male meant being defiant. To be black and female was to be defiant by being natural. For many blacks, hair, that part of our bodies so subject to transformation, became the mark of one's commitment to being real. The Nation of Islam temporarily embraced that position but ultimately turned against it, distinguishing themselves from the crowd of newcomers to nationalism. For most others, hair functioned as an important symbol. The politicization of hair is captured in Amiri Baraka's "Wig Poem," in which he repeats nine times the command, "take off the wig."[41] In each of the repetitions of the command an unspoken context can be heard. A man is issuing commands to women. The wig is a pretense that represents middle-class aspirations, rejection of a natural black self, shame, and subordination to whites.

"Natural" became, for many nationalists attempting to solve the nationalist's problem of building a collectivity, a useful ideological construct. Races, after all, are conventionally thought of as biological entities. One resolution to the question of where to find authentic blackness was to look to the body. The natural was born at the intersection of three ideological positions: the desire to eliminate white influence from black life, confidence in the goodness of nature, and the belief that race is a biological category. At a time when African Americans in social movement organizations sought a definition and location of an authentic black culture, the natural emerged as a simple symbol of black identity. It aided individual black women in accomplishing a different task: the daily project of making a self. Racial formation takes place as individuals reconstruct themselves as racial beings, giving life to socially constructed boundaries and meanings. The natural was an act and a symbol that bridged the collective and the individual projects. It was personal and collective, private and public. A movement and its constituents gave each other life. Pearl Marsh described what her natural meant to her: "You had to stop identifying with culture that was the oppressor culture. You know. I don't care how much I straighten my hair. I don't even care how much bleach cream I use. I was never going to be white. And even if I got white, my nose wasn't going to be little. There was just a limit and so you have to respect who you were."[42] Marsh believed her racial identity was an important part of who she was and that this identity was lodged in her natural body. She had been scorned for her blackness, and the establishment of her self-respect began with a defense of the body's natural state. Beneath an artifice that had become associated with "acting white" lay an authentic black person worthy of respect. Her sentiments are echoed in Myesha Jenkins's words: "I don't want [to] look like the oppressor. I don't need to assimilate. My nappy hair is fine. And there ain't nothing wrong with Africa and black people and blackness and who we are for real."[43] By 1966, straightened hair no longer signified being a well-groomed black woman. Its meaning had been transformed into "looking like the oppressor."

In September 1966, just months after Stokely Carmichael heralded a change in the movement in his "black power" speech, Abbey Lincoln published a pathbreaking article on black women.[44] "Who Will Revere the Black Woman?," which appeared in *Negro Digest*, asked why black women who have endured the brutality of racism were harshly criticized and rejected sexually by black men. *Negro Digest* received dozens of passionate responses, including one from a "T. Brown" in Omaha, Nebraska, who lashed out at black women for their disloyalty. He began with a denunciation of hair straightening and wigs and then focused on elite black women who, "after reaching a certain stage in their climb to become a celebrity, [bemoan] the fact that there are no Black men on their 'level.' This is the best alibi that they can fabricate in order to do what they had in mind all along: have white men."[45] In his argument, straightened hair is but the first step in a chain of betrayal that ends with sleeping with the enemy. The call to racial unity was used to stifle gender divisions. Brown's angry letter and Baraka's poem are representative of the many pleas made in the late 1960s to return to the truth and goodness of the natural black body. Exposing the physical self in all its glory was thought to be the first step of a militant. "Stop frying your hair" and political awareness will follow.

In a time when hair became a highly racialized symbol, a hairdo could be experienced as a political statement. Black women could show agreement with the Black Power Movement simply by cutting their hair into Afros. In an interview, an Oakland woman recalled the meaning of her Afro: "It was a statement. I was saying something. I was making a political statement. I was saying that, yeah, I'm black and I'm proud. Say it loud. You know. That was me. It wasn't none of this Negro, colored . . . stuff. I was a black woman. I was proud. I just used to thank God I was black. I said I know we suffering and everything but thank you for making me a black person!"[46]

As their bodies were objectified, wearing a natural became one of the ways in which black women could take part in the symbolic process of racial rearticulation, community building, and differentiation. A woman remembered the warm greeting she was given by a total stranger when she walked out of a beauty shop wearing an Afro for the first time:

> There was a place in Harlem called Black Rose. It was on 125th Street. I heard about it and took the subway up there and got off, went in, and cut my hair off. And as I walked out, there was a little black man, on the sidewalk, and he said, "Sister, you're looking good!" I remember putting my head up and just . . . I was shocked. But I mean literally he said it as soon as I stepped outside the beauty parlor. I literally took a foot out and he said it. I was so glad he said it. That's why I remember it. And just how he said it.[47]

Myesha Jenkins described what she felt were the differences between women who straightened their hair and women who did not:

> Straightened was respectable. It was what was, what we did. Decent people. We don't look like . . . unkempt. If you are riding freedom buses and getting water hosed down on you, you ain't going to keep your hair straight. So then the symbol of a person who fights for their rights, a person who can be self-determining and self-defining and proud of themselves, which grows out of that period, gets its expression in a black is beautiful movement. I'm black and I'm proud. And I'm equal and you know I don't have to press my hair. And I

don't have to be light. And the women who were afraid of that . . . didn't do it. Not everybody did do naturals. And it was a political statement where many people who were more on the fringe, more you know, willing to go to jail, more willing to throw a brick. Say something to a cop. Call a pig a pig [laughs]. Those women as opposed to the women who were going to school and getting the jobs and you know had another track in mind were more likely to have naturals. And [women with Afros] look[ed] askance at those women, who they didn't necessarily think were willing to fight for their rights.[48]

Actually, many women who wore naturals went to school, got jobs, and were afraid of or were uninterested in throwing bricks. The symbols were more polarized than the lives of the people who wore them. "Black is beautiful" was an assertion of the dignity and self-possession of one's body, but as the natural became the mark of a proud black woman, the hair on women's heads became a public matter. For many women, having their kinky hair and brown skin celebrated in public was absolutely wonderful. Shame and invisibility were replaced by joyous presence. Exclusion from all that was good was supplanted by membership in the community of proud brothers and sisters. Particularly in the years when the natural was new and the movement was still strong, "sisters" with naturals knew they were special and acknowledged one another on the street.

As the natural became widespread and demands to be natural proliferated, disenchantment with the power of the style grew. Some black women resented being called beauties in black power rhetoric when they were still not treated as desirable by the black men they knew. Women activists saw the attention given to their hair as evidence of the limited role they were being asked to play in the movement.

Yet there is a generation of black women who will never again straighten their hair. These women discovered relief and self-love when they threw away their hot combs. Others have memories of joy mixed with disenchantment. They enjoy an expanded beauty standard but straighten their hair when it pleases them. These women did not find a lasting sense of membership in a community through the style or the stance of black and beautiful.

The new black identity was variably defined as a quality that was natural and lodged in the body, or performed or felt, something called "soul." Black was southern rural poverty. Black was urban poverty. Black was elegance. Black was communal. Black was angry. Black was not white. Black was African. These elements were not arbitrarily imagined. They reflected demographic reality and black diversity and were shaped by the aims and experience of the Civil Rights and Black Power movements. Black as natural was one of many attempts to forge racial unity. Linked with a highly visible if fragmented and troubled movement, "black is beautiful" appeared to be new. It seemed as new as black nationalism, itself detached from the nationalism of previous African American generations.

The intensity of activism of the late 1960s did not last. Black students won victories that were institutionalized in black studies departments, and then the level of student activism declined. Kwanzaa, the holiday created by Karenga was broadly accepted by black families as an important new tradition, but US, the organization he led, ceased to grow. The Black Panther Party was crushed by a combination of government repression and internal collapse. The Nation of Islam survived as a strong black institution but worked primarily outside of political arenas. The beautiful and natural black body had served as a symbol as each of these groups tried to establish a collective identity. Without a movement, any woman's body was just her own—not a symbol of unity, just a person.

In 1992, I interviewed an African American woman who had recently straightened her hair after more than twenty-five years of wearing it in a natural. I asked her what wearing a natural meant in the 1990s. Her answer was that "it totally says how old we are." Her natural did nothing but give away her age, identify her as someone who had come of age in the 1960s. In 1966, an Afro signified a break with the past and became part of a movement's effort to build a politically effective collective identity. Without an active social movement, the natural was just a haircut, not a symbol of defiance or even a symbol of blackness. Both the natural and an identifiable movement disappeared together.

Chapter Nine

AN ONGOING DIALOGUE

Entering Mrs. Williams's beauty shop in 1994, I recognized a pre-1966 smell, the smell of something sweet and fragile burning. Barbara Williams, the proprietor of Barbara's Beauty Spot, was straightening an elderly woman's hair the old way, using a hot comb and grease, tools she has used professionally since 1959. Mrs. Williams wore her hair elegantly styled, dyed light blonde and swept upward into a tall, motionless arrangement of curls. The shop was decorated with six or seven landscapes and portraits painted by Mrs. Williams's brother in the early 1970s. Admiring them, I felt a jolt of recognition when I saw one that depicted a young man bound and gagged in a courtroom. It was a painting of Black Panther Bobby Seale during the Chicago Seven trial. In another beauty shop along Oakland's MacArthur Boulevard, a poster of Malcolm X watches over the hair straightening stations. Portraits of black rebels decorate shops where old ladies and young women get their hair straightened because the legacy of black insurgency has become a part of the everyday life of African Americans. This chapter considers that legacy and what it demonstrates about the dynamics of racial rearticulation.

In the late 1960s, the words "black is beautiful" were an exuberant break from the past and the latest expression of something very old. Call it prepolitical resistance, self-love, early nationalism, racial pride, racial rearticulation, or common sense, some African Americans since coming to these shores have been able to love themselves and their race despite the difficulty of their circumstances or the ways in which the race has been represented. Under the conditions of racial ascription and domination, self-love is a daily, person-by-person project of racial redefinition.

Black self-love and efforts to find ways to instill pride in black children have taken many forms. Most directly antecedent to "black is beautiful" were the efforts by black parents to teach their children to love brown skin. Ruth Beckford, born in Oakland in the mid-1920s, and Pearl Marsh, born in the rural Northwest in the 1940s, both told me of their parents' efforts to obtain pretty black dolls for them through mail order. Beckford's father was a Garveyite and nurtured his daughter with Garvey's message that black women were the most beautiful. Not a Garveyite, Marsh's mother was simply determined to raise a daughter who could appreciate her own brown skin.

The practice of making distinctions among black people, who whites treated as indistinguishable, was another manifestation of black racial pride. Brenda Travis, born into a very poor family in McComb, Mississippi, in the mid-1940s, remembered her grandmother's efforts to instill in her a sense of self-respect using the language available to her in rural Mississippi. She told her granddaughter, "You're colored. You're Negro, and American. And you can never be a nigger. Because nigger doesn't run in my blood."[1] "Nigger" was the word that racist whites used to malign blacks. She taught her granddaughter that she was an American and accordingly deserved the rights and privileges due any citizen. Brenda could choose among the polite terms for the race—Negro and colored—but she was not a "nigger." The strategy Travis's grandmother employed was one that blacks, regardless of income, used in order to maintain a personal sense of dignity and convey that sentiment to their children. Within black communities, one could be poor but have social standing based on one's conduct. The ability to maintain an autonomous sense of social rankings was another of the ways black communities undermined a white racial order that denigrated all blacks.

Black social institutions fostered racial pride by creating safe social spaces that could not be violated by white racism. They did not challenge segregation but created separate social worlds that fostered an appreciation of black life. Robert Curry recalled that in the 1950s an uncle took him to events sponsored by a black fraternal order in New York City where he learned to separate militancy from racial pride. They taught him "how to stay out of harm's way and have pride in your blackness."[2]

Products of their time, these various lessons in black dignity incorporated elements that could not fit into later conceptualizations of black pride. In the early 1960s in southern California, in her mother's kitchen, Myesha Jenkins learned racial pride and the importance of a straightened head of hair at the same time: "I learned the Negro National Anthem sitting between my mama's legs while she pressed my hair. She would sing that to me when she pressed my [hair]. I would have her [sing]. 'Sing me songs, Mama.' Cause it takes an hour, an hour and a half to do your hair. And that's how I learned the Negro National Anthem."[3]

"Lift Every Voice and Sing," known as the Negro National Anthem and easily recognized within black communities, was written in 1900 by James Weldon Johnson and set to music by his brother J. Rosamond Johnson. Prior to the Civil Rights Movement, gifts of black dolls, use of the word "Negro" and insistence on its capitalization, proud use of the word "black," the popularity of "Lift Every Voice and Sing," identification with Africa, and jokes about the stupidity of whites existed in African American communities alongside robust sales of bleaching creams, avoidance of the word "black," feelings of shame about having dark skin, and the popular use by blacks of expressions of black racial deprecation. Neither uniform racial pride and resistance nor internalized shame adequately characterizes pre–civil rights era black communities. The meanings about race that circulated within black communities were the remnants of prior struggles. Ruth Beckford's father drew upon remnants of Garveyism to raise his daughter; Jenkins's mother sang a Negro anthem created in the context of the unrestrained racism of turn-of-the-century America. The way in which the meanings and practices of racial pride incorporate remnants of past struggles and integrate prevailing hierarchies of class and gender suggests a general model for the dynamics of racial rearticulation. The process of incorporating familiar and dominant cultural themes and stretching the interlocking boundaries of race, class, and gender is what I have described as top-down and bottom-up racial rearticulation. It is a dialogue between actions taken at the institutional and individual levels. Racial rearticulation occurred at the institutional level as the media and social movement organizations promoted new meanings of race and at the individual level as men and women embodied or rejected and, as a result, altered those meanings. Day-to-day racial rearticulation at the individual level occurred in dialogue with a continually changing larger environment. These institutional and individual acts of racial rearticulation were products of the heterogeneous black habitus. They reflected the embedded agency of the black men and women who used them as what seemed, from where they stood, to be the best strategies for winning dignity. Social movements accelerated and redirected the process of racial rearticulation by changing the contexts in which everyday racial rearticulation occurred. They produced new strategies, meanings, and practices, altering the heterogeneous black habitus that had initially given the movement form.

We can begin to look at the process of racial rearticulation at a time of movement abeyance. At that point, the social hierarchy is stable and has broad acceptance (though I would argue that there will always be some members of dominated groups who challenge it). A movement builds, organizing around issues that are not necessarily cultural. Yet social movements open a space for the reassessment of cultural hierarchies. In Bourdieu's language they expose doxa (the rules so accepted that they go unsaid) as orthodoxy. In the process of organizing, new identities emerge within the movement that are elaborated in the day-to-day practices of movement participants. The new identities and related practices soon transcend the boundaries of the movement and shape culture outside of it as well. New identities and practices become the basis for new doxa. New things are taken for granted. The meanings associated with practices are sustained by the movement. If the movement declines, fragments of identities and practices of resistance remain. Consider the model in relation to the emergence of "black is beautiful."

"Black is beautiful" was the product of a mixture of inadvertent cultural transformations and deliberate cultural interventions. Some civil rights leaders were concerned about the image of the race and made cultural representations the focus of their demands. They picketed beauty pageants, pressured advertising agencies to employ black models, and promoted alternative representations of black women in order to counter humiliating portrayals of the race. However, a large part of the transformation in the meaning of black and particularly the emergence of unstraightened hair as a symbol of racial pride was an unintended consequence of a decade of activism. The experience of participating in the Civil Rights Movement prompted a transformation of identity among the youths who dedicated their lives to the movement. Black movement communities were centers of intensive exploration in which activists questioned existing meanings of black identity, reevaluated conventional practices, and created new ways of living day-to-day life. A dominant ideology that disparaged black people and especially disparaged black bodies permeated majority and minority cultures. This began to change in 1960, when a few women who were involved actively in the Civil Rights Movement began to view their bodies differently as a result of the emerging culture of the movement. They began wearing unstraightened hair and faced ridicule and insult within African American communities. Before long, women within the movement began to see the natural hairstyle as the obvious way to wear their hair. The natural became established within the social movement field as the new doxa. For a period of several years, the Afro expressed a sense of solidarity. It became the hallmark of a woman who participated in or identified with the Civil Rights Movement. As more and more women adopted naturals, a profound change occurred. In time, naturals were not just a way to express pride. They were, quite simply, a way to be beautiful.

The dialogue that was racial rearticulation had effects inside and outside of black communities. The cultural shifts initiated by the Civil Rights and Black Power movements were not just changes in the representation of blacks by whites. Of equal or greater importance, the movements stimulated an internal critique of black culture. As a by-product of these movements, African Americans reevaluated their own cultural practices. While African Americans challenged misrepresentation of blacks in the media and exclusion of blacks from white cultural institutions, recasting the meanings of black and beautiful *out-*

side of black communities, they also reconsidered African American cultural practices and reshaped meanings of black and beautiful *inside* black communities. Black women had learned dominant standards within their childhood homes from the grooming instruction given by their mothers and the teasing of their friends. In the 1950s, an adult black woman proudly wearing "nappy" hair was unfathomable to most people within African American communities. Almost all African American women straightened their hair as a part of what was considered routine grooming. The youths who sought to establish the recognition of beauty in what had previously been considered ugly met some of the most stubborn resistance within black communities. There were generational splits between mothers accustomed to seeing unstraightened hair as nappy and daughters who had learned to associate straightened hair with shame. There were large numbers of black men and women who had not seen kinky hair or dark skin called beautiful frequently enough to be able to recognize their beauty. In time, the rapid rearticulation of the meaning and performance of black identity that developed within black movement communities spread beyond their confines. The cultural message developed within the Civil Rights Movement was focused and communicated nationally by the black and the white media. When dark-skinned female models wearing Afros were shown in *Ebony*, blacks outside of the movement learned to see beauty where they had not seen it before.

The inadvertent cultural exploration that began in the Civil Rights Movement developed into a more deliberate rethinking of the meaning of black in the Black Power Movement. Black power organizations had to address the nationalist's dilemma. They organized on the basis of an identity that was at once self-evident and needed definition. Within different organizations, black was variously defined as African, revolutionary and communal, urban and poor, or Muslim. The beautiful black woman was an important symbol that could stand as the authentic representation of any of these variations. The meanings, symbols, and practices generated within black power organizations also disseminated through black communities, leading to new orientations toward Africa, the adoption of Kwanzaa as a black holiday, and the addition of black militants and martyrs of the 1960s in a revised pantheon of black heroes.

The forms that expressions of pride took at any historical moment reflected prevailing opportunities, levels of racist repression, levels of political activism, and class trajectories within black communities. They incorporated and stretched the boundaries of common meanings of race, class, and gender. Prevailing understandings of male and female roles constituted a fundamental context for projects of racial rearticulation. Racial projects occasionally challenged but more often incorporated and reinforced existing gender norms. Middle-class "race men" of the nineteenth century and Elijah Muhammad in the twentieth century called on women to make racial projects real through their bodies and behavior. A frequent strategy employed by race leaders was to gain social honor for the race by incorporating conventional representations of gender into newly articulated representations of the race. On contest runways, black beauty queens paraded alternative and hegemonic visions with each step.

Women were not just represented but also participated in creating representations. Negro clubwomen promoted images of black women as upstanding and chaste symbols of the race's character. Contestants in the black beauty contests in the era of segregation and the Negro beauties who entered white beauty contests at the dawn of racial integration used the beauty of their bodies to represent the magnificence of black people. Black Panther women wrote newspaper columns and poems instructing their sisters in how to be revolutionary women and denouncing bourgeois black female traitors. In the early calls for women to "elevate the race," in celebrations of Negro beauty queens, and in demands that black women restore dignity to the black race by remaining subordinate to men, black women were told by male and female black leaders that their carriage, demeanor, appearance, and behavior embodied the dignity of the race. The call to queendom was hard to resist, when the alternative was the wider culture's disparagement.

The cultural transformation initiated by the Civil Rights Movement had considerable effects outside of black communities. In the 1960s, African Americans primarily entered the national picture as subjects of the nightly news. Gradually, white producers of films, television programs, advertisements, beauty contests, and toys expanded their imagery to include portrayals of blacks that went beyond grotesque stereotypes. The presence of beautiful black women in national venues is no longer newsworthy but is, nonetheless, a relatively recent phenomenon. Before 1974, every *Vogue* cover had featured a white woman. Before 1983, every Miss America was white. Advertisers, magazine editors, casting directors, and television programmers responded to the demands of a black movement and also began to recognize the profitability of marketing to black consumers. African Americans succeeded in winning dramatic changes in the frequency and character of their representation in images created by the makers of mass media and industrial production. From Barbie dolls to MTV to Afrocentric pages on the World Wide Web, African Americans are included in mass representation. As a direct and indirect consequence of the Civil Rights and Black Power movements, images of African Americans have been diversified in the mass media. While these images fit into new (and newly limited) patterns of representation, they are nonetheless better than the monolithic, degrading portrayals of blacks that characterized earlier years. As beautiful black women were included with increasing frequency in television programs, fashion magazines, and films, the generally held standard of beauty grew more inclusive. Recognition of the beauty of dark brown skin is no longer a nonconformist view. Contemporary images of beauty presented by the mass media include at least a few dark-skinned models and film stars. A more inclusive aesthetic makes it more possible for young black women to escape the shame felt by many dark-skinned women of past generations.

When practices and products developed inside of black communities were mirrored outside of black communities, their meanings changed. As expressions of black pride were incorporated into fashion, their value as expressions of racial pride and of defiance faded. The case of the natural hairstyle demonstrates this effect most dramatically. By the late 1970s, wearing a natural had lost its importance to all but a dedicated cadre of women who recognized that—though the style remained meaningful to them as individuals—it was no longer the singular expression of black pride. The radical meaning of an Afro could not be sustained at a time when black social movements were declining.

Many of the specific cultural practices associated with the Civil Rights and Black Power movements have fallen out of favor. Few black parents give their newborns African names and no one wears a big Afro. The legacy of the activism of the 1960s remains in the broad acceptance of race as an analytical frame for understanding one's predicament in life. It lives in a rearticulated concept of what it means to be black that structures common-sense categories of race employed in day-to-day life. It shapes assumptions about what constitutes acting black or acting white. Black identity continues to takes up temporary residence in objects of material culture—home grown and mass produced—that gain and lose racial meaning as they travel across racial borders.

In the contemporary context of low levels of black political activism and a bifurcated black class structure, African Americans find ways to say, "I choose blackness," and claim dignity, autonomy, and authority in their daily lives. This legacy of the black consciousness era lives on in the daily lives of African Americans in the absence of an organized social movement. Particular practices that are deemed authentically, proudly black change, but an underlying and widespread commitment to assertions of racial pride endures. Employing narratives of racial pride that are products of black power politics, African Americans even reclaim pre–black power era practices. Mary O'Neal, who was willing to endure insults to wear her hair natural at Howard University in the early 1960s, fondly recalled the bleached-blonde, straightened-hair black women she saw in black "juke joints" of the 1950s as women who, she believed, were ostentatiously proud of their dark skin.

> I can remember when I was growing up and sneaking into the juke joints. There were these women—black, black, black women who would have blonde hair. They were the most exciting and the most beautiful women I'd ever seen. And it wasn't about them trying to look white. It was like they were lighting their faces as if you take a photograph with an over light. They were wonderful. Wonderful!

People have assumed that when they bleached their hair they wanted to look white. They bleached their hair because they looked fabulous. You know it was like this funny white hair against this black skin. A black, black woman who's got this bleached hair is not saying, "I'm white." She's not saying that at all. She's saying "But look at me." As if you put a big red sign on your shirt and said "Look at me!"[4]

And Lee Gilliam, a black hairstylist who operates a shop in Oakland, reassures his customers that the hairstyles they are choosing are black styles, with origins in Egypt, even though they are now featured in hair-styling magazines on white models: "I have to pick the [style] book up and explain to them, forget the white face. Don't think that we're copying off Caucasian women because we're not copying off them. All their A-shapes come from Egypt and beyond. We're just copying back from ourselves."[5] Bound by a discourse of racial pride, Gilliam establishes what he feels is a necessary direct link between contemporary black choices and the continent of Africa. And another hair-straightening practitioner in Oakland can decorate his shop with a poster of Malcolm X, whose autobiography stigmatized hair straightening for a generation, because contemporary articulations of racial pride accept all black hair care practices as expressions of black creativity. In the contemporary African American discourse of racial pride, specific styles are less connected to political meanings than they were during the late 1960s.

Articulations of racial pride are personally sustaining and maintain everyday critical readings of a social structure that continues to reproduce racial inequality. But does racial pride serve as a barrier to continued racial domination? Identities, like grievances, are plentiful wherever there is inequality. A proud black identity implies no particular set of demands nor does an identity guarantee a definite political vision. Laclau and Mouffe describe identity-based antagonisms as "floating signifiers" that become political projects when articulated with other social antagonisms.[6] The "partial character" of identity-based struggles "can be articulated to very different discourses. It is this articulation which gives them their character, not the place from which they come."[7] The evidence of the preceding chapters demonstrates that black political identity, a product of the Civil Rights Movement, gave no predetermined strategic direction to the movement. Black identity was leveraged into a variety of political projects, none of which flowed automatically from black racial identity but instead reflected black identity articulated with class trajectories and particular understandings of gender. Black identity provided a base for black capitalism, for the development of black consumers as a market segment for capitalists of any hue, for the celebration of imaginary monarchies, for the defense of black communities against police brutality, for the development of black political clout, for assertions of patriarchy, and for challenges to a culture of white supremacy that would have excluded Toni Morrison from undergraduate syllabi and limited Arthur Mitchell to endlessly dancing the solo role of death in ballet companies where all the ballerinas were white.[8] A stance of pride does not chart a particular political course, turn into particular demands, or ensure power.

The experience of the Black Power Movement cautions against optimism about the effectiveness of cultural politics. White supremacy expressed itself through culture. Black cultural interventions were successful in creating and sustaining counterhegemonic views. But, as it turns out, culture is just a field in which power plays. Cultural practices are not power's source. Culture proved to be an accommodating field, able to sustain both racial pride and continued domination. In 1966, natural hairstyles and the vibrant colors of African fabrics were new to a generation of young African Americans. The pride with which they were worn was sustained by the wider culture's hostility toward these styles and by the existence of an organized black movement with which to identify. Within a few years, the pressures against these particular expressions of militancy faded. When styles gained broad acceptance across racial and generational boundaries, they lost their ability to communicate defiance or even black identity. An African American woman I interviewed who maintains a strong identification with African culture was explicit about the problem of ownership of black culture. She complained of "Afro sheen that was owned by somebody other than black, Afro Cola was owned by somebody other than black. Dashikis coming from France."[9] The value of particular styles as expressions of black identity could not be maintained once they circulated outside of social movement communities.

Where is black pride and black identity today? For Benetton, an upscale clothing manufacturer, multiculturalism is what the billboard was to Burma Shave: the best new way to get attention. Peter Fressola, Benetton's director of communications, went so far as to say, "We own multiculturalism."[10] The Black Panthers were the heroes of a big-budget Hollywood movie directed by second-generation black filmmaker Mario Van Peebles. Spike Lee's dramatization of the life of Malcolm X, available on video, is shelved in the documentary section of home video stores. Across the country, small black entrepreneurs produce and sell countless black pride T-shirts, bookmarks, bridal gowns, jewelry, and art in neighborhood shops, at home, at flea markets, and at black trade expositions. These goods sell for their beauty or their style, but most of all they sell because the men and women who buy them are proud of being black and want to say so. That is, these objects constitute a meaningful set of symbols with which to convey racial pride. Discount store managers in the major cities understand the value in the meaning of these products and stock their shelves with queens of Africa posters and Kwanzaa greeting cards.

These commodities are, quite literally, the products of social movements in the terrain of everyday life.

Black pride has settled into the new racial landscape as a site of difference that does little to move the unmarked, raceless position of whites. In the past decade, historians and sociologists have begun to define white racial identity as something other than the absence of race.[11] Their scholarship has yet to influence day-to-day life where multiculturalism has become the inclusion of racial "others" alongside a norm that is white but has no race. The almost entirely white Joffrey Ballet is a raceless dance company, while the almost entirely black Alvin Ailey company is a black dance company. A stance of neutrality protects white privilege without recourse to racial discourse.

Political strategists too often confuse expressions of identity and political action. There is good reason for the confusion. Dignity as well as access to material well-being was at stake in the Civil Rights and Black Power movements. Aldon Morris argues that the Civil Rights Movement fought a "tripartite system of domination" that consisted of economic, political, and personal domination.[12] His study of the Civil Rights Movement concluded that the movement's significant victories were in the realms of politics and personal freedom. The new racial balance achieved was won through the sacrifices, love, hope, and energy of those who gave themselves to the Civil Rights and Black Power movements. But these movements succeeded in winning greater dignity without securing sufficient economic ground. It is a better state than that which existed prior to the movements, when black disenfranchisement and social and economic exclusion of blacks were unquestioned norms, southern whites could murder blacks with impunity, and depictions of African Americans as stupid and ugly were widespread. Yet, to this day, too many young African Americans grow up in communities destroyed by joblessness.

The current racial balance was won through the activities of a social movement. In the absence of a movement, there is no guarantee that the current balance can be maintained. Conservative forces, representing themselves as grassroots outsiders while operating from centers of power, are dismantling the liberal racial compromises of the 1960s. Cultural representations matter because racial demonization in the media provides a popular rationale for the continued deprivation of blacks and the neglect of the urban infrastructure. But culture is a slippery medium. Cultural domination is never complete and resistance never final. Battles will continue to be fought in and through culture because it is the material through which we live our daily lives. These battles, when successful, will win dignity and change the texture of everyday life. Evidence from the Civil Rights Movement demonstrates that very often cultural battles are won most effectively as inadvertent prizes of battles over other issues. Negro civil rights workers, seeking in 1960 to end disenfranchisement and racist terror, discovered in the process that they were black and beautiful.

NOTES

ABBREVIATIONS

SCF   Schomburg Clipping File, Schomburg Center for Research in Black Culture, New York Public Library

TNCF   Tuskegee Institute News Clipping File, Tuskegee Institute, Tuskegee, Alabama.

CHAPTER 1

1. "Negroes Plan Show to Rival Contest for Miss America," *New York Times*, 29 August 1968, 38; Charlotte Curtis, "Miss America Pageant Is Picketed by 100 Women," *New York Times*, 8 September 1968, 81; Charlotte Curtis and Judy Klemesrud, "Along with Miss America, There's Now Miss Black America," *New York Times*, 9 September 1968, 54; Jack Gould, "TV: Profile of Mike Todd; Promoter Extraordinary," *New York Times*, 9 September 1968, 93; "Women with Gripes Lured to Picket 'Miss America,'" *Pittsburgh New Courier*, 21 September 1968, 3; "The Price of Protest," *New York Times*, 28 September 1968, 25.

2. "The Price of Protest," *New York Times*, 28 September 1968, 25. Morgan, *Sisterhood Is Powerful*, 585.

3. "Saundra Williams of Philly Winner," *Philadelphia Afro-American*, 14 September 1968, 1–2.; "Beauty Accepts Tan Winner Idea," *Baltimore Afro-American*, 14 September 1968, 12; "The Fashionable Scene," *Pittsburgh New Courier*, 14 September 1968, 11; "There's Now 'Miss Black America' along with White 'Miss America,'" *Jet*, 26 September 1968, 26–27. An exception was a derisive article published in the *New Courier* two weeks after the Women's Liberation protest: "Women with Gripes Lured to Picket 'Miss America,'" *Pittsburgh New Courier*, 21 September 1968, 3.

4. Evans, *Personal Politics*.

5. Charlotte Curtis, "Miss America Pageant Is Picketed by 100 Women," *New York Times*, 8 September 1968, 81. In the feminist anthology *Sisterhood Is Powerful*, published two years after the Miss America protest, Robin Morgan described herself as a poet who had been "active in the male-dominated Left for about six or seven years, and has been working solely in the Women's Liberation Movement for the past three years" (648).

6. Charlotte Curtis, "Miss America Pageant Is Picketed by 100 Women," *New York Times*, 8 September, 1968, 81.

7. Crenshaw, "Whose Story Is It, Anyway," 406.

8. Chapkis, *Beauty Secrets*; Lakoff and Scherr, *Face Value*; Wolf, *The Beauty Myth*.

9. Banet-Weiser, "Fade to White," 171.

10. hooks, *Feminist Theory*, 1–4.

11. Palmer, "White Women/Black Women." 151–155.

12. Painter, *Sojourner Truth*, 164–178.

13. For the racist construction of images of white womanhood, see Frankenberg, *White Women, Race Matters*; Feldstein, "I Wanted the Whole World to See"; and Palmer, *Domesticity and Dirt* and "White Women/Black Women."

14. Charlotte Curtis and Judy Klemesrud, "Along with Miss America, There's Now Miss Black America," *New York Times*, 9 September 1968, 54.

15. For the portrayal of black women in white popular culture, see Bogle, *Toms, Coons, Mulattoes, Mammies and Bucks*; Bond, "The Media Image"; Dates and Barlow, *Split Image*; Fredrickson, *The Black Image in the White Mind*; Harley and Terborg-Penn, *The Afro-American Woman*; Jewell, *From Mammy to Miss America and Beyond*; and Smith, *Images of Blacks in American Culture*. For her portrayal in academic writing, see Gilman, "Black Bodies, White Bodies"; Jordan, *White over Black*; Morton, *Disfigured Images*; and Schiebinger, *Nature's Body*. Bogle's *Toms, Coons, Mulattoes, Mammies and Bucks* and Morton's *Disfigured Images* are exceptional in that their research considers work produced by blacks as well as whites.

16. The following works document and analyze the social construction of black and white as racial categories in the United States. Allen, *The Invention of the White Race*; Blumer and Duster, "Theories of Race and Social Action"; Dominguez, *White by Definition*; Frankenberg, *White Women, Race Matters*; Gossett, *Race*; Jordan, *White over Black*; Omi and Winant, *Racial Formation in the United States*; Palmer, *Domesticity and Dirt*; Roediger, *The Wages of Whiteness*; and Schiebinger, *Nature's Body*.

17. Omi and Winant developed the concept of rearticulation in relation to race in *Racial Formation in the United States*.

18. Swidler, "Culture in Action."

19. For a discussion of the relationship between social movements and culture, see Taylor and Whittier, "Analytical Approaches to Social Movement Culture."

20. Nancy Whittier makes a similar argument in her study of the radical feminist movement. Women who participated in the movement retained lifelong identities as radical feminists. See *Feminist Generations*, especially chapter 3.

21. Bourdieu has developed his analysis through a substantial body of work that has primarily looked at the role of culture in social reproduction. The interviews with Bourdieu in Bourdieu and Wacquant, *An Invitation to Reflexive Sociology*, can serve as an introduction to and clarification of his analysis of social reproduction. His model of social reproduction is presented in *Distinction*.

22. Sociologist Craig Calhoun notes that Bourdieu acknowledges the possibility of social change but does not offer an explanation of why such change might arise. See Calhoun, "Habitus, Field, and Capital," especially 70–75.

23. I have developed this argument in relation to my research on resistance to racial oppression. The same analysis may apply to resistance by other subordinated groups such as sexual, ethnic, or religious minorities who live in similarly semiautonomous social locations. Such an extension of the argument is beyond the scope of this book.

24. This argument is most characteristic of Bourdieu's early work. See "Cultural Repro-

duction and Social Reproduction." The argument is not contradicted by and has been considered foundational to his later writing. See Bourdieu and Wacquant, *An Invitation to Reflexive Sociology*, 12.

25. Bourdieu, "What Makes a Social Class?," 4.
26. Bourdieu, *The Logic of Practice*, 55.
27. Higginbotham, *Righteous Discontent.*
28. Similarly, sociologists Rick Fantasia and Eric Hirsch describe how French colonial segregation of Algerians created "movement havens" that provided a firm base for the anticolonial guerilla movement. See "Culture in Rebellion."
29. Political scientist Bonnie Honig makes a similar argument about the social sources of agency in "My Culture Made Me Do It," 39–40.
30. Mosse, *Nationalism and Sexuality*, 134.
31. A number of historians have demonstrated that popular white images of blacks went through several substantial revisions. See Allen, *The Invention of the White Race*; Gossett, *Race*; Jordan, *White over Black*; and Sommerville, "The Rape Myth in the Old South Revisited."
32. Bogle, *Toms, Coons, Mulattoes, Mammies and Bucks*; Fredrickson, *The Black Image in the White Mind*; Jewell, *From Mammy to Miss America and Beyond*.
33. Jefferson, "Notes on the State of Virginia," reprinted in *The Portable Thomas Jefferson*, 187.
34. Ibid., 192–193.
35. Johnson, Rush, and Feagin, "Doing Anti-Racism," 98.
36. Bourdieu, *Outline of a Theory of Practice*, 184.
37. For an excellent collection of articles about parallel struggles relating to the image of the African American male, see Hine and Jenkins, *A Question of Manhood*.
38. Lisa Jones, *Bulletproof Diva*, 11–12.
39. This term is an adaptation of Nancy Whittier's use of "women's movement community" (*Feminist Generations*, 26). My use of the term "community" is not meant to imply homogeneity among the community's members. Black movement community members shared a commitment to fighting racism but differed in many ways. In the earlier, "civil rights" days of the movement, white civil rights activists could be considered part of what I am calling the black movement community.
40. For studies of the uses of women as symbols in political rhetoric, see Nader, "Orientalism, Occidentalism, and the Control of Women"; and Ryan, *Women in Public*.
41. Norbert Elias discusses this concept in "The Social Constraint towards Self-Constraint," in *Norbert Elias*, 49–66.
42. Michele Norris, "Nappy Hair Flap," ABCNEWS.com [Online]. Available: http://204.202.137/onair/worldnewstonight/general/wnt_nappyhair981204_story.html [19 June 2000]. Liz Leyden, "N.Y. Teacher Runs into Racial Divide," *Washington Post*, 3 December 1998, A3. [Online]. Available: http://washingtonpost.com/wp_srv/national/frompost/dec98/hair3.htm [19 June 2000].
43. Herron, *Nappy Hair.*
44. See my earlier study of conflicting standards of beauty among contemporary African American young women. Young women who were raised to believe that black is beautiful and that true beauty must be natural find ways to talk about artificial hair as natural and continue to make jokes about dark skin. Leeds, "Young African-American Women and the Language of Beauty."

45. I conducted interviews with fifty-six black men and women between 1992 and 1995 in California, Mississippi, New York, Pennsylvania, and Washington, D.C.

CHAPTER 2

1. Bogle, *Toms, Coons, Mulattoes, Mammies and Bucks*; Joseph Boskin, "Sambo and Other Male Images in Popular Culture," in Smith, *Images of Blacks in American Culture*, 257–272; Dates and Barlow, *Split Image*; Gilman, "Black Bodies, White Bodies"; Jewell, *From Mammy to Miss America and Beyond*; Jordan, *White over Black*; Morton, *Disfigured Images*; Janet Sims-Wood, "The Black Female," in Smith, *Images of Blacks in American Culture*, 235–256; Schiebinger, *Nature's Body*.

2. See Chapkis, *Beauty Secrets*; Lakoff and Scherr, *Face Value*; and Wolf, *The Beauty Myth*, for studies of the role of beauty ideals in women's lives. Basing their claims upon experimental research, Dion, Berscheid, and Walster, in "What Is Beautiful Is Good," and Webster and Driskell, in "Beauty as Status," argue that attractiveness equally affects the life chances of men and women. However, these experiments, in which college students were asked to rate the personalities and abilities of "attractive" and "unattractive" men and women in photographs, artificially encouraged the subjects to evaluate men exclusively on the basis of appearance. Outside of experimental situations, women more frequently than men are judged by a standard that favors youthful good looks.

3. Adams, *An Uncommon Scold*, 37.

4. Banner, *American Beauty*, 205–206.

5. Juadine Henderson, interview by author, 22 October 1993.

6. Anonymous, interview by author, 1993.

7. Anonymous, interview by author, 1992.

8. Pearl Marsh, interview by author, 16 June 1992.

9. Anonymous, interview by author, 1992.

10. See White and White, *Stylin'*, 169–172, and Peiss, *Hope in a Jar*, 230–232, for discussions of the spread of the practice of hair straightening among African American women in the early twentieth century.

11. Sheila Head, interview by author, 13 October 1994.

12. Linda Burnham, interview by author, 16 April 1992.

13. Brenda Winstead, interview by author, 20 October 1993.

14. Jean Wiley, interview by author, 26 January 1993.

15. Letisha Wadsworth, interview by author, 11 October 1993.

16. Sociologist K. Sue Jewell has written about "the dozens" as an African American practice that incorporates negative images of black women. Jewell, *From Mammy to Miss America and Beyond*, 62.

17. Levine, *Black Culture and Black Consciousness*, 352.

18. Pearl Marsh, interview by author, 16 June 1992.

19. For additional discussions of the role of women in racial projects, see Gates, "The Trope of a New Negro," 138–141; Higginbotham, *Righteous Discontent*; Hine, "Rape and the Inner Lives of Black Women in the Middle West"; Giddings, *When and Where I Enter*; Jacqueline Jones, *Labor of Love, Labor of Sorrow*; Terborg-Penn, "Black Male Perspectives on the Nineteenth Century Woman"; and White, *Too Heavy a Load*. W. H. Crogman, one of the two authors of this section's epigraph, was

black. H. F. Kletzing and W. H. Crogman, *Progress of a Race . . . or . . . The Remarkable Advancement of the Afro-American from the Bondage of Slavery to the Freedom of Citizenship, Intelligence, Affluence, Honor and Trust* (Cincinnati: Ferguson, 1900).

20. Omi and Winant, in *Racial Formation in the United States*, define a racial project as "simultaneously an interpretation, representation, or explanation of racial dynamics and an effort to reorganize and redistribute resources along racial lines" (56).

21. Jacquelyn Dowd Hall, "'The Mind That Burns in Each Body'"; Hine, "Rape and the Inner Lives of Black Women in the Middle West."

22. Giddings, *When and Where I Enter*, 31.

23. Brumberg, *The Body Project*, 149.

24. See Gossett, *Race*, 47–48, for a description of the museum display of black penises, and Gilman, "Black Bodies, White Bodies," 232–235, for the pseudoscientific living display of African women's bodies.

25. Hine, "Rape and the Inner Lives of Black Women in the Middle West."

26. Mary Church Terrell, "The Progress of Colored Women," quoted in Guy-Sheftall, *Words of Fire*, 64.

27. Carby, "Policing the Black Woman's Body in an Urban Context."

28. Quoted in Higginbotham, *Righteous Discontent*, 206–207.

29. See Jacqueline Jones, *Labor of Love, Labor of Sorrow.* For an analysis of the myth of the "mammy," see White, *Ain't I a Woman?*, 46–61.

30. G. W. Rigler, "School for Girls," *Opportunity* 1 (April 1923): 15–16.

31. *Baltimore Afro-American*, TNCF, reel 30, frame 15; *Boston Guardian*, 29 January 1927, TNCF, reel 30, frame 7.

32. U.S. Bureau of the Census, *Negroes in the United States.*

33. Jacqueline Jones, *Labor of Love, Labor of Sorrow*, 234–235.

34. For a discussion of the meaning of appearance within African American communities, see White and White, *Stylin'*, especially 161–169.

35. *The Madam C. J. Walker Year Book: 1944* [p. 1], National Archives for Black Women's History, Mary McLeod Bethune Council House National Historic Site. For an extended discussion of the advertising campaigns developed by Madam C. J. Walker, see Rooks, *Hair Raising.*

36. For further examples of the ways in which late twentieth-century black women worked to maintain respect in their communities, see Abrahams, "Negotiating Respect," 80.

37. Barbara Christian, interview by author, 12 November 1992.

38. Peiss, *Hope in a Jar*, 256.

39. Letisha Wadsworth, interview by author, 11 October 1993.

40. Shirley A. Drake, letter to the editor, *Ebony*, March 1968, 17.

41. K. E. Williams, letter to the editor, *Ebony*, March 1968, 17.

42. Adele Jones and Cenen Moreno, quoted in "Ebony Minds, Black Voices," in Bambara, *The Black Woman*, 182.

43. Linda Burnham, interview by author, 16 April 1992.

44. Frances Beal, interview by author, 26 September 1993.

45. Anonymous, interview by author, 1994.

46. Clark and Clark, "Racial Identification and Preference in Negro Children." I describe the Clarks' work as foundational because of its impact outside of the discipline of psy-

chology. In *Shades of Black*, William E. Cross, Jr., traces the intellectual history of the Clarks' work and shows its roots in earlier studies.

47. For a discussion of the role of the Clarks' research in the *Brown v. Board of Education of Topeka* decision, see Williams, *Eyes on the Prize*, 23.

48. For the impact of Fanon's work on activists, see King, *Freedom Song*, 169, and Van Deburg, *New Day in Babylon*, 60.

49. Udry, Bauman, and Chase, "Skin Color, Status, and Mate Selection," 772.

50. Clark and Clark, "Racial Identification and Preference in Negro Children."

51. Ibid., 611.

52. *Time*, 5 November 1951; "Negro Doll Makes Friends," *New York Post* [undated clipping]. Both clippings are found in SCF, "Dolls and Doll Houses."

53. Banks, "White Preference in Black"; Brand, Padilla, and Ruiz, "Ethnic Identification and Preference."

54. Spencer, "Black Children's Race Awareness, Racial Attitudes and Self-Concept."

55. Cross, *Shades of Black*.

56. Ibid., 46.

57. Drake and Cayton, *Black Metropolis*.

58. Goering, "Changing Perceptions and Evaluations of Physical Characteristics among Blacks."

59. Himes and Edwards, "Hair Texture and Skin Color in Mate Selection among Negroes."

60. Anderson and Himes, "Dating Values and Norms on a Negro College Campus."

61. Goering, "Changing Perceptions and Evaluations of Physical Characteristics among Blacks."

62. Goering did not analyze these data by sex of respondent.

63. Freeman et al., "Color Gradation and Attitudes among Middle-income Negroes."

64. Udry, Bauman, and Chase, "Skin Color, Status, and Mate Selection."

65. Mullins and Sites, "The Origins of Eminent Black Americans."

66. Ransford, "Skin Color, Life Chances and Anti-white Attitudes."

67. Keith and Herring, "Skin Tone and Stratification in the Black Community," 773.

68. Johnson and Farrell, "Race Still Matters," A48.

CHAPTER 3

1. Cowan and Maguire, *Timelines of African American History*, 143.

2. Armistead S. Pride, "A Register and History of Negro Newspapers in the United States: 1827–1950" (Ph.D. diss., Northwestern University, 1950), quoted in Wolseley, *The Black Press*, 444; U.S. Department of Education, National Center for Education Statistics, *The Traditionally Black Institutions of Higher Education*, 13.

3. Scott, *Domination and the Arts of Resistance*, 120.

4. "Beauty Contest," *Chicago Appeal: A National Afro-American Newspaper*, 31 January 1891, 2.

5. Fredrickson, *The Black Image in the White Mind*, 276.

6. Gutman, *The Black Family in Slavery and Freedom*, 532.

7. Banner, *American Beauty*, 256–257.

8. "Women's Beauty Will Win Prizes," *New York Age*, 23 July 1914, 1.

9. "Photos Come in Large Numbers," *New York Age*, 13 August 1914, 1.

10. Ibid.

11. "More Interest in Race Beauty," *New York Age*, 20 August 1914, 1.

12. Banet-Weiser, "Fade to White," 168; Gates, "The Trope of a New Negro," 143.

13. "Ideal Type of Negro Beauty," *New York Age*, 6 August 1914, 1.

14. Moses, *The Golden Age of Black Nationalism*, 10.

15. Peiss, "Making Faces," 157.

16. "Photos Come in Large Numbers," *New York Age*, 13 August 1914, 1.

17. Autumn Expo Is Great Show," *New York Age*, 1 October 1914, 1.

18. "Beauty Contest Awards Made," *New York Age*, 8 October 1914, 1.

19. "Isaac Fisher and the *Age* Beauty Contest," *New York Age*, 13 October 1914. Booker
T. Washington was the driving force behind Alabama's Tuskegee Institute but also had
substantial influence nationwide. The *Negro Farmer* regularly advertised in the *New
York Age*.

20. Bogle, *Toms, Coons, Mulattoes, Mammies and Bucks*, 10.

21. "Mrs. Helen Rich," *Chicago Defender*, 2 May 1925, TNCF, reel 24, item 498.

22. White and White, *Stylin'*, 203.

23. For the racial identity of the Golden Brown Chemical Company, see Peiss, *Hope in
a Jar*, 111, 117–118, 215. For additional information on the National Golden Brown
Beauty Contest, see White and White, *Stylin'*, 198–201.

24. "America's Miss Golden Brown," *Norfolk Journal and Guide*, 3 October 1925, 8.

25. "Ladies, Girls Rescued at Last by Alluring Offer," *Oakland (Calif.) Western American*, 4 February 1927, 1.

26. "Miss Golden State Contest Swings into Action," *Oakland (Calif.) Western American*, 11 February 1927, 1.

27. "Miss Adams Wins," *Oakland (Calif.) Western American*, 8 April 1927, 1.

28. "Miss Fine Brown Frame," *Ebony*, May 1947, 47–50.

29. "Lighter Brighter for You!" *Ebony*, May 1947, 48.

30. Daniel, *Black Journals in the United States*, 312–314.

31. "Ten Most Beautiful Negro Women," *Our World*, November 1950, cover, 15–19.

32. Peiss, "Making Faces," 164.

33. "Ten Most Beautiful Negro Women," *Our World*, November 1950, 15, 17–19.

34. Lee Gilliam, interview by author, 19 October 1994.

35. "Miss Africa Crowned in New York," *Africa Weekly* 1, no. 24 (21 August 1957): [3].

CHAPTER 4

1. "Detroit Beauty Queen," *Ebony*, September 1962, 23–28.

2. *New York Age*, 12 April 1924, 1; Lincoln News Service, April 1924, TNCF, reel 21, item 892.

3. "Colored and White Girls Entered in New York's First International Beauty Contest," *Pittsburgh Courier*, 10 September 1938, TNCF, reel 59, item 790.

4. "Honored by Schoolmates," *Chicago Defender*, 4 March 1944, TNCF, reel 90, item 154.

5. Lee Gilliam, interview by author, 19 October 1994.

6. Sheila Head, interview by author, 6 November 1994.

7. Mary Lovelace O'Neal, interview by author, 4 October 1994.

8. "Negro Girl in Miss America Race," *Ebony*, July 1965, 76.

9. Bill Chase, " 'Miss Subway' Selected after Six-Year Campaign," *New York Amsterdam News*, 24 April 1948, TNCF, reel 103, item 339; "From the Readers: Pretty Girls Wanted," TNCF (1947), reel 102, frame 273; "Miss Subways for April," *Crisis*, May 1948, cover, 131; "Historic," *New York Amsterdam News*, 2[4?] April 1948, TNCF (1948), reel 103, item 340.

10. "Airlines Agree to Hire Negro Pilots, Hostesses," *New York Daily News*, 13 October 1956, SCF, Airlines Employment SC 000, 186.

11. "Airline Bias Case Will Get Hearing," *New York Times*, 10 June 1957; "TWA Faces Hearing after Rejecting Negro Hostess," *Daily Worker*, 10 June 1957; "Negro Girl Denied a Job by Airline, SCAD Hearing Set," *New York Post*, 10 June 1957, SCF, Airlines Employment SC 000, 156.

12. "Miss Festival," *Ebony*, August 1960, 93–95.

13. "Plan to Integrate Miss America Fete," *New York Post*, 27 August 1966, SCF, Beauty Contests SC 000, 476.

14. "Court Drops Bias Charges of Negro Beauty Queen," *Jet*, 9 August 1962, 6.

15. "Freedom Riders Marry, Settle in Mississippi," *Jet*, 11 January 1962, 23.

16. "Popular Girl on Campus," *Jet*, 17 January 1963, 24.

17. "Along with Miss America, There's Now Miss Black America," *New York Times*, 9 September 1968, 54.

18. "Antiwar Miss Montana Gave up Title Gladly," *New York Times*, 20 July 1970, 21.

19. "Beauty Contestant Denounces the 'Indignities,' " *New York Times*, 16 June 1988, 18.

20. "Black Beauty Queens at White Schools," *Jet*, 30 November 1967, 44.

21. "100 Arrested in Mobile," *New York Times*, 2 May 1969.

22. Quoted in Daniel, *Black Journals in the United States*, 161–162.

23. "Miss Weusi," SCF, S–C 9–C Beauty Contest 000, 476.

24. I reviewed *Jet, Ebony,* and the Tuskegee and Schomburg subject-arranged collections of clipping files and found no comments on the shade of the complexion of a black contestant between 1951 and 1966.

25. Chester Higgins, "People Are Talking About," *Jet*, 9 March 1967, 43.

26. "Black Beauty Queens at White Schools," *Jet*, 30 November 1967, 42.

27. "Howard University Queen's 'Natural' Hair Style Creates Controversy," *New York Amsterdam News*, 12 November 1966, 15.

28. "Says Miss America Biased; Wants Black Pageant," *Jet*, 25 January 1968, 60.

29. "Cheryl Browne: Black Miss America?," *Newsweek*, 29 June 1970.

30. "Miss Black America Gets $8,000 Cash, TV Role, Other Awards," *Jet*, 11 September 1969, 54–55; "Colored Women to Sponsor Miss Black America," *Jet*, 10 April 1969, 58–59.

31. SCF, S-C 9-C Beauty Contest 000, 476

32. "Cheryl Browne: Black Miss America?" *Newsweek*, 29 June 1970.

33. "Black Leaders Praise Choice of First Black Miss America," *New York Times*, 19 September 1983, B4; *Current Biography Yearbook 1984*, s.v. "Vanessa Williams," 455–457.

CHAPTER 5

1. For early critiques of Eurocentric beauty standards within African American communities, see Peiss, *Hope in a Jar,* 204–210.

2. Du Bois, *The World of W. E .B. Du Bois,* 10–11.
3. Russell, Wilson, and Hall, *The Color Complex,* 33.
4. Several examples can be found in Alain Locke's 1925 Harlem Renaissance anthology *The New Negro.*
5. "African Beauties," *Ebony,* April 1954, 33.
6. Essien-Udom, *Black Nationalism,* 72.
7. Elijah Muhammad, *The Supreme Wisdom,* vol. 2. N.p. [1957].
8. Nat B. Williams, "Down on Beale," *Pittsburgh Courier,* 19 January 1958, 5.
9. Ruth Beckford, interview by author, 14 April 1992; Margot Dashiell, interview by author, 5 November 1992.
10. Ruth Beckford, interview by author, 14 April 1992.
11. Gloria King Jackson, interview by author, 13 September 1994.
12. Jean Wiley, interview by author, 25 January 1993.
13. Sellers, *The River of No Return,* 57–59.
14. Cleveland Sellers, interview by author, 24 June 1994.
15. H. Rap Brown was not a Howard University student. Carson, *In Struggle,* 252.
16. Cleveland Sellers, interview by author, 24 June 1994.
17. Mary Lovelace O'Neal, interview by author, 4 October 1994.
18. Muriel Tillinghast, interview by author, 17 October 1993.
19. Jean Smith Young, interview by author, 23 October 1993.
20. Carson, *In Struggle,* 9–11; Williams, *Eyes on the Prize,* 126–139.
21. Sellers, *The River of No Return,* 44.
22. Quoted in Crawford, "Beyond the Human Self," 22.
23. Juadine Henderson, interview by author, 22 October 1993.
24. Ibid.
25. Ingrid Monson, "Abbey Lincoln's 'Straight Ahead.' "
26. "The Soul of Soul," *Ebony,* December 1961, 116.
27. *Jet,* 30 March 1961, 43.
28. "Hairdo of the Week," *Jet,* 21 September 1961, 28.
29. "Will Naturally '62 Be the New Hair-do?," *New York Amsterdam News,* 10 March 1962, 12; "Au Naturelle Revue Sparks Controversy," *Pittsburgh Courier,* 9 March 1963, 9; *Liberator,* July 1963, 13.
30. "Wigs Make Comeback," *Ebony,* December 1962, cover, 132.
31. Margaret Burroughs, "Down the Straight and Narrow," *Urbanite,* May 1961, 15, 34; "Natural Hair: Yes," *Liberator,* July 1963, 13–14; "Hot Irons and Black Nationalism," *Liberator,* July 1963, 21–22; "Should Negro Women Straighten Their Hair?," *Negro Digest,* August 1963, 65–71; Eldridge Cleaver, "As Crinkly as Yours, Brother," *Muhammad Speaks,* June 1962, 4, 16; Cleaver, "As Crinkly as Yours."
32. Burroughs, "Down the Straight and Narrow," *Urbanite,* May 1961, 15.
33. John Lewis, quoted in *Negro Protest Thought in the Twentieth Century,* ed. Broderick and Meier, 318–319.
34. Fantasia, *Cultures of Solidarity,* 236.
35. Jean Smith, "I Learned to Feel Black," 209.
36. "Racial Pride Called Key to Negro Enigma," *Pittsburgh Courier,* 12 November 1963, 5.
37. King, *Freedom Song,* 169.
38. Ibid., 170.

39. Margot Dashiell, interview by author, 5 November 1992.

40. Jean Wiley, interview by author, 26 January 1993.

41. Anonymous, interview by author, 1992.

42. Anonymous, interview by author, 1992.

43. Brenda Travis, interview by author, 8 August 1994.

44. Carson, *In Struggle*, 209–210.

45. Ibid., 217.

46. Jean Wiley, interview by author, 26 January 1993.

47. Emory Douglas, interview by author, 15 September 1993.

48. Pearl Marsh, interview by author, 16 June 1992.

49. Emory Douglas, interview by author, 15 September 1993.

50. Scott, *Domination and the Arts of Resistance*, 226.

51. Anonymous, interview by author, 1992.

52. Sheila Head, interview by author, 13 October 1994.

53. This use of "bad," while characteristic of late 1960s black slang, was by no means new. Clarence Major, in a dictionary of African American slang, notes that "bad" was used by African Americans from the 1700s to the 1990s to mean "positive to the extreme." Major, *Juba to Jive*, 15.

54. Pearl Marsh, interview by author, 16 June 1992

55. Jean Wiley, interview by author, 26 January 1993.

56. Phil Gardiner, interview by author, 30 July 1993.

57. James Brown and Alfred James Ellis, "Say It Loud, I'm Black and I'm Proud," ©1968 (Renewed) Dynatone Publishing Company. All rights reserved on behalf of Dynatone Publishing Company. Administered by Unichappell Music, Inc. All rights reserved. Used by permission. Warner Bros. Publications U.S. Inc., Miami, Fla. 33014.

58. "James Brown Goes 'Natural' to Give Kids True Black Identity," *Jet*, 19 September 1968, 52–53.

59. Anonymous, interview by author, 1994.

60. Imshi Atkins, interview by author, 8 September 1994.

61. Michelle Bailey, interview by author, 20 October 1994.

62. "Poster of Cleaver, Angela, 'Rap' Leads to Suspension," *Jet*, 15 October 1970, 47; "Challenge 'Free Angela' Posters in Faculty Lounge," *Jet*, 18 March 1971, 16.

63. Davis, "Black Nationalism," 320.

64. "Police Picking up Angela Look Alikes," *Jet*, 3 September 1970, 21; "People Are Talking About," *Jet*, 17 September 1970; "Words of the Week," *Jet*, 18 March 1971, 30.

65. Barbara Williams, interview by author, 14 September 1994.

66. Lee Gilliam, interview by author, 19 October 1994.

67. Gloria King Jackson, interview by author, 13 September 1994.

68. "New Order Allows Black Marines to Have More 'Soul,'" *Jet*, 18 September 1969, 22–25; "Afro Jeopardizes Ft. Hood G.I.s," *Ebony*, January 1970, 15–16; "TWA OKs Naturals for Black Hostesses," *Jet*, 23 July 1970, 50.

69. "Guns in Their Hair," *Black Panther*, 10 June 1972, 8, 16.

70. *Ebony*, August 1970, 29.

71. Quoted in Chester Higgins, "People Are Talking About," *Jet*, 7 September 1967, 42. "Processed" was a popular black term for straightened hair. It usually, but not always, referred to a male hairstyle.

72. Anonymous, interview by author, 1992.

73. Paris Williams, interview by author, 5 July 1992.

74. Melucci, "The Process of Collective Identity."

CHAPTER 6

1. Yvonne is a pseudonym.

2. Gilroy, *Black Atlantic*, 85.

3. Malcolm X, *The Autobiography of Malcolm X*, 39.

4. Ibid., 53–54.

5. For discussions of the conk as a style for black hipsters, see Kelley, "The Riddle of the Zoot," in his *Race Rebels*, 161–181, and Mercer, "Black Hair/Style Politics," 247–264.

6. Emory Douglas, interview by author, 15 September 1993.

7. Lee Gilliam, interview by author, 19 October 1994.

8. Anonymous, interview by author, 1994.

9. Barbara Williams, interview by author, 14 September 1994.

10. Mary Lovelace O'Neal, interview by author, 4 October 1994.

11. Eldridge Cleaver, interview by author, 10 January 1995.

12. Landry, *The New Black Middle Class*, 24.

13. Synnott, "Shame and Glory," 405.

14. Connell, *Gender and Power*, 183.

15. Brenda Travis, interview by author, 8 August 1994.

16. A. S. Young, "Should Negro Men Marcel Their Hair?" *Jet*, 24 September 1953, 58–61. Marcel is another term for hair straightening.

17. Sara Slack, "Should Teen Boys 'Konk' Their Hair?" *New York Amsterdam News*, 2 November 1957, 1.

18. "Judge 'Declares War' on 'Processes': 'Natural' Hair-dos Ordered," *Baltimore Afro-American*, 5 November 1960, 8. The *Afro-American*, founded in 1892, is one of the oldest African American newspapers. In 1960, its pages carried the motto, "When you finish reading your Afro, pass it along to a friend."

19. "Woman Judge Touches off 'Konktroversy' with Hair Order," *Jet*, 11 November 1960, 6–7.

20. "Judge 'Declares War' on 'Processes': 'Natural' Hair-dos Ordered," *Baltimore Afro-American*, 5 November 1960, 8.

21. Men who work conks often wore a piece of cloth called a "du-rag" around their head to hold the curls of the conk in place.

22. Landry, *The New Black Middle Class*, 70.

23. Kelley, "Nap Time."

24. Karenga, *The Quotable Karenga*, 2.

25. Julia Fields, "Not your Singing, Dancing Spade," *Negro Digest* 16, no. 4 (1967): 54–59.

26. Emory Douglas, interview by author, 15 September 1993.

27. "Bald Head," written by Henry Roeland Byrd, ©1950 Professor Longhair Music, All rights reserved, used by permission.

28. Juadine Henderson, interview by author, 22 October 1993.

29. Ruth Beckford, interview by author, 14 April 1992.

30. Linda Burnham, interview by author, 16 April 1992.

31. Pearl Marsh, interview by author, 16 June 1992.
32. Anonymous, interview by author, 1992.
33. Juadine Henderson, interview by author, 22 October 1993.
34. Zoharah Simmons, interview by author, 24 October 1993.
35. Kelley, "Nap Time," 344.
36. Ibid., 347.
37. *Jet*, 31 August 1967, 54.
38. D. E. Wilson, "Back to the Hot Comb," *Ebony*, November 1969, 19.
39. The straightened hairstyle's primary competition is the addition of braided extensions to the hair. This hairstyle, whose exquisite variations are testimony to the vast creativity of black beauticians, satisfies the demands of dominant constructions of gender by creating long, moving hair but does so through a distinctly black idiom. Beauticians and their clients can claim braids as a black or African style.
40. Zoharah Simmons, interview by author, 24 October 1993.
41. Anonymous, interview by author, 1992.
42. Chinosole, interview by author, 6 April 1992.

CHAPTER 7

1. Higginbotham, *Righteous Discontent,* 196–200.
2. Carby, "Policing the Black Woman's Body in an Urban Context," 153; White, *Too Heavy a Load,* 128–131.
3. Frazier, *The Black Bourgeoisie,* 222.
4. See, for example, White, *Too Heavy a Load.*
5. The Montgomery Bus Boycott, which was organized in response to Rosa Parks's arrest for sitting in the whites only section of a bus, is an example of the care with which test cases were chosen. The local Women's Political Council, a group that was key in organizing the boycott, had considered rallying around an earlier victim of Montgomery's segregated transportation laws. When they discovered that the arrested unmarried teenage woman was pregnant, they decided not to proceed with a boycott. Morris, *The Origins of the Civil Rights Movement,* 53.
6. James M. Lawson, Jr., "We Are Trying to Raise the 'Moral Issue,'" reprinted in *Negro Protest Thought in the Twentieth Century*, ed. Francis L. Broderick and August Meier, eds. 280.
7. Quoted in Lerone Bennett, "The Mood of the Negro," *Ebony*, July 1963, 32.
8. Williams, *Eyes on the Prize,* 137; Broderick and Meier, eds., *Negro Protest Thought in the Twentieth Century,* 274.
9. Lawson, "We Are Trying to Raise the 'Moral Issue,'" 276.
10. White, *Too Heavy a Load,* 69–71; Higginbotham, *Righteous Discontent,* 204–205.
11. Edwards, "Occupational Trends and New Lifestyles," 18.
12. Ibid.; Landry, *The New Black Middle Class,* 67, 70; Wilson, *The Declining Significance of Race,* 129.
13. Smith and Horton, *Historical Statistics of Black America,* 851.
14. Jean Wiley, interview by author, 26 January 1993.
15. Zoharah Simmons, interview by author, 24 October 1993.
16. Hardy Frye, interview by author, 12 May 1993.
17. Martha Norman, interview by author, 25 October 1993.

18. "Are Negro Girls Getting Prettier?" *Ebony*, February 1966, 25–28, 30–31.

19. "Letters to the Editor," *Ebony*, April 1966, 18.

20. Evelyn Rodgers, "Is *Ebony* Killing Black Women?" *Liberator*, May 1966, 12–13.

21. Phyl Garland, "The Natural Look," *Ebony*, June 1966, 142–144, 146, 148.

22. Carmichael and Hamilton, *Black Power*, 53.

23. For residential patterns of the black middle class, see Landry, *The New Black Middle Class*, 183–185; and Massey and Eggers, "The Ecology of Inequality."

24. Landry, *The New Black Middle Class*, 114–115.

25. Ibid., 87–88.

26. U.S. Bureau of the Census, *Statistical Abstract of the United States: 1974*, 95th ed., 1974, 116.

27. Banner-Haley, *The Fruits of Integration*, 44; Wilson, *The Declining Significance of Race*, 168–169.

28. Van Deburg, *New Day in Babylon*, 64–82.

29. Brenda Payton, interview by author, 9 September 1993.

30. "Warning to So-called 'Paper Panthers,'" *Black Panther*, 14 September 1968, 10.

31. See, for example, Imamu Ameer Baraka [Amiri Baraka], "The Coronation of the Black Queen," *Black Scholar*, June 1970, 46–48.

32. Marsha, "To the Women of Babylon," *Black Panther*, 19 July 1969, 24.

CHAPTER 8

1. Garvey, *Garvey and Garveyism*, 29.

2. Essien-Udom, *Black Nationalism*, 48.

3. Ruth Beckford, interview by author, 14 April 1992.

4. Pearl Marsh, interview by author, 16 June 1992.

5. *San Francisco CORElator*, July 1962, Bancroft Library, University of California, Berkeley, Social Protest Pamphlet file 3:46.

6. Karenga, *The Quotable Karenga*, 5.

7. Anonymous, interview by author, 1992.

8. McAdam, *Political Process and the Development of Black Insurgency*, 190.

9. Lieberson, *A Piece of the Pie*, 9.

10. Karenga, *The Quotable Karenga*, 7.

11. Myesha Jenkins, interview by author, 12 June 1992.

12. Anonymous, interview by author, 1992.

13. Anonymous, introduction to *The Quotable Karenga*, by Maulana Ron Karenga, iii.

14. Majied, *Muhammad Speaks*, 5 November 1965, 5.

15. "Racial rearticulation" is a term I have adapted from Omi and Winant, *Racial Formation*. The term "collective identity" is drawn from Alberto Melucci, who argues that in the context of social movements collective identity is always a process and not a stable actor. Melucci, "The Process of Collective Identity."

16. Essien-Udom, *Black Nationalism*, 68.

17. Ibid., 169. By 1962, the name had been shortened to *Muhammad Speaks*.

18. Edwin Moss, "Wallace Muhammad Says Women Not Forbidden to 'Make-up.'" *Mr. Muhammad Speaks*, special edition [n.d., c. January 1961], 7.

19. Peiss, "Making Faces," 146.

20. Essien-Udom, *Black Nationalism*, 24.

21. Ibid., 78.

22. Julius Vincent, "So-Called Negroes Waste Billions of Dollars Yearly in Hair Preparations," *Muhammad Speaks*, January 1962, 24.

23. Cleaver, "As Crinkly as Yours," 127–132; "As Crinkly as Yours, Brother," *Muhammad Speaks*, June 1962, 4, 16.

24. See, for example, "Natural Beauties," *Muhammad Speaks*, 31 August 1962, 24.

25. Leroy E. Mitchell, Jr., "Writer Rips Alleged 'Bad' and 'Good' Hair Standards," *Muhammad Speaks*, 30 September 1962.

26. Historians White and White documented the establishment of the African American fashion show in the post–World War I years as an institution used by members of the black middle class to define themselves. White and White, *Stylin'*, 212.

27. Sylvester Leeks, "Coiffure Creations: The Natural Look Is Reborn in Brilliant New Show," *Muhammad Speaks*, 4 February 1963, 13.

28. "Many Negro Women Favor New African-Type Hairdos," *Muhammad Speaks*, 15 April 1963, 17.

29. "Letter to Mr. Muhammad from the Wife of the Late Marcus Garvey," *Muhammad Speaks*, 15 January 1965, 6; "Route of Ace Salesman from Marcus Garvey to the Messenger," *Muhammad Speaks*, 9 October 1964, 20; Hubert X, "Marcus Garvey Said a Messenger Will Follow Me," *Muhammad Speaks*, 5 June 1964, 7.

30. "Women's News and Notes," *Muhammad Speaks*, 21 June 1963, 16; "Four Years Later, the Natural Look African Styles Still Popular," *Muhammad Speaks*, 27 August 1965, 18; "The African Look," *Muhammad Speaks*, 27 August 1965, 19; "Black Begins to Look Better Than Ever," *Muhammad Speaks*, 5 August 1966, 21; "Ex-CORE Chief Farmer Lauds College Students' Turn towards Black Identity," *Muhammad Speaks*, 21 April 1967, 17.

31. "Blessings of Islam Include Dignity and Self Respect," *Muhammad Speaks*, 14 May 1965, 8; "An Examination of Negro's Self-Hate Image," *Muhammad Speaks*, 19 August 1966, 17.

32. Sylvester Leeks, "The Revolution in Hair Grooming: Is the Black Beautician Losing Fight for Life?," *Muhammad Speaks*, 26 February 1965, 21.

33. Minister Roy, "Beauty Dollar Waste; Could Fight Poverty," *Muhammad Speaks*, 26 March 1965, 15; "In Business for Self," *Muhammad Speaks*, 26 March 1965, 15.

34. "Beautician Shares Recipe for Delicious Lamb Chops," *Muhammad Speaks*, 26 March 1965, 16.

35. "Confessions of a Male Beautician," *Muhammad Speaks*, 8 October 1965, 21–22.

36. Leo P. X. McCallum, "Finds 'Black Is Beautiful' Inherent in the Messenger's Teachings," *Muhammad Speaks*, 26 April 1968, 18.

37. Abdul Basit Naeem, "Gives View of Muhammad's Warning against Foreign Garb, Intermarriage," *Muhammad Speaks*, 26 July 1968, 14.

38. Van Deburg, *New Day in Babylon,* 17–18.

39. *Muhammad Speaks*, 26 July 1968, and reprinted the following week, 2 August 1968.

40. "Whites Buying 'African Hair' Wigs as 'Natural' Hair Style Gains Popularity," *Muhammad Speaks*, 19 July 1968, 31.

41. Amiri Baraka, n.d., "Wig Poem," in *Selected Poetry of Amiri Baraka/LeRoi Jones*, 139.

42. Pearl Marsh, interview by author, 16 June 1992.

43. Myesha Jenkins, interview by author, 12 June 199.

44. Lincoln, "Who Will Revere the Black Woman?"

45. T. Brown, "Black Woman" [letter to the editor], *Negro Digest*, July 1967, 98.

46. Anonymous, interview by author, 1992.

47. Anonymous, interview by author, 1992.

48. Myesha Jenkins, interview by author, 12 June 1992.

CHAPTER 9

1. Brenda Travis, interview by author, 8 August 1994.

2. Robert Curry, interview by author, 19 October 1994.

3. Myesha Jenkins, interview by author, 12 June 1992.

4. Mary Lovelace O'Neal, interview by author, 4 October 1994.

5. Lee Gilliam, interview by author, 19 October 1994. An "A-shape" is a common American haircut, sometimes called a "pageboy."

6. Laclau and Mouffe, *Hegemony and Socialist Strategy*, 141.

7. Ibid., 169.

8. Tired of performing these roles, Arthur Mitchell founded the Dance Theater of Harlem in 1969 as a black company that would perform the classical ballet repertoire, thereby articulating black identity with an elite European cultural tradition.

9. Anonymous, interview by author, 1992.

10. Quoted in Penelope Green, "World Hues," *New York Times Magazine*, 18 August 1991, 38.

11. Allen, *The Invention of the White Race*; Frankenberg, *White Women, Race Matters*; Palmer, *Domesticity and Dirt*; Roediger, *The Wages of Whiteness*.

12. Morris, *The Origins of the Civil Rights Movement*, 1.

SELECTED BIBLIOGRAPHY

Abrahams, Roger D. "Negotiating Respect: Patterns of Presentation among Black Women." *Journal of American Folklore* 88 (1975): 58–80.

Adams, Abby. *An Uncommon Scold.* New York: Simon and Schuster, 1989.

Allen, Theodore W. *The Invention of the White Race.* Vol. 1. New York: Verso, 1994.

Anderson, Charles, and Joseph S. Himes. "Dating Values and Norms on a Negro College Campus." *Marriage and Family Living* 21 (August 1959): 227–229.

Bambara, Toni Cade, ed. *The Black Woman: An Anthology.* New York: Penguin, 1970.

Banet-Weiser, Sarah. "Fade to White: Racial Politics and the Troubled Reign of Vanessa Williams." In *Women Transforming Politics: An Alternative Reader,* edited by Cathy J. Cohen, Kathleen B. Jones, and Joan Tronto, 167–184. New York: New York University Press, 1997.

Banks, W. Curtis. "White Preference in Blacks: A Paradigm in Search of a Phenomenon." *Psychological Bulletin* 83 (1976): 1179–1186.

Banner, Lois. *American Beauty.* New York: Knopf, 1983.

Banner-Haley, Charles T. *The Fruits of Integration: Black Middle-Class Ideology and Culture, 1960–1990.* Jackson: University Press of Mississippi, 1994.

Baraka, Amiri. *Selected Poetry of Amiri Baraka/LeRoi Jones.* New York: William Morrow, 1979.

Blumer, Herbert, and Troy Duster. "Theories of Race and Social Action." In *Sociological Theories: Race and Colonialism,* 211–238. Paris: UNESCO, 1980.

Bogle, Donald. *Toms, Coons, Mulattoes, Mammies and Bucks: An Interpretive History of Blacks in American Films.* New York: Continuum, 1992.

Bond, Jean Carey. "The Media Image of Black Women." *Freedomways* 15 (1975): 34–37.

Bourdieu, Pierre. "Cultural Reproduction and Social Reproduction." In *Knowledge, Education, and Cultural Change,* edited by Richard Brown, 71–112. London: Tavistock, 1973.

———. *Distinction: A Social Critique of the Judgement of Taste.* Cambridge: Harvard University Press, 1984.

———. *The Logic of Practice.* Cambridge, Mass.: Polity, 1990.

———. *Outline of a Theory of Practice.* New York: Cambridge University Press, 1977.

———. "What Makes a Social Class? On the Theoretical and Practical Existence of Groups." *Berkeley Journal of Sociology* 32 (1987): 1–18.

Bourdieu, Pierre, and Loic J. D. Wacquant. *An Invitation to Reflexive Sociology.* Chicago: University of Chicago Press, 1992.

Brand, Elaine S., A. M. Padilla, and R. A. Ruiz. "Ethnic Identification and Preference: A Review." *Psychological Bulletin* 81 (1974): 860–890.

Broderick, Francis L., and August Meier, eds. *Negro Protest Thought in the Twentieth Century.* New York: Bobbs-Merrill, 1965

Brumberg, Joan J. *The Body Project: An Intimate History of American Girls.* New York: Random House, 1997.

Calhoun, Craig. "Habitus, Field, and Capital: The Question of Historical Specificity." In *Bourdieu: Critical Perspectives*, edited by Craig Calhoun, Edward LiPuma, and Moishe Postine, 61–88. Chicago: University of Chicago Press, 1993.

Carby, Hazel V. "Policing the Black Woman's Body in an Urban Context." *Critical Inquiry* 18 (Summer 1992): 738–755.

Carmichael, Stokely, and Charles V. Hamilton. *Black Power: The Politics of Liberation in America.* New York: Vintage, 1967.

Carson, Clayborne. *In Struggle: SNCC and the Black Awakening of the 1960s.* Cambridge: Harvard University Press, 1981.

Chapkis, Wendy. *Beauty Secrets: Women and the Politics of Appearance.* Boston: South End, 1986.

Clark, Kenneth B., and Mamie P. Clark. "Racial Identification and Preference in Negro Children." In *Readings in Social Psychology*, 3rd ed., edited by Eleanor Maccoby, Theodore Newcomb, and Eugene Hartley, 602–611. New York: Holt, 1958.

Cleaver, L. Eldridge. "As Crinkly as Yours." *Negro History Bulletin* 25 (March 1962): 127–132.

Connell, R. W. *Gender and Power: Society, the Person and Sexual Politics.* Stanford, Calif: Stanford University Press, 1987.

Cowan, Tom, and Jack Maguire. *Timelines of African American History: 500 Years of Black Achievement.* New York: Perigee, 1994.

Crawford, Vicki. "Beyond the Human Self: Grassroots Activists in the Mississippi Civil Rights Movement." In *Women in the Civil Rights Movement: Trailblazers and Torchbearers, 1941–1965*, edited by Jacqueline Anne Rouse and Barbara Woods, 13–26. Brooklyn: Carlson, 1990.

Crenshaw, Kimberlé. "Whose Story Is It, Anyway? Feminist and Antiracist Appropriations of Anita Hill." In *Race-ing Justice, En-gendering Power: Essays on Anita Hill, Clarence Thomas, and the Construction of Social Reality*, edited by Toni Morrison, 402–440. New York: Random House, 1992.

Cross, William E., Jr. *Shades of Black: Diversity in African American Identity.* Philadelphia: Temple University Press, 1991.

Cruse, Harold. *The Crisis of the Negro Intellectual.* New York: William Morrow, 1967.

Daniel, Walter C. *Black Journals in the United States.* Westport, Conn.: Greenwood, 1982.

Dates, Jannette L., and William Barlow, eds. *Split Image: African Americans in the Mass Media.* Washington, D.C.: Howard University Press, 1990.

Davis, Angela Y. "Black Nationalism: The Sixties and the Nineties." In *Black Popular Culture*, a project by Michele Wallace, edited by Gina Dent, 317–324. Seattle: Bay, 1992.

Dion, Karen K., Ellen Berscheid, and Elaine Walster. "What Is Beautiful Is Good." *Journal of Personality and Social Psychology* 24 (1972): 285–290.

Dominguez, Virginia R. *White by Definition: Social Classification in Creole Louisiana.* New Brunswick, N.J.: Rutgers University Press, 1986.

Drake, St. Clair, and Horace R. Cayton. *Black Metropolis: A Study of Negro Life in a Northern City.* Vol. 2. New York: Harper and Row, 1962.

Du Bois, W. E. B. *The World of W. E. B. Du Bois*, edited by Meyer Weinberg. Westport, Conn.: Greenwood, 1992.

Edwards, G. Franklin. "Occupational Trends and New Lifestyles." In *Dilemmas of the New Black Middle Class,* edited by Joseph R. Washington, Jr., 15–25. N.p., c. 1980.

Elias, Norbert. *Norbert Elias: On Civilization, Power, and Knowledge: Selected Writings,* edited by Stephen Mennell and Johan Goudsblom. Chicago: University of Chicago Press, 1998.

Essien-Udom, E. U. *Black Nationalism: The Rise of the Black Muslims in the U.S.A.* New York: Penguin, 1966.

Evans, Sara. *Personal Politics: The Roots of Women's Liberation in the Civil Rights Movement and the New Left.* New York: Vintage, 1979.

Fanon, Frantz. *The Wretched of the Earth.* Translated by Constance Farrington. New York: Grove, 1963.

Fantasia, Rick. *Cultures of Solidarity: Consciousness, Action, and Contemporary American Workers.* Berkeley: University of California, 1988.

Fantasia, Rick, and Eric L. Hirsch. "Culture in Rebellion: The Appropriation and Transformation of the Veil in the Algerian Revolution." In *Social Movements and Culture,* edited by Hank Johnston and Bert Klandermans, 144–159. Minneapolis: University of Minnesota Press, 1995.

Feldstein, Ruth. "I Wanted the Whole World to See": Race, Gender, and the Construction of Motherhood in the Death of Emmett Till." In *Not June Cleaver: Women and Gender in Postwar America, 1945–1960,* edited by Joanne Meyerowitz, 263–303. Philadelphia: Temple University Press, 1994.

Frankenberg, Ruth. *White Women, Race Matters: The Social Construction of Whiteness.* Minneapolis: University of Minnesota Press, 1993.

Frazier, E. Franklin. *The Black Bourgeoisie: The Rise of a New Middle Class.* New York: Free Press, 1957.

Fredrickson, George. *The Black Image in the White Mind.* New York: Harper and Row, 1971.

Freeman, Howard E., Michael Ross, Davis Armor, and Thomas Pettigrew. "Color Gradation and Attitudes among Middle-income Negroes." *American Sociological Review* 31 (June 1966): 365–375.

Garvey, Amy Jacques. *Garvey and Garveyism.* New York: Macmillan, 1970.

Gates, Henry Louis, Jr. "The Trope of a New Negro and the Reconstruction of the Image of Black." *Representations* 24 (Fall 1988): 129–155.

Giddings, Paula. *When and Where I Enter: The Impact of Black Women on Race and Sex in America.* New York: William Morrow, 1984.

Gilman, Sander L. "Black Bodies, White Bodies: Toward an Iconography of Female Sexuality in Late Nineteenth Century Art, Medicine and Literature." In *"Race," Writing, and Difference,* edited by Henry Louis Gates, Jr., 223–240. Chicago: University of Chicago Press, 1986.

Gilroy, Paul. *Black Atlantic: Modernity and Double Consciousness.* Cambridge, Mass.: Harvard University Press, 1993.

Goering, John M. "Changing Perceptions and Evaluations of Physical Characteristics among Blacks: 1950–1970." *Phylon* 33 (1972): 231–241.

Gossett, Thomas F. *Race: The History of an Idea in America.* New York: Schocken, 1965.

Grier, William H., and Price M. Cobbs. *Black Rage.* New York: Basic, 1968.

Gutman, Herbert. *The Black Family in Slavery and Freedom.* New York: Vintage, 1976.

Guy-Sheftall, Beverly, ed. *Words of Fire: An Anthology of African-American Feminist Thought.* New York: New Press, 1995.

Hall, Jacquelyn Dowd. "'The Mind That Burns in Each Body': Women, Rape and Racial Violence." In *Powers of Desire: The Politics of Sexuality*, edited by Ann Snitow, Christine Stansell, and Sharon Thompson, 329–349. New York: Monthly Review, 1983.

Harley, Sharon, and Rosalyn Terborg-Penn, eds. *The Afro-American Woman: Struggles and Images*. Port Washington, N.Y.: Kennikat, 1978.

Herron, Carolivia. *Nappy Hair*. New York: Knopf, 1997.

Higginbotham, Evelyn Brooks. *Righteous Discontent: The Women's Movement in the Black Baptist Church, 1880–1920*. Cambridge: Harvard University Press, 1993.

Himes, Joseph S., and R. E. Edwards. "Hair Texture and Skin Color in Mate Selection among Negroes." *Midwest Journal* 4 (1952): 80–85.

Hine, Darlene Clark. "Rape and the Inner Lives of Black Women in the Middle West: Preliminary Thoughts on the Culture of Dissemblance." *Signs* 14 (Summer 1989): 912–920.

Hine, Darlene Clark, and Earnestine Jenkins, eds. *A Question of Manhood: A Reader in U.S. Black Men's History and Masculinity*. Vol. 1. Bloomington: Indiana University Press, 1999.

Honig, Bonnie. "My Culture Made Me Do It." In *Is Multiculturalism Bad for Women?*, edited by Susan Okin, 35–40. Princeton, N.J.: Princeton University Press, 1999.

hooks, bell. *Feminist Theory: From Margin to Center*, 2d ed. Boston: South End, 2000.

Hull, Gloria, Patricia Bell Scott, and Barbara Smith, eds. *All the Women Are White, All the Blacks Are Men, but Some of Us Are Brave*. New York: Feminist Press, 1982.

Jefferson, Thomas. *The Portable Thomas Jefferson*. New York: Viking, 1975.

Jewell, K. Sue. *From Mammy to Miss America and Beyond: Cultural Images and the Shaping of U.S. Social Policy*. New York: Routledge, 1993.

Johnson, Jacqueline, Sharon Rush, and Joe Feagin. "Doing Anti-Racism: Toward an Egalitarian American Society." *Contemporary Sociology* 29 (2000): 95–110.

Johnson, James H., and Walter C. Farrell. "Race Still Matters." *Chronicle of Higher Education*. 7 July 1995. A48.

Johnston, Hank, and Bert Klandermans, eds. *Social Movements and Culture*. Minneapolis: University of Minnesota Press, 1995.

Jones, Jacqueline. *Labor of Love, Labor of Sorrow: Black Women, Work and the Family from Slavery to the Present*. New York: Basic, 1985.

Jones, Lisa. *Bulletproof Diva: Tales of Race, Sex, and Hair*. New York: Doubleday, 1994.

Jordan, Winthrop. *White over Black: American Attitudes toward the Negro, 1550–1812*. New York: Norton, 1977.

Karenga, Maulana Ron. *The Quotable Karenga*, edited by Clyde Halisi and James Mtume. Los Angeles: US Organization, 1967.

Keith, Verna M., and Cedric Herring. "Skin Tone and Stratification in the Black Community." *American Journal of Sociology* 97 (1991): 760–778.

Kelley, Robin D. G. "Nap Time: Historicizing the Afro." *Fashion Theory* 1, no. 4 (1997): 339–351.

———. *Race Rebels: Culture, Politics, and the Black Working Class*. New York: Free Press, 1994.

King, Mary. *Freedom Song: A Personal Story of the 1960s Civil Rights Movement*. New York: William Morrow, 1987.

Laclau, Ernesto, and Chantal Mouffe. *Hegemony and Socialist Strategy: Towards a Radical Democratic Politics*. Thetford, Norfolk, U.K.: Thetford, 1985.

Lakoff, Robin, and Raquel Scherr. *Face Value: The Politics of Beauty.* London: Routledge and Kegan Paul, 1984.

Landry, Bart. *The New Black Middle Class.* Berkeley: University of California Press, 1987.

Leeds, Maxine. "Young African-American Women and the Language of Beauty." In *Ideals of Feminine Beauty: Philosophical, Social, and Cultural Dimensions,* edited by Karen Callaghan, 147–159. Westport, Conn.: Greenwood, 1994.

Levine, Lawrence. *Black Culture and Black Consciousness: Afro-American Folk Thought from Slavery to Freedom.* New York: Oxford University Press, 1977.

Lieberson, Stanley. *A Piece of the Pie: Blacks and White Immigrants since 1880.* Berkeley: University of California Press, 1980.

Lincoln, Abbey. "Who Will Revere the Black Woman?" *Negro Digest* (September 1966): 16–20.

Locke, Alain, ed. *The New Negro.* 1925. Reprint, with a preface by Robert Hayden, New York: Atheneum, 1968.

Major, Clarence, ed. *Juba to Jive: A Dictionary of African-American Slang.* New York: Penguin, 1994.

Malcolm X, and Alex Haley. *The Autobiography of Malcolm X.* New York: Ballantine, 1965.

Massey, Douglas S., and Mitchell L. Eggers. "The Ecology of Inequality: Minorities and the Concentration of Poverty, 1970–1990." *American Journal of Sociology* 95 (1990): 1153–1188.

McAdam, Doug. *Political Process and the Development of Black Insurgency, 1930–1970.* Chicago: University of Chicago Press, 1982

Melucci, Alberto. "The Process of Collective Identity." In *Social Movements and Culture,* edited by Hank Johnston and Bert Klandermans, 41–63. Minneapolis: University of Minnesota Press, 1995.

Mercer, Kobena. "Black Hair/Style Politics." In *Out There: Marginalization and Contemporary Cultures,* edited by Russell Ferguson, Martha Gever, Trinh T. Minh-ha, and Cornel West, 247–264. Cambridge, Mass.: MIT Press, 1990.

Monson, Ingrid. "Abbey Lincoln's 'Straight Ahead': Jazz in the Era of the Civil Rights Movement." In *Between Resistance and Revolution: Cultural Politics and Social Protest,* edited by Richard Fox and Orin Stern, 171–194. New Brunswick, N.J.: Rutgers University Press, 1997

Morgan, Robin. *Sisterhood Is Powerful: An Anthology of Writings from the Women's Liberation Movement.* New York: Vintage, 1970.

Morris, Aldon. *The Origins of the Civil Rights Movement: Black Communities Organizing for Change.* New York: Free Press, 1984.

Morrison, Toni. *The Bluest Eye.* New York: Washington Square, 1970.

Morton, Patricia. *Disfigured Images: The Historical Assault on Afro-American Women.* New York: Greenwood, 1991.

Moses, Wilson. *The Golden Age of Black Nationalism: 1850–1925.* Hamden, Conn.: Archon, 1978.

Mosse, George L. *Nationalism and Sexuality: Middle-Class Morality and Sexual Norms in Modern Europe.* Madison: University of Wisconsin Press, 1985.

Muhammad, Elijah. *The Supreme Wisdom.* Vol. 2. N.p. [1957].

Mullins, Elizabeth I., and Paul Sites. "The Origins of Eminent Black Americans: A Three-Generation Analysis of Social Origin." *American Sociological Review* 49 (1984): 672–685.

Nader, Laura. "Orientalism, Occidentalism, and the Control of Women." *Cultural Dynamics* 2, no. 3 (1989): 323–355.

Omi, Michael, and Howard Winant. *Racial Formation in the United States: From the 1960s to the 1990s.* 2d ed. New York: Routledge, 1994.

Painter, Nell. *Sojourner Truth: A Life, a Symbol.* New York: Norton, 1996.

Palmer, Phyllis Marynick. *Domesticity and Dirt.* Philadelphia: Temple University Press, 1989.

———. "White Women/Black Women: The Dualism of Female Identity and Experience in the United States." *Feminist Studies* 9 (1983): 151–170.

Peiss, Kathy. *Hope in a Jar: The Making of American Beauty Culture.* New York: Metropolitan, 1998.

———. "Making Faces: The Cosmetics Industry and the Cultural Construction of Gender, 1890–1930." *Genders* 7 (Spring 1990): 143–169.

Ransford, Edward H. "Skin Color, Life Chances and Anti-white Attitudes." *Social Problems* 18 (1970): 164–178.

Roediger, David R. *The Wages of Whiteness: Race and the Making of the American Working Class: 1776–1865.* New York: Verso, 1991.

Rooks, Noliwe. *Hair Raising: Beauty, Culture, and African American Women.* New Brunswick, N.J.: Rutgers University Press, 1996.

Russell, Kathy, Midge Wilson, and Ronald Hall. *The Color Complex: The Politics of Skin Color among African Americans.* New York: Anchor, 1992.

Ryan, Mary P. *Women in Public: Between Banners and Ballots, 1825–1880.* Baltimore: Johns Hopkins University Press, 1990.

Schiebinger, Londa L. *Nature's Body: Gender in the Making of Modern Science.* Boston: Beacon, 1993.

Scott, James C. *Domination and the Arts of Resistance: Hidden Transcripts.* New Haven, Conn.: Yale University Press, 1990.

Sellers, Cleveland. *The River of No Return: The Autobiography of a Black Militant and the Life and Death of SNCC.* Jackson: University Press of Mississippi, 1973.

Smith, Jean. "I Learned to Feel Black." In *The Black Power Revolt: A Collection of Essays,* edited by Floyd B. Barbour, 207–218. Boston, Mass.: Extending Horizons Books, 1968.

Smith, Jessie Carney. *Images of Blacks in American Culture.* Westport, Conn.: Greenwood, 1988.

Smith, Jessie C., and Carrell P. Horton, eds. *Historical Statistics of Black America.* New York: Gale Research, 1995.

Sommerville, Diane Miller. "The Rape Myth in the Old South Revisited." In *A Question of Manhood: A Reader in U.S. Black Men's History and Masculinity,* edited by Darlene Clark Hine and Earnestine Jenkins, 438–472. Vol. 1. Bloomington: Indiana University Press, 1999.

Spencer, Margaret B. "Black Children's Race Awareness, Racial Attitudes and Self-Concept: A Reinterpretation." *Journal of Child Psychology* 23 (1984): 433–441.

Swidler, Ann. "Culture in Action: Symbols and Strategies." *American Sociological Review* 51 (April 1986): 273–286.

Synnott, A. "Shame and Glory: A Sociology of Hair." *British Journal of Sociology* 38 (1987): 381–413.

Taylor, Verta, and Nancy Whittier. "Analytical Approaches to Social Movement Culture:

The Culture of the Women's Movement." In *Social Movements and Culture*, edited by Hank Johnston and Bert Klandermans, 163–187. Minneapolis: University of Minnesota Press, 1995.

Terborg-Penn, Rosalyn. "Black Male Perspectives on the Nineteenth Century Woman." In *The Afro-American Woman: Struggles and Images*, edited by Sharon Harley and Rosalyn Terborg-Penn, 28–42. Port Washington, N.Y.: Kennikat, 1978.

Thurman, Wallace. *The Blacker the Berry.* 1929. Reprint, New York: AMS Press, 1972.

Udry, J. Richard, Karl E. Bauman, and Charles Chase. "Skin Color, Status, and Mate Selection." *American Journal of Sociology* 76 (1971): 722–733.

U.S. Bureau of the Census. *Negroes in the United States: 1920–1932.* Washington, D.C.: Bureau of the Census, 1935.

U.S. Department of Education, National Center for Education Statistics. *The Traditionally Black Institutions of Higher Education: 1860 to 1982*, by Susan T. Hill. Washington, D.C.: GPO, 1985.

Van Deburg, William L. *New Day in Babylon: The Black Power Movement and American Culture, 1965–1975.* Chicago: University of Chicago Press, 1992.

Webster, Murray, and James Driskell. "Beauty as Status." *American Journal of Sociology* 89 (1983): 140–165.

White, Deborah Gray. *Ain't I a Woman? Female Slaves in the Plantation South.* New York: Norton, 1985.

———. *Too Heavy a Load: Black Women in Defense of Themselves, 1894–1994.* New York: Norton, 1999.

White, Shane, and Graham White. *Stylin': African American Expressive Culture from Its Beginnings to the Zoot Suit.* Ithaca, N.Y.: Cornell University Press, 1998.

Whittier, Nancy. *Feminist Generations: The Persistence of the Radical Women's Movement.* Philadelphia: Temple University Press, 1995.

Williams, Juan. *Eyes on the Prize: America's Civil Rights Years, 1954–1965.* New York: Viking, 1987.

Wilson, William Julius. *The Declining Significance of Race.* 2d ed. Chicago: University of Chicago Press, 1980.

Wolf, Naomi. *The Beauty Myth.* New York: William Morrow, 1991.

Wolseley, Roland. *The Black Press, U.S.A.* 2d ed. Ames: Iowa State University Press, 1990.

INDEX